The Mystical and Magical Paths of Self and not-self

Volume 2

A Comprehensive Guide toward
Unveiling the Past, Emphasising the Present and Blueprinting the Future

Bringing forth the Kaballistic and Ha Kha Teachings
Of the Supreme Grand Hierophant Tehuti

Paul Simons

Second Edition

TamaRe House Publishers
Web: www.TamaReHouse.com
Email: info@TamaReHouse.com

The Mystical and Magical Paths of Self and not-self

Volume 2

A Comprehensive Guide toward
Unveiling the Past, Emphasising the Present and Blueprinting the Future

Bringing forth the Kaballistic and Ha Kha Teachings
Of the Supreme Grand Hierophant Tehuti

First Published in 2006
By TamaRe House Publishers Ltd, London, UK

Printed and Bound by Lightning Source, Milton Keynes, UK

Authored by Paul Simons aka Nebu Ka Ma'at

Copyright © 2006 Paul Simons

Cover design by Marilyn Mitchell

ISBN 978-1-906169-01-5

Dedication

To my 3 Sons

Levelle, and the twins Sahleem and Sahlee

The MMSN 3-part Series

The Mystical and Magical Paths
of Self and not-self

Volume 1

An Introduction to Christ Consciousness
and the Fourth Dimension

True Love, Peace and Joy of the Annus Magnus
NOW

The Mystical and Magical Paths
of Self and not-self

Volume 2

A comprehensive Guide toward
Unveiling the Past, Emphasising the Present and Blueprinting the Future

Bringing forth the Kaballistic and Ha Kha Teachings
of the Supreme Grand Hierophant Tehuti

The Mystical and Magical Paths
of Self and not-self

Volume 3

Nuwaubu
The Afro-Conscientric Curriculum for Life in the 21st Century

Taking the practical steps necessary for Self-Empowerment

Contents

Chapter 3: The Science of Love in the Making

Chapter 4: Sacred Geometry

Chapter 5: Melanin and the Nubian Black Box

Chapter 6: Ancestral Ontology and Cosmology

Chapter 9:   Merkaba Energy

Acknowledgements

Special thanks to the following people for their reliability in assistance, support and encouragement throughout my work toward completing both volumes 1 and 2 of the MMSN series:

Charles Oduro
Bolanle Adebanjo
Reginald Enyi
Grace Martin
Emanuel Prempeh
Stephen Griffith
Nenda & Joan Lofters
Simon Spence
Dennis Liverpool

Preliminaries

As an aspiring student of the Creator, it is imperative that one must continue to educate, inspire and to be an exemplified example for others who are also on the mystical path toward Self-enlightenment. Great students will no doubt assume the role of becoming great teachers by default. On the contrary, it is an irony that many devout religious persons of today lack the ability to become great teachers. They are obliviously unable to motivate and inspire others to achieve great things within their lives – as far as <u>true human potential</u> is concerned. Why is this? I believe it is due to the lack of practicality or application within most modern religious doctrines. For instance, in ancient **Khemet** (Egipt[1]), not only did the religious priesthood have a system of initiation and a sound cosmogony of Creation and of existence, but the results achieved by the application of the latter were so far empowering for the neophyte,[2] that the information had to be kept secret/ sacred.

One rule of thumb to note hereon is that the quality of information that one possesses will determine the quality of life they lead. This will also determine their abilities to motivate and inspire others and so on. We must understand however that a person who is a committed Christian may well speak of how their life has been changed for the better as a result of becoming a Christian. But we also must become aware that the propagators and puppeteers of the doctrine have already set the standard/ bar or level of achievable spiritual enlightenment. This

---

[1] In volume 1, I defined Egipt spelled with an 'I' to create a distinction between the invading Egyptians (Persians, Greeks and Romans etc), and the original Nilotic/ Neolithic Blacks of that region of North Afrokha. Also the word Afrokha was coined from Afro and Khan meaning *'wooly haired rulers'* or *'wooly haired civilizers.'*

[2] A neophyte is a person who has initiated her/ his self into the Khemetian mystery systems – of Ascension and Enlightenment.

means that Christians, Muslims and Jews alike are unknowingly being lead-on to only achieve a certain level of spiritual enlightenment. This makes difficult a task for a true spiritual Master or teacher to even begin to educate one who has been conditioned to think only at certain levels. I have noticed however, that Christianity, as well as some Islamic sects of today, have actually raised the standard on the level of propagated information of their doctrines. They are quietly trying to keep their congregations afloat. This is because there is a frenzy of empowering information available publicly today as we are now at the fringe of the *Information Age* – the Age of *Aquarius*. This has obviously caused today's religious zealots to raise their eyebrows with despair, and with the fright of being disrobed.

The approach of the Aquarian Age represents a time of enlightenment, re-alignment, cleansing, replenishing and purging of the entire galactical system. This reality will also affect all plant and animal life, as well as the Collective-Consciousness of humans on planet earth (all Creatures great and small). This is why advanced information is absolutely necessary in this day and time.

In volume 1 of *'The Mystical and Magical Paths of Self and not-self,'* I presented an introduction to **'Christ-Consciousness'** and the **Fourth Dimension**. It is the intention of this volume to provide pointers in the direction of the levels of spiritual enlightenment or levels of Consciousness and awareness that one <u>must</u> achieve in order to continue to exist as we approach and enter the Christ-Consciousness realm – the Fourth Dimension. This phenomenon will be explained in proceeding chapters, but you may also refer to volume 1, Ch9 of Part1. I must point out at this time that it is not in my intention to encourage people to stop being Christians, Muslims or Jews – that would be arrogant and selfish of me. I am however suggesting that we need to raise the standard on our levels of acquiring knowledge, wisdom and understanding of our belief systems. To be blunt, I am also presenting the admonition that we

<u>must</u> replace belief with knowing, because belief is the acceptance of things we do not actually know. It is an emotion that enforces acceptance of an experience we did not actually experience. A belief by definition therefore, is an emotion – a weak excuse for certainty of what something means, whereas knowing comes from experience and from union with **Conscience**.[3]

The standpoint and context that this work takes is an Introduction to Afrocentric Ontology and Fourth Dimensional Awareness and living. The work also encourages one to consistently strive to unveil, and close, the mysteries of the ancient past; thereby enabling her or him to emphasise the Present-Now, thus blueprinting a possible future based upon the future, – not the past. This is an absolute must, because the ancient Afrokhan, as well as most ancient Eastern thinkers are those that perpetually persist to recognise the underlining interconnectedness of all aspects of nature. Our religion <u>must</u> therefore be at the centre of our society – as religion is not what we practice, it is what we are. Afrokhan religion and culture embraces the reality of the Oneness of the Spirit of God by way of its people's ability to intertwine all aspect of their societies. Religion, economics, government, education, astronomy, medicine and socialism were all centred, based on the One Eternal Spirit of the Creator. The Afrokhan person could not fathom a separation of any of the latter – to her/ him this was impossible. This is why today's Eurocentric societies are crumbling. Western philosophy, routed in all of its society's faculties has become the cause of its own demise and destruction – because, western philosophy can only educate people to think in terms of fragments of the collective, or segments of Reality. This causes people to become limited in terms of their mental powers, their aptitude and overall human potential.

---

[3] The Conscience is the highest aspect of the Self; it is the all-knowing faculty of God

The Christ-Consciousness zone is engaged by applying the Doctrine of Unity-Consciousness – as opposed to the Doctrine of Polarity[4] in 3-D. It is to be ushered in with the vibration of Love – as in Unconditional Love for all aspects of nature. This 4th dimensional awareness zone is analogous to the much awaited for *Christ/ Messiah* that the Christian community is waiting for. The term *Messiah* is synonymous with the Monasic radiation of the photon belt, which I will be elaborating on. However, a Messiah in person is one that has been initiated into the order of Melchizadeck,[5] and has raised her/ his self into Unity-Consciousness by way of the Love vibration – just as Jesus was made a High Priest after the order of Melchizadeck:

> *'Though he were a Son, yet learned he obedience by things which he suffered; and being made perfect, he became the author of eternal salvation unto all that obeyed him; Called of God a high priest after the order of Melchizadeck.'*
>
> Heb 5v7-10

The 4th dimensional zone is the much awaited for heaven also. There will be no wars, diseases, hate, envy, natural disasters etc. There will therefore be none but True Love, Peace and Joy, for some 2,000 years; completely void of Polarity and Duality-Consciousness.

~

---

[4] The Doctrine of Polarity is explained in volume 1
[5] The Order of Melchizadeck is also called the Order of Tehuti

Introduction

Computer Analogy

Planet earth, – Tamare, Taneen, Shan, Ta, Kush, Tiwawat, Tiamat, Qi, Gaea, Dunya or by whatever name we choose to call it, is analogous to a computer hard-drive that is incorporated with various peripheral systems controlled by a CPU (or central processing unit). There comes a time when the computer may require de-fragmenting, or its memory may need to be completely erased followed by a rebooting of the system. This is usually because after long-term usage, the system may have become corrupted with all types of viruses and unwanted software application programs etc., or maybe some of its peripherals need updating to accommodate larger memory requirements. However it may be – planet earth is currently experiencing these exact scenarios as you read this paragraph. As we approach the Monasic radiation ring (or the photon belt), earth/ Tamare[1] – meaning *'planet of land, water and sun,'* is preparing for a major de-fragmentation of its entire ecosystem. It needs to be cleansed of its 'almost completely negative crystallised energy grid' first and foremost, in order for it to be allowed to enter the 4th dimension. Just like the computer, Tamare has been infested with all types of software and application viruses (literally) – which manifest themselves to us in forms of devilish activities, hatred amongst people, wars and diseases; as economical breakdowns, dwindling social structures and failing education systems; as well as in many other forms. The rest I will leave for your own imaginations or your own experiences to figure out.

---

[1] Taken from <u>Ta</u>-earth, <u>Ma</u>-water and <u>Re</u>-sun – ancient Khemet, the term Tamare is actually with respect to *Pangaea,* the Greek term for the planet before the continental drifts (i.e. one landmass).

Planet earth has petitioned to move into a higher frequency vibration in order to escape these flaws. And guess what… the request has been granted, as ascension is long overdue – perhaps by hundreds of thousands of years. The entering of the Monasic ring, which is also called the **Christ-Consciousness zone**, may effectively cause the temporary suspension of the planetary electromagnetic grid system as the north and south poles reposition themselves. Some scientists postulate that there will be a complete reversal of the poles. The **Mayans**, in a manner of writing, complements this thesis by stating that the planet will halt and proceed to revolve in the opposite direction – all to happen over a 3-4 day period. As bizarre as this may sound at first, as it did to me initially, this is actually a routine phenomenon that happens to earth every twelve to thirteen thousand years or so. Much information on the Monasic ring and the photon belt will be presented in Ch8. The temporary suspension of the planetary grid system will drastically affect the collective memory of the planet. In fact, there is also a possibility that we could loose memory all together. This is because the electromagnetic grid system is responsible for keeping the information of planet earth in tact – if this goes, all goes. Just as the computer has an electrical supply system that it uses to maintain its functions and memory, humans have electrical systems also. In fact, the human body is nothing but a multi-function capacitor that stores and processes energy in the form of electric and magnetic currents. As humans we also have an electromagnetic field surrounding our bodies, emanated by our Chakra energies, which enables us to retain our faculties as well as our individual memory.

As far as earth's collective memory is concerned, it requires a certain number of individuals to act as memory disks to hold its information until it is rebooted in the 4th dimension. Could this number of individuals be referring to the 144,000 rapturees' (souls) mentioned in the book of Revelation? Either way, humans are no doubt the memory disks that Tamare requires to hold its memory in the interim – In particular the **Melanated Afrokhan**. Equally, as the computer operator prepares to de-fragment the hard-drive, she/ he may also have to re-format several floppy disks, CD ROMs or Zip disks in order to store operation software programs as well as application software programs. The re-formatting of these storage devices is analogous with the fact that earth's humans will have to be re-formatted in order to once again become compatible with the earth's CPU. Or at least, a certain amount of souls are required to become zip drives etc. Do you follow? Imagine trying to run an Apple Mac software application program within Microsoft Windows. It simply would not happen. This is like an Afrokhan ancestor such as Nyame of the Asante people of Ghana trying to communicate or correspond with his human children. But the deity is unsuccessful in his attempts because his subjects are now operating under another faculty; another language, another code of conduct etc., having nothing to do with their own genetic lineage or legacy. The people would have to become reprogrammed or re-aligned with their own culture, language and natural way of being in order to correspond accordingly. Today however, we have computer wizards who have created programs that can allow Apple Mac software programs to be run on Microsoft Windows and visa versa. Unfortunately with earth, it doesn't quite pan out that way. We are faced with a situation simile to a computer programmer who is trying to write a program for a particular application, and is randomly being forced to change from Pascal to Cobal or to Basic etc., or even combinations of the latter, without warning. This will inevitably cause confusion to the writer, and may also cause problems within the CPU itself. And so humans today are faced with various different operation programs all interpolated with each other – as in the various forms of religion, different cultural roots and different educational backgrounds and so on.

In volume 1, we looked at various archetypal and metaphorical triggers that have been set up by the Ancient Ones to awaken us to the call for ascension prior to entering the Christ-Consciousness zone; scenarios, such as the Yoruba God Obatala and his Orisha-nla pantheon (angelic host), returning to earth to rapture his lost souls. We also looked at other Creator deities such as Andromedas, Athena, Ra, Tehuti, Ptah, Khnum, Asaru, Olodumare, Nyame and more. Throughout the proceeding chapters of MMSN volume 2, I will of course shed more light on these metaphoric triggers, in order for us to raise the bar and standard of our awareness of Self. Christ-Consciousness, which is in contrast to Afrocentric-Consciousness, never minding the different connotations, is the main theme of this volume, and will enable the rapturees to become unified, under one operating system. In the legendary **Lemurian** culture, this doctrine is referred to as the '**Law of One**.' The 'Law of One' embodies the Doctrine of Unity-Consciousness or Fourth Dimensional Awareness where all aspects of the society are governed by the acknowledgement of the One Universal Spirit of God that underpins All *things*. From a scientific perspective it is the realm of which matter and antimatter particles are perceived as one complete experience. So-called positive and negative characteristics will no longer 'be' – *persons, places* and *things* will manifest exactly as they are without the tendency to be polarised in expression. The 'Law of One' unites us with our twin flame or twin Soul – the merging of the lower self with the Higher Self. But there is a catch… In order for us to handle this type of energy, one must first learn to stand in a space of Pure Unconditional Love for all.

Therefore, this work attempts to re-establish Love and Integrity within our Black communities, and throughout the many differing cultural communities of the world. A clear definition of Love, coupled with Divine Integrity, Oneness with Nature and, Unity with 'All that Is,' will be realised on completing this course of study. You will find within, a number of concepts, from old and of new, all within the context of Unity-Consciousness. This work has been inspired by the Ancient Egiptian Order, and by its approach toward the re-establishment of Godliness and Power of Be*ing*, within the Afrokhan woman and man of the West. The purpose of the AEO is to present a doctrine that unveils, and closes, the past; to emphasise the Present-Now; and, to blueprint a possibility based upon the future. The AEO propagates the ancient spiritual science of Nuwaubu.

How to reference this work

- Some pages will present an appendix via footnotes, shown at the bottom of the said page. These appendixes may provide further elaboration on some terms or phrases.
- Each chapter will provide references via endnotes. These references provide a bibliography for further research. Publication dates and ISBN numbers are toward the back of the book.
- Each page's footnote is sequenced as A, B, C, etc.
- Each chapter's endnote is sequenced as 1, 2, 3, etc.

~

Flower of Life

Sacred Pattern of Creation

Chapter 1
Involution Vs Evolution

Children of the Black Dot

The <u>Supreme Grand Hierophant</u>[A] **Tehuti** and his celestial siblings come to us as the transmutable blue flame from the auratic field of the Great Central Sun, **NTR**.[B] The Conscientious NTR; the source of all of Creation – is the great Providence existing before the original **Nuqta**,[1] expressing itself from the Great Central Vortex; as the Great Central Sun of our seven universes. The Nuqta or '**Black Dot**' is the ultimate point of reckoning – it is the Alpha and the Omega – the point of which **The All**, God, merges and proceeds to manifest all that now '*Is,*' and, the point of which The All shall return. The Great Creator NTR, the Omnipotent Subjective, through objective meditation *caused* the original Nuqta to move – as <u>e</u>nergy in <u>motion</u> (or e-motion) from the Substantial Presence of Unconditional Love. We have all heard the saying that '*God, created the world out of Love,*' of which earthly love is only a reflection.[2] God is not essentially NTR, but is rather the creative Conscience of NTR. Therefore God, the aspect of NTR that creates, exists as Deity of deities, and biblically speaking, He is the collective Elohim. This energy of Unconditional Love began to rotate at speeds unimaginable by us mere mortals, for it is beyond Mind. The spin of the Nuqta, the birth of emotion, spiralled through the void and darkness bringing light to its attention as the perfect mathematical *pi*, expressed in manifested *things* as the Golden Mean *phi* ratio (more in Ch4).

[A] The term Hierophant is relating to an ascended spiritual master, such as the well-known Tehuti/ Thoth.

[B] NTR is the Khemetian term for the undifferentiated substantial essence of matter. NTR in all respect must therefore represent the Godhead of all mysticism.

1

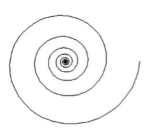

Fig1.1:
The spiralling motion of
the first Nuqta

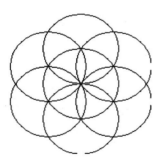

Fig1.2:
The Egg of Life

The birth of emotion is the birth of light, or rather, NTR *caused* light to merge from the void and darkness, by mentally willing the original Nuqta to spin, move and collide with other Nuqta positions – thus creating space and time. NTR increased the original single-spiral of the Nuqta to seven spirals, which collided with seven other Nuqta co-ordinates and *caused* them to move and spiral in duplication – all by way of its own will and mental projection. Each collision represents a *'Big Bang,'* where the process duplicated itself indefinitely in accordance with what was intended by the Universal Mind.

Each of the seven created vortexes formed our seven universes – these are therefore children of NTR, symbolised as the Egg of Life in Sacred Geometry. The Sumerian cosmology propagates this creation story as the differentiation of **Sal**, where Sal, the root of the word *Soul* is comparative to NTR. Sal and its mate **Arina**, produces seven children who in turn produced many children of their own. These children are the many galaxies or star clusters we currently marvel at.

Creative Forces

9-ether,[A] the highest composition of spiritual energies; the duplications of NTR, exists in pure space as sparks of light; forever existing as sparks of intelligence. With unlimited potential and creativity, 9-ether gasses proceed to create life as is intended by the Creator. These 9-ether energies, the Involutionary forces of the Universe, are presented to us in the Khemetian mystery system as the 99NTRU; western science calls them the 99elements of earth; and the Islamic religion calls them the 99attributes of Allah. The four Supreme Grand Hierophants (ascended masters), according to the ancient Khemetian mystery teachings, are the gods that are responsible for assisting us, humans, to remember our spiritual heritage. We once existed as sparks of light, 9-ether, *Chi*, *Sekhem*, with unlimited power – sadly, we have forgotten. We have suffered cosmic amnesia due to our denial of the eternal Spirit that binds All of Creation as One. Our participation within the world of material *things* under the auspices of the ego-self, has afforded us to disregard our conscientious-Self. We did however, aeon after aeon, record and store our experiences so we may be prompted to remember Conscience when the time comes for the quickening of Spirit, the ultimate rapture. One of our greatest scribes of the latter was Tehuti.

Table 1:	The 4 Supreme Grand Hierophants
Tehuti -	Scribe of the Neteru
Khnum -	God of the Potter's Wheel
Khonsu -	The Divine Spirit
Anubu -	Angel of Rapture

Conscience, the highest aspect of the Self, also called the 'I AM Presence,' never forgets us – it constantly remembers that its lower

[A] 9-ether, as taught by Dr Malachi, is the combination of all spiritual forces – the most powerful creative gas within the Universe.

nature, now governed by the ego-self, called the 'I Me Presence,' has but undergone a period of denial of Reality. *'The ego, the self-arrogating aspect of the mind'* [Dr Malachi],[3] deludes and obscures the 'I Me Presence' from who we are in Reality; for that is exactly its purpose – a faculty of Mind created for the sole purpose of schooling us within the lower planes of spiritual life and living. The greatest of all schools, with the greatest of lessons for souls to learn and prosper from, is the school of earth, a domain of negativity and illusion, nine planes of existence away from the bosom of the Creator. The earth, or Material Plane, is but the lowest vibration of existence within the created matrix of The All. Our lower nature – governed by the ego-self, whereas, our Higher Nature is governed by the Conscience-Self, – you choose…

Table 2: creativity Vs destructivity

Involution	Vs	Evolution
9-ether (Creative force)	Vs	6-ether (Destructive force)
Conscience-Self	Vs	Ego-self
I AM Presence	Vs	I ME Presence
Subjective Reality	Vs	Objective manifestation

Fig1.3:
Neter Tehuti

Tehuti – the Divine Scribe

Brother Tehuti, one of the many grand children or grand creations of NTR – is but a differentiated effect of the interconnected spirals of many a Nuqta. This conscientious entity is thus a manifestation of several attributes of the unseen Creator.

The attributes of the Creator are therefore expressed as the many creator-Deities that are created of its-self – or, the Creator is recognised by way of its pantheon of creator-Gods who collectively represent its characteristics.

Tehuti is assigned the task by NTR of helping and assisting us humans in the physical as well as spiritual evolution of our specie. He is the master scribe of the NTRU, the recording angel that keeps the Akasha – the Collective Unconscious of our Universe, the Cosmos. He was not sent alone on this great mission. Many other creator deities are also present throughout the seven universes and throughout the many galaxies of them – such as **Khnum** and **Ptah**. Tehuti brings us good tidings and blessings as he prepares us for the next stage of our spiritual evolution. His very Presence, which superimposes our reality approximately every 25,000years, accommodates the conscientious Subjective aspect of our collective corporeal ancestry and existence. He is the head of our divine chronicle. As the blue flame, he also represents the alpha and the omega, as the Supreme Melchizadeck of our current matrix and reality – for the colour blue represents transformation and ascension. The Hopi Native American tribes hold this truth as the 'Blue Star Kachina,' relating to the tri star system Sirius – a celestial triad of solar deities that governs our earthly reality. The Khemetian mystery system called these deities Atum, Atun and Amun; the Sumerians called them Utu, Apsu and Shamash; and modern astronomers call them Sirius A, B and C. These Stars, Suns, or 'Sons of God' just as Tehuti, are indeed children of the Black Dot. They are Self-created and are androgynous existing in and of their be*ing*, just as they are created by NTR, which exists in and of itself as NTRU, the collective of the deities. All mystical schools ancient, medieval and new have taken from the teachings of the Great Tehuti. As a God, who incarnated and walked the earth during Lemurian and Atlantaen times, he established the teachings of '**Ha Kha**,' of which the so-called seven Hermetic Truths are based. Many of the latter-day Egiptian doctrines were also centred on his

5

teachings, such as the 'Order of Amun' and the 'Ausarian/ Osirian Religion.' The Initiate or '**Neophyte**'[A] would enter the 'Grand Lodge,' as the ultimate stepping-stone toward achieving Self-mastery and Self-realisation. The main purpose of these Egiptian mystical schools was to educate the neophyte; that is to assist her/ him; to draw out the best of their spiritual characteristics, qualities, attributes of God etc.

The people of the Egiptian city Annu, with its Greek term Heliopolis, considered the deity **Aset** and her counterpart **Asaru** to be the metaphorical archetypal body of God, and, the student must develop herself or himself to become an emblem of Aset or Asaru respectively. Thus we have the emergence of the 'Osirian Religion.' Aset and Asaru, though are two distinct deities, are actually essentially one complete deity expressing its twin flames through gender within the material world as female and male. This is why in the Khemetian cosmogony the two are depicted as wife and husband, or as sister and brother. Meaning, they express the underlying faculty of duality, from the standpoint of the 'Law of One.'[B] They underlay the Principles of life and death, with their son **Haru** underlying the Principles of re-birth and regeneration.

Fig1.4:
Neter Khnum

Khnum – the Divine Potter

Khnum, the creator deity of the potter's wheel, marvelled within the torah as the God that fashions man from mud; or from the dust of the ground, is forever present. With Satet and Atet, as the triad of Sudan/ Aswan, they are worshipped and revered as creators of man, and together represent the animative forces of NTR.

[A] The word Neophyte, as explained by George G.M. James means student, one who has initiated her/ him self into any of the mystical orders.
[B] The 'Law of One' was the religion of the Lemurian and Atlantean cultures.

Khnum's triad, represent the 'us' and the 'our' in the bible, who created man within their own image:

'And God said, let <u>us</u> make man in <u>our</u> image, after <u>our</u> likeness.'
Gen 1v26

'And the Lord God formed man from the <u>dust of the ground</u>, and breathed in his nostrils the breath of life; and man became a living soul.'
Gen 2v7

Khnum is the fashioner of the evolutionary man, but Tehuti is the deity who writes and records the formula for this intervention, into mankind's evolution. Khnum's job was to ensure that the fashioned man was developed in order to procreate and reproduce his own kind. He also assisted the Neteru in creating the seven spheres that protect mankind from the damaging UV rays of the sun. He is therefore also known as *'God of the Rainbow.'* He created each being and allocated them with 120years of physical life in the light. And now the next stage of man's spiritual evolution is nigh. In the Khemetian mysteries, it was Khnum who created the cosmic egg; *'The Goose that laid the Golden Egg,'* comes from this story.

'I am Khnum, your creator; my arms are around you, to steady your body, to safeguard your limbs. I bestow on you ores with precious stones since antiquity (existing) that were not worked before to build temples, rebuild ruins, and sculpt chapels for his master. I am master of creation. I have created myself, the great ocean which came into being in past times, according to whose pleasure the Nile rises. For I am the master who makes, I am he who makes himself exalted in Nun, who first came forth, Hapi who hurries at will; fashioner of everybody, guide of each man to their hour. I am Tenen, father of Gods, the great Shou living on the shore.' [Taken from the Famine Steel][4]

Fig1.5:
Neter Khonsu

Khonsu – the Holy Spirit

Khonsu, son of Amun and Mut, are the triad deities of the Egiptian City of Nu Amun, called Thebes by the invading Greeks. Khonsu is the aid of Tehuti; he is the master healer of the sick and protector against evil. He is called the *'Holy Spirit'* in the New Testament of the Christian doctrine and, he represents the descending dove that carries the Spirit of Jesus.

Khonsu – with one of his attributes 'The Traveller' is depicted as a youth standing on a plinth and mummified, (very much like Ptah) and, having the princely side-lock, a beard, and a crescent moon headdress. He is especially associated with the moon (hence possibly the origins of his name), as his father Amun is with the sun. In later times, Khonsu became identified closely with **Haru-Sa-Aset** and **Haru-Pa-Khered** as the 'divine son' of the 'King of the Neteru.' In the 19th Dynasty, Rameses II sent a statue of Khonsu with great fame for miraculous healing powers to the kingdom of the Bactrians (Bekhten in Khemet), to heal the Bekhteny king's daughter; supposedly of a demon possession. The story of this healing and the statue's part in it can be read in anthologies of many ancient texts.

Fig1.6:
Neter Anubu

Anubu – the Angel of Rapture

Anubu (Anupu; Anpu; Anubis), 'The Royal Child,' a title of pre-dynastic origins; depicted either as a full jackal or as a jackal-headed man, originally known as both embalmer and caretaker of the deceased. He is also known as the guardian of royal burial tombs and of the necropolis. He is the son of Asaru and Nebthet.

8

Masks of Anubu were routinely worn by the priests officiating at funerals and the 70-day mummification processes. Images of him wrapping bandages, pouring oils or embracing the coffin are generally not actually images of the Neter himself, but of his servants doing his work. In later times Anubu, just like Tehuti would be synchronized with the Greek god Hermes, and seen as a messenger or guide of the deceased soul. In Khemetic iconography, he can be seen leading the deceased person into the 'Hall of Double Truth,' where he then weighs the deceased's heart against the feather of Ma'at. Ma'at is the principle of justice and rightness whereas Isfet is the principle of injustice. These are just some of the deities that are echoed in the various Egiptian cosmogonies of Creation. They are of the Involutionary Beings that came with the original Black Dot – Nuqta – El Qubt – Big Bang etc., out of Chaos. But… what exactly is Involution, and how does it compare with the more common term 'evolution?'

9-*ether* & Involution

Involution in creation is to bring about the new. It is to bring *things* into existence for the first time from the essential stuff – with Unconditional Love – or, from that which underlies all that we perceive as parts of creation. This essential stuff called 9-ether, the forces of Creation from out of chaos, the bringing about of *things* for the first time into spiritual embodiment, must be called Involution, as it utilises the undifferentiated essence of Mind. The atom as we know it is but an effect of Involution. It is by far not the first point or act of creation, as it is preceded by planes of sub-atomic particles; the sub-atomic levels of Spirit. The hydrogen atom came at the end of Involution and thus represents the birth of evolution, which ironically is the first sign of a dying Universe – entropy. Evolution is therefore Involution in reverse, the return of infinite Nuqta spirals back into Chaos – Supreme Blackness (see Ch8). Involution is to enwarp; it is to spiral outward from a single point; from the Black Dot – **El Qubt**,[A] the axis of creation. The Black Dot exists only in and of itself; it is self-existing and is self-governing, as the first and last point of reckoning, yet non-existent until manifested as 'All that Is.' NTR, in its undifferentiated Presence also exists only in and of itself, yet non-existent until manifested as Creation itself. Paradoxical? Indeed. Beloved, truth at this level can never really be explained or taught.

The neophyte has to elevate her/ him Self in order to experience and appreciate the latter. The ancients used metaphors as platforms to stand on, which only serve as pointers toward the truth. Involution is the science of spiritual manifestation and embodiment. This phenomenon then proceeds into the physical as evolution, utilising the *phi* ratio based numbers as brought to European attention by Leonardo Fibonacci (which will be exemplified in Ch4). The projection of this perfect mathematical ratio is carried out by Conscience, which is the highest perceivable state of the Self. Contra to Conscience is the ego, where this faculty of Mind is about obscuring our Consciousness from who and what we really are. By realigning with Conscience, one will be blessed to experience existence from within the bosom of the Creator. Conscience utilises Unconditional Love or, it utilises the Undifferentiated NTR to manage, maintain and heal all aspects of creation. *'All we need is Love'* [John Lennon].

Ptah – the Divine Opener

Ptah, pronounced P-taa, (not to be confused with Ta, – the collective term for earth; the 99elements), is the Creative principle that opens and paves the way for 9-ether forces to manifest on this terrain from the Canis Major constellation (fig5.2).

[A] El Qubt is an Arabic term relating to the North and South poles and their relative points. In this context it is relating to the original pole of which all manifested poles are derived from.

Fig1.7: Neter Ptah

The Creator Ptah is one of the many children of NTR, whom are all 9-ether creative forces. He is also the essence of the original Involuted Adam of the original 9-ether black-skinned Afrokhan Melanated peoples of Tamare/ earth. And very much later, the deity Khnum fashioned the Adam of the Hindu and Aryan races through evolution, where their animative Spirit is from Nirvana – a planet of the star Procyon in the Canis Minor constellation (fig5.3).

Ptah is one of the oldest gods of Khemet's many cosmogonies. He was worshipped at Memphis in the first dynasty and probably before that. Ptah was the god of craftsmanship, and therefore the inventions of the arts were attributed to him. One of the first attributes of Ptah was *'Lord of the Master Craftsman.'* By the Pyramid Age, he had assumed the position of Creator God. He created by means of his heart and tongue, as duplications of residual divine rhythmic tones from NTR, thus fashioning the world by the power of his words – vibrations.[5] Ptah was regarded as the ancient one who united in his person the entity Nun, the masculine aspect, and Nunet the feminine aspect. The Ancient Ones knew Ptah as the sculptor of the earth, who, like the god Khnum, created all beings on a potter's wheel. Ptah assimilated the nature of Asaru through his connection with the Memphite earth and mortuary deity, Seker (as Ptah-Seker-Ausar). According to the Memphite theology, Ptah in the form of a hill was the first to emerge from the primeval waters of Nun. He was followed by Atum (Atom) who rose up out of the waters and rested upon the hill. Ptah also represented Divine Mind and Thought, since he conceived of every created thing in his heart and gave utterance to it, bringing it into be*ing*. The actual work of creating was done by Atum, who carried out the utterance of Ptah. Ptah is also represented as a man wrapped as a mummy from below his neck. His

11

hands protrude from a single opening in the front. He holds a scepter composed of the symbols for strength, life, and stability. So, 9-ether and Involution is subsequently existence, before what is known as the '**Event-Horizon**,' which is then proceeded by 6-ether and evolution.

Table 3: triad Principles of Involution and Evolution

9-ether triad Principles of the Involutionary cycle

Atum–Atun–Amun:	the triad forces of Sirius that govern earth
Re–Nun–Atum:	the tri-stages of embodiment (Kaballion, fig2.1)
Ptah–Seker–Asaru:	the tri-stages of manifestation of man through Asaru
Aset–Asaru–Heru:	the trinity of 'life, death and resurrection'

6-ether triad Principles of the evolutionary cycle

Utu–Apsu–Shamash:	from the Babylonian epic of creation
Brahma–Vishnu–Siva:	from the East Indian doctrine
Kronos–Rhea–Zeus:	Greek mythology
Father–Son–Ghost:	from the Christian doctrine

The Event-Horizon

The Event-Horizon on the Universal level is the point of no return as we transit from Involutionary cycles onto evolutionary ones. However, on the Galactical level, scientists and physicists postulate that black holes are the only phenomenon within the Cosmos that can have an Event-Horizon. It is the theorised point of the first increase of entropy[A] – the evidence of the destruction of the Universe.

> '*The event horizon is the one-way 'membrane' that surrounds a black hole. Anything that falls through – whether matter or light – can never get out again.*[6]

Marcus Chown

[A] Entropy in one context is the term used in the measurement of the disordered Universe. In another context it is the measurement of unavailability of a system's thermal energy for conversion into mechanical work.

The Babylonian epic of creation, the Enuma Elish, though addresses creation of our solar system from an evolutionary point of view, was actually orchestrated by 9-ether beings, such as Utu, Apsu and Shamash. This means that despite the nature of evolution being that of entropy and, of the destruction of Involution, it requires a pantheon of super intelligent *Cyclopean*[7] entities to fine-tune the forces that underpin its growth. Once the Event-Horizon has been reached, retardation of the original creation sets in. Thus, we have a slow and sluggish vibration of bi-product forces thereby creating the material representation of the original spiritual Big Bang – the physical creation of the hydrogen atom. Oh yes, the hydrogen atom was indeed the first sign of entropy, as Dr Malachi enlightened us. He said: *"Evolution represents the slow decay of the Universe."*[8] The bi-product forces of 9-ether are that of 6-ether. 9-ether intelligence and Conscience therefore utilised the bi-product forces to create the material world as we know it. Dr Malachi also says that the nature of our world as we have it is destructive and, is of 6-ether intelligence, though it is underpinned by 9-ether intelligence. The nature of the earth is such that in order for one to build, something has to first be destroyed, says Dr Malachi. We merely looked at these implications in volume 1 of the MMSN series, so this is just a reminder for those who have read it… The food we eat had to be killed first – the chicken – the fish; the apple – the banana; the cabbage – the spinach etc. The house we live in and its constituents, are all made (not created!) of raw materials that had to be destroyed first. This way of life and living is consequent (con-sequential) to the result of passing the Universal Event-Horizon, the end of Creation – the regrouping of Conscience – NTR, Anu, Olodumare, Nkulu-Nkulu, Nyame etc. So evolution only occurs on this side of the Horizon of the Event – the return swing after the Events of Involution. The earth according to the Babylonian epic of creation, the Enuma Elish, was created and seeded by beings, after the accidental destruction of a larger planet, Tiamat (the original earth).

The Enuma Elish

The Babylonian 'Epic of Creation – Enuma Elish,' meaning *'When in the heights,'* is written on seven tablets; each is between 115 and 170 lines long, hence the seven days of creation. It supposedly was written no later than the reign of Nebuchadnezzar in the 12th century BCE. Drawing some new light on the ancients, Henry Layard found within the ruins of the library of the Assyrian King Ashurbanipal in Nineveh, texts that were not unlike the Genesis creation in the Bible. However, it is generally accepted that the Enuma Elish was written during the time of the Sumerians, obviously well before the book of Genesis. George Smith first published these texts in 1876 under the title *'The Chaldean Genesis.'* The Babylonian God finished his work within the span of six tablets of stone. The last and seventh stone exalted the handiwork and greatness of the deity's work. Thus the comparison must be made that the seven days of creation found in the Bible borrowed its theme from the Babylonians, who had borrowed it from the Sumerians. The Sumerian epic places Anu, Enlil and Ninurta as the heroes, but, the Babylonian epic stars Marduk. But there is also an Assyrian version, which exalts Yahweh. Some portions of the tablets are therefore illegible.

The First Tablet

When in the height, heaven was not named,
And the earth beneath did not yet bear a name,
And the primeval Apsu, who begat them,
And chaos, Tiamat, the mother of them both
Their waters were mingled together,
And no field was formed, no marsh was to be seen;
When of the gods none had been called into being,
And none bore a name, and no destinies were ordained;
Then were created the gods in the midst of heaven,
Lahmu and Lahamu were called into being...
Ages increased...
Then Anshar and Kishar were created, and over them....
Long were the days, then there came forth....
Anu, their son...
Anshar and Anu...

Fig1.8: Depiction of Anshar

And the god Anu...
Nudimmud, whom his fathers, his begetters....
Abounding in all wisdom...
He was exceeding strong...
He had no rival...
Thus were established and were... the great gods.
But Tiamat and Apsu were still in confusion...
They were troubled and...
In disorder...
Apsu was not diminished in might...
And Tiamat roared...
She smote, and their deeds...
Their way was evil...
Then Apsu, the begetter of the great gods,
Cried unto Mummu, his minister, and said unto him:
"O Mummu, thou minister that rejoicest my spirit,
Come, unto Tiamat let us go!
So they went and before Tiamat they lay down,
they consulted on a plan with regard to the gods, their sons.
Apsu opened his mouth and spake,
And unto Tiamat, the glistening one, he addressed the word:
...their way...
By day I can not rest, by night I can not lie down in peace.
But I will destroy their way, I will...
Let there be lamentation, and let us lie down again in peace."
When Tiamat heard these words,
She raged and cried aloud...
She... grievously...
She uttered a curse, and unto Apsu she spake:
"What then shall we do?
Let their way be made difficult, and let us lie down again in peace."
Mummu answered, and gave counsel unto Apsu,
...and hostile to the gods was the counsel Mummu gave:
"Come, their way is strong, but thou shalt destroy it;
Then by day shalt thou have rest, by night shalt thou lie down in peace."
Apsu harkened unto him and his countenance grew bright,
since he (Mummu) planned evil against the gods his sons.
... He was afraid...,
His knees became weak; they gave way beneath him,
Because of the evil which their first-born had planned.
... their... they altered.
... they...,
Lamentation they sat in sorrow...
Then Ea, who knoweth all that is, went up and he beheld their muttering.

Fig1.9: Depiction of Ea/ Enqi

[about 30 illegible lines]

... he spake:
... thy... he hath conquered and
... he weepeth and sitteth in tribulation.
... of fear,
... we shall not lie down in peace.
... Apsu is laid waste,
... and Mummu, who were taken captive, in...
... thou didst...
... let us lie down in peace.
... they will smite....
... let us lie down in peace.
... thou shalt take vengeance for them,
... unto the tempest shalt thou...!"

Fig1.10:
Tablets of Shamash

And Tiamat harkened unto the word of the bright god, and said:
... "Shalt thou entrust! Let us wage war!"
... the gods in the midst of...
... for the gods did she create.

They banded themselves together and at the side of Tiamat they advanced;
They were furious; they devised mischief without resting night and day.
They prepared for battle, fuming and raging;
They joined their forces and made war,
Ummu-Hubur [Tiamat] who formed all things,
Made in addition weapons invincible; she spawned monster-serpents,
Sharp of tooth, and merciless of fang;
With poison, instead of blood, she filled their bodies.
Fierce monster-vipers she clothed with terror,
With splendour she decked them, she made them of lofty stature.
Whoever beheld them, terror overcame him,
Their bodies reared up and none could withstand their attack.

She set up vipers and dragons, and the monster Lahamu,
And hurricanes, and raging hounds, and scorpion-men,
And mighty tempests, and fish-men, and rams;
They bore cruel weapons, without fear of the fight.
Her commands were mighty, none could resist them;
After this fashion, huge of stature, she made eleven [kinds of] monsters.
Among the gods who were her sons, inasmuch as he had given her support,
She exalted Kingu; in their midst she raised him to power.
To march before the forces, to lead the host,
To give the battle-signal, to advance to the attack,
To direct the battle, to control the fight,
Unto him she entrusted; in costly raiment she made him sit, saying:
"I have uttered thy spell, in the assembly of the gods I have raised thee to power.
The dominion over all the gods have I entrusted unto him.
Be thou exalted, thou my chosen spouse,
May they magnify thy name over all of them the Anunnaki."

She gave him the Tablets of Destiny, on his breast she laid them, saying:
"Thy command shall not be without avail, and the word of thy mouth shall be established."
Now Kingu, thus exalted, having received the power of Anu,
Decreed the fate among the gods his sons, saying:
"Let the opening of your mouth quench the Fire-god;
Whoso is exalted in the battle, let him display his might!"

Fig1.11:
Creation of first man by the Anunnaqi; Laboratory vessels and Tree of Life; and, Anu sent Enqi and his followers to Earth to live.

Fig1.12:
Enqi with the Gods and the Initiate. The Water of Life flowing into the laboratory glassware indicates alchemical circulations.

The Second Tablet

Tiamat made weighty her handiwork,
Evil she wrought against the gods her children.
To avenge Apsu, Tiamat planned evil,
But how she had collected her forces, the god unto Ea divulged.
Ea harkened to this thing, and
He was grievously afflicted and he sat in sorrow.
The days went by, and his anger was appeased,
And to the place of Anshar his father he took his way.
He went and, standing before Anshar, the father who begat him,
All that Tiamat had plotted he repeated unto him,
Saying, "Tiamat our mother hath conceived a hatred for us,
With all her force she rageth, full of wrath.
All the gods have turned to her,
With those, whom ye created, they go at her side.
They are banded together and at the side of Tiamat they advance;
They are furious, they devise mischief without resting night and day.
They prepare for battle, fuming and raging;
They have joined their forces and are making war.
Ummu-Hubur, who formed all things,
Hath made in addition weapons invincible; she hath spawned monster-serpents,
Sharp of tooth, and merciless of fang.
With poison, instead of blood, she hath filled their bodies.
Fierce monster-vipers she hath clothed with terror,
With splendour she hath decked them; she hath made them of lofty stature.
Whoever beholdeth them is overcome by terror,
Their bodies rear up and none can withstand their attack.
She hath set up vipers, and dragons, and the monster Lahamu,
And hurricanes and raging hounds, and scorpion-men,
And mighty tempests, and fish-men and rams;
They bear cruel weapons, without fear of the fight.
Her commands are mighty; none can resist them;
After this fashion, huge of stature, hath she made eleven monsters.
Among the gods who are her sons, inasmuch as he hath given her support,
She hath exalted Kingu; in their midst she hath raised him to power.
To march before the forces, to lead the host,
To give the battle-signal, to advance to the attack.
To direct the battle, to control the fight,
Unto him hath she entrusted; in costly raiment she hath made him sit, saving:
I have uttered thy spell; in the assembly of the gods I have raised thee to power,
The dominion over all the gods have I entrusted unto thee.
Be thou exalted, thou my chosen spouse,
May they magnify thy name over all of them
She hath given him the Tablets of Destiny, on his breast she laid them, saying:
"my command shall not be without avail, and the word of thy mouth shall be established."
Now Kingu, thus exalted, having received the power of Anu,

18

Decreed the fate for the gods, her sons, saying:
"Let the opening of your mouth quench the Fire-god;
Whoso is exalted in the battle, let him display his might!"
When Anshar heard how Tiamat was mightily in revolt,
he bit his lips, his mind was not at peace,
..., he made a bitter lamentation:
... battle,
... thou...
Mummu and Apsu thou hast smitten
But Tiamat hath exalted Kingu, and where is one who can oppose her?
... deliberation
... the ... of the gods, Nudimmud.

[A gap of about a dozen lines occurs here.]

Anshar unto his son addressed the word:
"... my mighty hero,
Whose strength is great and whose onslaught cannot be withstood,
Go and stand before Tiamat,
That her spirit may be appeased, that her heart may be merciful.
But if she will not harken unto thy word,
Our word shalt thou speak unto her, that she may be pacified."
He heard the word of his father Anshar
And he directed his path to her, toward her he took the way.
And drew nigh, he beheld the muttering of Tiamat,
But he could not withstand her, and he turned back.
... Anshar
... he spake unto him:

[A gap of over twenty lines occurs here.]

An avenger...
... valiant
... in the place of his decision
... he spake unto him:
... thy father
"Thou art my son, who maketh merciful his heart.
... to the battle shalt thou draw nigh,
he that shall behold thee shall have peace."
And the lord rejoiced at the word of his father,
And he drew nigh and stood before Anshar.
Anshar beheld him and his heart was filled with joy,
He kissed him on the lips and his fear departed from him.
"O my father, let not the word of thy lips be overcome,
Let me go, that I may accomplish all that is in thy heart.
O Anshar, let not the word of thy lips be overcome,
Let me go, that I may accomplish all that is in thy heart."

What man is it, who hath brought thee forth to battle?
... Tiamat, who is a woman, is armed and attacketh thee.
... rejoice and be glad;
The neck of Tiamat shalt thou swiftly trample under foot.
... rejoice and be glad;
The neck of Tiamat shalt thou swiftly trample under foot.
0 my son, who knoweth all wisdom,
Pacify Tiamat with thy pure incantation.
Speedily set out upon thy way,
For thy blood shall not be poured out; thou shalt return again."
The lord rejoiced at the word of his father,
His heart exulted, and unto his father he spake:
"O Lord of the gods, Destiny of the great gods,
If I, your avenger,
Conquer Tiamat and give you life,
Appoint an assembly, make my fate pre-eminent and proclaim it
In Upsukkinaku seat yourself joyfully together,
With my word in place of you will I decree fate.
May whatsoever I do remain unaltered,
May the word of my lips never be chanced nor made of no avail."

The Third Tablet

Anshar opened his mouth, and
Unto Gaga, his minister, spake the word.
"O Gaga, thou minister that rejoicest my spirit,
Unto Lahmu and Lahamu will I send thee.
... Thou canst attain,
... thou shalt cause to be brought before thee.
... let the gods, all of them,
Make ready for a feast, at a banquet let them sit,
Let them eat bread, let them mix wine,
That for Marduk, their avenger they may decree the fate.
Go, Gaga, stand before them,
And all that I tell thee, repeat unto them, and say:
That he may go and fight your strong enemy.
Gaga went, he took his way and
Humbly before Lahmu and Lahamu, the gods, his fathers,
He made obeisance, and he kissed the ground at their feet.
He humbled himself; then he stood up and spake unto them saying:
"Anshar, your son, hath sent me,
The purpose of his heart he hath made known unto me.
He saith that Tiamat our mother hath conceived a hatred for us,
With all her force she rageth, full of wrath.
All the gods have turned to her,
With those, whom ye created, they go at her side.

They are banded together and at the side of Tiamat they advance;
They are furious, they devise mischief without resting night and day.
They prepare for battle, fuming and raging;
They have joined their forces and are making war.
Ummu-Hubur, who formed all things,
Hath made in addition weapons invincible; she hath spawned monster-serpents,
Sharp of tooth and merciless of fang.
With poison, instead of blood, she hath filled their bodies.
Fierce monster-vipers she hath clothed with terror,
With splendour she hath decked them, she hath made them of lofty stature.
Whoever beholdeth them, terror overcometh him,
Their bodies rear up and none can withstand their attack.
She hath set up vipers, and dragons, and the monster Lahamu,
And hurricanes, and raging hounds, and scorpion-men,
And mighty tempests, and fish-men, and rams;
They bear merciless weapons, without fear of the fight.
Her commands are mighty; none can resist them;
After this fashion, huge of stature, hath she made eleven monsters.
Among the gods who are her sons, inasmuch as he hath given her support,
She hath exalted Kingu; in their midst she hath raised him to power.
To march before the forces, to lead the host,
To give the battle-signal, to advance to the attack, To direct the battle, to control the fight,
Unto him hath she entrusted; in costly raiment she hath made him sit, saying:
I have uttered thy spell; in the assembly of the gods I have raised thee to power,
The dominion over all the gods have I entrusted unto thee.
Be thou exalted, thou my chosen spouse,
May they magnify thy name over all of them...the Anunnaki.
She hath given him the Tablets of Destiny on his breast she laid them, saying:
Thy command shall not be without avail, and the word of thy mouth shall be established.
Now Kingu, thus exalted, having received the power of Anu,
Decreed the fate for the gods, her sons, saying:
"Let the opening of your mouth quench the Fire-god;
Whoso is exalted in the battle, let him display his might!"
I sent Anu, but he could not withstand her;
Nudimmud was afraid and turned back.
But Marduk hath set out, the director of the gods, your son;
To set out against Tiamat his heart hath prompted him.
He opened his mouth and spake unto me, saying:
"If I, your avenger,
Conquer Tiamat and give you life,
Appoint an assembly, make my fate pre-eminent and proclaim it.
In Upsukkinaku seat yourselves joyfully together;
With my word in place of you will I decree fate.
May, whatsoever I do remain unaltered,
May the word of my lips never be changed nor made of no avail."
Hasten, therefore, and swiftly decree for him the fate which you bestow,
That he may go and fight your strong enemy!

21

Lahmu and Lahamu heard and cried aloud
All of the Igigi [The elder gods] wailed bitterly, saying:
What has been altered so that they should
We do not understand the deed of Tiamat!
Then did they collect and go,
The great gods, all of them, who decree fate.
They entered in before Anshar, they filled...
They kissed one another, in the assembly...;
They made ready for the feast, at the banquet they sat;
They ate bread, they mixed sesame-wine.
The sweet drink, the mead, confused their...
They were drunk with drinking, their bodies were filled.
They were wholly at ease, their spirit was exalted;
Then for Marduk, their avenger, did they decree the fate.

The Fourth Tablet

They prepared for him a lordly chamber,
Before his fathers as prince he took his place.
"Thou art chiefest among the great gods,
Thy fate is unequalled thy word is Anu!
0 Marduk, thou art chiefest among the great gods,
Thy fate is unequalled, thy word is Anu!
Henceforth not without avail shall be thy command,
In thy power shall it be to exalt and to abase.
Established shall be the word of thy mouth,
irresistible shall be thy command,
None among the gods shall transgress thy boundary.
Abundance, the desire of the shrines of the gods,
Shall be established in thy sanctuary, even though they lack offerings.
O Marduk, thou art our avenger!
We give thee sovereignty over the whole world.
Sit thou down in might; be exalted in thy command.
Thy weapon shall never lose its power; it shall crush thy foe.
O Lord, spare the life of him that putteth his trust in thee,
But as for the god who began the rebellion, pour out his life."
Then set they in their midst a garment,
And unto Marduk,- their first-born they spake:
"May thy fate, O lord, be supreme among the gods,
To destroy and to create; speak thou the word,
and thy command shall be fulfilled.
Command now and let the garment vanish;
And speak the word again and let the garment reappear!
Then he spake with his mouth, and the garment vanished;
Again he commanded it, and the garment reappeared.
When the gods, his fathers, beheld the fulfilment of his word,
They rejoiced, and they did homage unto him, saying, " Marduk is king!"

They bestowed upon him the scepter, and the throne, and the ring,
They give him an invincible weaponry which overwhelmed thee foe.
Go, and cut off the life of Tiamat,
And let the wind carry her blood into secret places."
After the gods his fathers had decreed for the lord his fate,
They caused him to set out on a path of prosperity and success.
He made ready the bow, he chose his weapon,
He slung a spear upon him and fastened it...
He raised the club, in his right hand he grasped it,
The bow and the quiver he hung at his side.
He set the lightning in front of him,
With burning flame he filled his body.
He made a net to enclose the inward parts of Tiamat,
The four winds he stationed so that nothing of her might escape;
The South wind and the North wind and the East wind and the West wind.
He brought near to the net, the gift of his father Anu.
He created the evil wind, and the tempest, and the hurricane,
And the fourfold wind, and the sevenfold wind,
and the whirlwind, and the wind which had no equal;
He sent forth the winds which he bad created, the seven of them;
To disturb the inward parts of Tiamat, they followed after him.
Then the lord raised the thunderbolt, his mighty weapon,
He mounted the chariot, the storm unequalled for terror,
He harnessed and yoked unto it four horses,
Destructive, ferocious, overwhelming, and swift of pace;
... were their teeth, they were flecked with foam;
They were skilled in..., they had been trained to trample underfoot.
.... mighty in battle,
Left and right....
His garment was... , he was clothed with terror,
With overpowering brightness his head was crowned.
Then he set out, he took his way,
And toward the raging Tiamat he set his face.
On his lips he held ...,
... he grasped in his hand.
Then they beheld him, the gods beheld him,
The gods his fathers beheld him, the gods beheld him.
And the lord drew nigh, he gazed upon the inward parts of Tiamat,
He perceived the muttering of Kingu, her spouse.
As Marduk gazed, Kingu was troubled in his gait.
His will was destroyed and his motions ceased.
And the gods, his helpers, who marched by his side,
Beheld their leader's..., and their sight was troubled.
But Tiamat... , she turned not her neck,
With lips that failed not she uttered rebellious words:
"... thy coming as lord of the gods,
From their places have they gathered, in thy place are they!"

23

Then the lord raised the thunderbolt, his mighty weapon,
And against Tiamat, who was raging, thus he sent the word:
Thou art become great, thou hast exalted thyself on high,
And thy heart hath prompted thee to call to battle.
... their fathers...,
... their... thou hatest...
Thou hast exalted Kingu to be thy spouse,
Thou hast... him, that, even as Anu, he should issue decrees.
Thou hast followed after evil,
And against the gods my fathers thou hast
contrived thy wicked plan.
Let then thy host be equipped, let thy weapons be girded on!
Stand! I and thou, let us join battle!
When Tiamat heard these words,
She was like one possessed; she lost her reason.
Tiamat uttered wild, piercing cries,
She trembled and shook to her very foundations.
She recited an incantation, she pronounced her spell,
And the gods of the battle cried out for their weapons.
Then advanced Tiamat and Marduk, the counsellor of the gods;
To the fight they came on, to the battle they drew nigh.
The lord spread out his net and caught her,
And the evil wind that was behind him he let loose in her face.
As Tiamat opened her mouth to its full extent,
He drove in the evil wind, while as yet she had not shut her lips.
The terrible winds filled her belly,
And her courage was taken from her,
and her mouth she opened wide.
He seized the spear and burst her belly,
He severed her inward parts, he pierced her heart.
He overcame her and cut off her life;
He cast down her body and stood upon it.
When be had slain Tiamat, the leader,
Her might was broken, her host was scattered.
And the gods her helpers, who marched by her side,
Trembled, and were afraid, and turned back.
They took to flight to save their lives;
But they were surrounded, so that they could not escape.
He took them captive, he broke their weapons;
In the net they were caught and in the snare they sat down.
The ... of the world they filled with cries of grief.
They received punishment from him, they were held in bondage.
And on the eleven creatures which she had filled with the power of striking terror,
Upon the troop of devils, who marched at her...,
He brought affliction, their strength he...;
Them and their opposition he trampled under his feet.
Moreover, Kingu, who had been exalted over them,

24

He conquered, and with the god Dug-ga he counted him.
He took from him the Tablets of Destiny that were not rightly his,
He sealed them with a seal and in his own breast he laid them.
Now after the hero Marduk had conquered and cast down his enemies,
And had made the arrogant foe even like...
And had fully established Anshar's triumph over the enemy
And had attained the purpose of Nudimmud,
Over the captive gods he strengthened his durance,
And unto Tiamat, whom he bad conquered, he returned.
And the lord stood upon Tiamat's hinder parts,
And with his merciless club he smashed her skull.
He cut through the channels of her blood,
And he made the North wind bear it away into secret places.
His fathers beheld, and they rejoiced and were glad;
Presents and gifts they brought unto him.
Then the lord rested, gazing upon her dead body,
While he divided the flesh of the ... , and devised a cunning plan.
He split her up like a flat fish into two halves;
One half of her he established as a covering for heaven.
He fixed a bolt, he stationed a watchman,
And bade them not to let her waters come forth.
He passed through the heavens, he surveyed the regions thereof,
And over against the Deep he set the dwelling of Nudimmud.
And the lord measured the structure of the Deep,
And he founded E-Sara, a mansion like unto it.
The mansion E-Sara which he created as heaven,
He caused Anu, Bel, and Ea in their districts to inhabit.

The Fifth Tablet

He (Marduk) made the stations for the great gods;
The stars, their images, as the stars of the Zodiac, he fixed.
He ordained the year and into sections he divided it;
For the twelve months he fixed three stars.
After he had ... the days of the year ... images,
He founded the station of Nibiru
to determine their bounds;
That none might err or go astray,
He set the station of Bel and Ea along with him.
He opened great gates on both sides,
He made strong the bolt on the left and on the right.
In the midst thereof he fixed the zenith;
The Moon-god he caused to shine forth, the night he entrusted to him.
He appointed him, a being of the night, to determine the days;
Every month without ceasing with the crown he covered him, saying:
"At the beginning of the month, when thou shinest upon the land,
Thou commandest the horns to determine six days,

25

And on the seventh day to divide the crown.
On the fourteenth day thou shalt stand opposite, the half...
When the Sun-god on the foundation of heaven...thee,
The ... thou shalt cause to ..., and thou shalt make his...
... unto the path of the Sun-god shalt thou cause to draw nigh,
And on the ... day thou shalt stand opposite, and the Sun-god shall...
... to traverse her way.
... thou shalt cause to draw nigh, and thou shalt judge the right.
... to destroy..."

[Nearly fifty lines are lost from here.]

The gods, his fathers, beheld the net which he had made,
They beheld the bow and how its work was accomplished.
They praised the work which he had done...
Then Anu raised the ... in the assembly of the gods.
He kissed the bow, saving, "It is...!"
And thus he named the names of the bow, saving,
'Long-wood' shall be one name, and the second name shall be ...,
And its third name shall be the Bow-star, in heaven shall it...!"
Then he fixed a station for it...
Now after the fate of...
He set a throne...
...in heaven...

[The remainder of this tablet is missing]

The Sixth Tablet

When Marduk beard the word of the gods,
His heart prompted him and he devised a cunning plan.
He opened his mouth and unto Ea he spake that which he had conceived in his heart he imparted unto him:
"My blood will I take and bone will I fashion
I will make man, that man may...
I will create man who shall inhabit the earth,
That the service of the gods may be established,
and that their shrines may be built.
But I will alter the ways of the gods, and I will change their paths;
Together shall they be oppressed and unto evil shall they...
And Ea answered him and spake the word:
"... the ... of the gods I have changed
... and one...
... shall be destroyed and men will I...
... and the gods.
... and they..."

[The rest of the text is lacking, with the exception of the last few lines of the tablet, which read as follows.]

They rejoiced...
In Upsukkinaku they set their dwelling.
Of the heroic son, their avenger, they cried:
"We, whom he succoured.... !"
They seated themselves and in the assembly they named him...,
They all cried aloud, they exalted him...

The Seventh Tablet

O Asaru, [Marduk] "Bestower of planting," "Founder of sowing"
"Creator of grain and plants," "who caused the green herb to spring up!"
O Asaru-alim, [Marduk] "who is revered in the house of counsel," "who aboundeth in counsel,"
The gods paid homage, fear took hold upon them!
O Asaru-alim-nuna, [Marduk] "the Mighty One," "the Light of the father who begat him,"
"Who directeth the decrees of Anu, Bel, and Ea!"
He was their patron, be ordained their...;
He, whose provision is abundance, goeth forth...
Tutu [Marduk] is "He who created them anew";
Should their wants be pure, then are they satisfied;
Should he make an incantation, then are the gods appeased;
Should they attack him in anger, he withstandeth their onslaught!
Let him therefore be exalted, and in the assembly of the gods let him...;
None among the gods can rival him!
15 Tutu [Marduk] is Zi-ukkina, "the Life of the host of the gods,"
Who established for the gods the bright heavens.
He set them on their way, and ordained their path;
Never shall his ... deeds be forgotten among men.
Tutu as Zi-azag thirdly they named, "the Bringer of Purification,"
"The God of the Favouring Breeze," "the Lord of Hearing and Mercy,"
"The Creator of Fullness and Abundance," " the Founder of Plenteousness,"
"Who increaseth all that is small."
In sore distress we felt his favouring breeze,"
Let them say, let them pay reverence, let them bow in humility before him!
Tutu as Aga-azag may mankind fourthly magnify!
"The Lord of the Pure Incantation," " the Quickener of the Dead,"
"Who had mercy upon the captive gods,"
"Who removed the yoke from upon the gods his enemies,"
"For their forgiveness did he create mankind,"
"The Merciful One, with whom it is to bestow life!"
May his deeds endure, may they never be forgotten,
In the mouth of mankind whom his hands have made!
Tutu as Mu-azag, fifthly, his "Pure incantation" may their mouth proclaim,
Who through his Pure Incantation hath destroyed all the evil ones!"
Sag-zu, [Marduk] "who knoweth the heart of the gods," " who seeth through the innermost part!"

"The evil-doer he hath not caused to go forth with him!"
"Founder of the assembly of the gods," who ... their heart!"
"Subduer of the disobedient," "...!"
"Director of Righteousness," "...,"
" Whose rebellion and...!"
Tutu as Zi-si, "the ...,"
"Who put an end to anger," "who...!"
Tutu as Suh-kur, thirdly, "the Destroyer of the foe,"
"Who put their plans to confusion,"
"Who destroyed all the wicked," "...,"
... let them... !

[A gap of sixty lines exists here. The following fragments belong among the lost lines.]

who...
He named the four quarters of the world, mankind he created,
And upon him understanding...
"The mighty one...!"
Agil...
"The Creator of the earth...!"
Zulummu...
"The Giver of counsel and of whatsoever...!"
Mummu, "the Creator of...!"
Mulil, the heavens...,
"Who for...!"
Giskul, let...,
"Who brought the gods to naught....!"
... "the Chief of all lords,"
... supreme is his might!
Lugal-durmah, "the King of the band of the gods," " the Lord of rulers."
"Who is exalted in a royal habitation,"
"Who among the gods is gloriously supreme!
Adu-nuna, "the Counsellor of Ea," who created the gods his fathers,
Unto the path of whose majesty
No god can ever attain!
... in Dul-azag be made it known,
... pure is his dwelling!
... the... of those without understanding is Lugaldul-azaga!
... supreme is his might!
... their... in the midst of Tiamat,
... of the battle!

[Here follows the better-preserved ending.]

... the star, which shineth in the heavens.
May he hold the Beginning and the Future, may they pay homage unto him,

Saying, "He who forced his way through the midst of Tiamat without resting,
Let his name be Nibiru, "the Seizer of the Midst!"
For the stars of heaven he upheld the paths,
He shepherded all the gods like sheep!
He conquered Tiamat, he troubled and ended her life,
In the future of mankind, when the days grow old,
May this be heard without ceasing; may it hold sway forever!
Since he created the realm of heaven and fashioned the firm earth,
The Lord of the World, the father Bel hath called his name.
This title, which all the Spirits of Heaven proclaimed,
Did Ea hear, and his spirit was rejoiced, and he said:
"He whose name his fathers have made glorious,
Shall be even as I, his name shall be Ea!
The binding of all my decrees shall he control,
All my commands shall he make known!"
By the name of "Fifty" did the great gods
Proclaim his fifty names, they, made his path pre-eminent.

Epilogue

Let them [i.e. the names of Marduk] be held in remembrances and let the first man proclaim them;
Let the wise and the understanding consider them together!
Let the father repeat them and teach them to his son;
Let them be in the ears of the pastor and the shepherd!
Let a man rejoice in Marduk, the Lord of the gods,
That he may cause his land to be fruitful, and that he himself may have prosperity!
His word standeth fast, his command is unaltered;
The utterance of his mouth hath no god ever annulled.
He gazed in his anger, he turned not his neck;
When he is wroth, no god can withstand his indignation.
Wide is his heart, broad is his compassion;
The sinner and evil-doer in his presence...
They received instruction, they spake before him,
... unto...
... of Marduk may the gods...;
... May they ... his name... !
... they took and...

Summary of the epics

There is more than enough information throughout the seven tablets that indicates the extremely high probability of the origins of the biblical accounts of creation. For example in volume 1, I wrote of the Sumerian accounts of the four angels and the four winds, which is found

29

in the books of Ezekiel and Revelation. This is with respect to the creation or recreation as it were, of our solar system and its formation of planets according to the Sumerians and Babylonians. Here, as presented above, the reader will be able to see and scrutinise one transliteration of what is actually written on these tablets. Only by diligent study of the accounts presented here, and by comparing it with other writers of Sumerian and Babylonian antiquity, then having revisit to the books of Genesis, Ezekiel and Revelation, will you be able to get the context of the bigger picture. And, for those of us whom are highly intuitive, our Higher Self, Conscience, will give us the desired level of understanding as we ask.

Fig1.13:
Cylinder seal VA/243 from a museum in Germany, about 2,500BCE. The upper left corner has a picture of a solar system. What is in the center? Were you told in school that the ancients knew the sun was in the center? Count the orbiting planets around the sun. Include our moon and one extra planet and you will notice the number is correct for our solar system. There are 9 known planets all represented in this seal. When were Pluto and Neptune discovered? When you count the sun, moon and Nibiru as part of our solar system the number of objects is 12.

Evolution, on the more accepted academic levels; of anthropology for instance, teaches us of the growth and development of earth's species of plant life, aquatic and marine life, fowls and birds of the air etc., and of course mammalian life, including mankind. These are all 6-ether based phenomenons, existing by the laws of entropy, as we move toward a total Ghostation of these bi-product forces, heading toward the ultimate Black Hole. Entropy, associated with the 'plank constant,' is the second law of thermodynamics. This law states that energy is never created nor destroyed. Energy (ether) has always existed – it transforms from phenomenon to phenomenon – it is a phantasmagoria of be*ing* that can only be scrutinised by beings experiencing the Magical Paths of not-self, within the realms of 6-ether and evolution. For, a spiritual entity that has never had a corporeal embodiment will not understand or know energy – therefore, material existence is imperative for such a privilege of learning of Self.

6-ether & Evolution

According to Richard Gerber, Creation and everything within it is underpinned by one essential substance, which is energy, and is a regardless fact whether one chooses to accept a creationist theory or an evolutionist one. Therefore, the evolution of matter on into *things* is but a crystallisation of light and energy of the Creator, which itself is Pure Consciousness. [Paraphrased].

Evolution in creation is to cause spiritual forces to grow into material manifestation within the Physical Plane, the plane of evolutionary forces. It is the results of Involution; the final stages of Involution; and, is also the reciprocal of Involution. Evolution is the process of which spiritually created *things,* after their manifesting physically, are regrouped back into the essential stuff. Evolution on earth therefore begins at its relative Event-Horizon.[A] The Principles of evolution in creation constitute the attributes of growth. The word 'growth' means to <u>change</u> the form or composition of a created *thing*. And so evolution means to grow or develop a system over a period, to the point of full enlightenment. Another way to view it is like this: Involution from a primary source (NTRU) toward physical embodiment, can cause the 'conscientious being' to suffer amnesia if she/ he gets caught up in the meddling of earthly or material *things*. But then evolution, on the adverse provides a vehicle for the now 'egoic being' to unburden its soul and re-establish cosmic memory.

The physical god-body is a vessel of much learning and enlightenment. It allows for us humans to live a life of spiritual development whilst residing within a materialistic domain. Though we are living in a three-dimensional world, our consciousness ought to be at least fourth dimensional, and above. We can therefore be *'within the world but not of it,'* as taught by Brother Sananda,[B] another celestial sibling of Tehuti and them. Both the Mystical and Magical Paths for the neophyte present cosmic dances, with which the ebb and fro from chaos to order and back again, channels the student to realise an all-inclusive system.

Fig1.14: Order Vs Chaos

The creation of the hydrogen atom and its evolution toward many other atomic structures signifies the end of Involution, because, the

---

[A] Although Dr Malachi does not speak much of the Event-Horizon, he does speak of 6-ether evolution and its beginnings on earth some 17,250,000years ago.
[B] Sananda is the Galactical name for Christ Jesus.

physical manifestations of creation signifies the fact that God/ Conscience has completed its work. Physical manifestation through evolution represents the reverse of Involution, the entropy of the Universe... the swinging pendulum, or the reclining dance of yin and yang forces toward stillness. Though the material world appears to be well ordered, it is in fact a complete disorder of Divine order. Divine order is chaos – as in the Presence of Consciousness and Be*ing*, without any manifestation; the absence of mental thought; existence as the 'I AM Presence.' Fig1.14 expresses chaos, the mist of 9-ether forces prior to Involution and without intention, as the 'I AM Presence.' Anticipation however, creates intention and thus Involution begins by virtue of the fact that a Mental thought occurred. Then on the contrary we eventually have material manifestation, order, and a crystallisation of 9-ether bi-product energies, glued together by Spirit. Manifestation and order in this manner brings chaos to the Universal Mind – paradoxically. The bi-product energies of these 9-ether forces are that of 6-ether energies or forces. 6-ether, the death of 9-ether is utilised by the Universal Mind to create the entropy of the created Universe, the reversal of created *things* back into the Nuqta via its corresponding Black Hole (fig8.1). So therefore we have evolution by way of 6-ether forces.

6-ether in turn will reach its own degrees of an Event-Horizon, where its energies reach the point of ensuing Ghostation. The Universe, on all levels, is analogous to the birth, development, growth and eventual decay of the human body. I.e., there comes a point when the rate of which our cells replicate has become much, much slower than the rate of which living cells decay. This means that we have reached a point of no return – we will inevitably die as a result of rapid increases in bodily entropy. This is only true since we have forgotten that death is but an illness. In such a situation, 6-ether gives off a bi-product of itself – this Dr Malachi has termed 3-ether or, the Ghostation of ether – also called ghost-spirit.

3-ether & Ghost

To substantiate the above according to Dr Malachi, in nature there are two types of spirit – 'ether-spirit' and 'ghost-spirit.' Ether spirit he says: is "the spirit of the Etherians," of which there are 2 levels – 9-ether and 6-ether, as already explained. The second of the two types of spirit, 3-ether or ghost-ether, is of the third level of creation, which is called 'tertiary creation,'[9] produced by the bi-products of 6-ether forces. This we have as the manifestation of the Caucasian race. Also note that most if not all root races of the planet have in their antiquity, writings that speak of the creation of the White race, as a manifestation of a degenerated recessive gene, from within their own DNA. The first question you might ask yourself is "which one of the stories is the correct one?" Well, they all are inasmuch that they all produced a ghosted or Caucasoid version of themselves, based on the hereditary genetic traits of melanin recessive genes within the DNA of that said people. Other names for the original 'White man' include the *Hallubeans* (who later became known as the Neanderthal man, who were over-ridden by the Cro-Magnon man) and the *Flugelrods*. The most common term however is the *Caucasian*. One strain of the Flugelrods, after migrating from the Caucasus Mountains onto Russia, became known as the Khazars. The Khazars of today are the unseen writers and rulers of our western societies. In chapter 7 we will look more into the Khazars and the 24 protocols of Zion – stemming from the code of Hammurabi. Some of the ancient cultures of antiquity also speak of how their elder scientists actually created, laboratory style (through gene splicing), the White race, such as Yaquub's graftation of the Caucasian from the Asiatic Black man. The biblical account of the origin of the White race, though not completely obvious on the face of it, is none other than the descending tribes of Ham via Canaan – the Canaanites. Not all Canaanites are White however; there are Black Canaanite tribes as well, descending from Hammath. Gene splicing...? Graftations...? Is this *truth* in reality, or would nature have produced them anyway? Would the White man and his descendant Mulattos be predetermined by the forces of nature?

The latter is inescapably correct and ineluctable since 6-ether forces subsequently grew all physically existing species of mankind of planet earth. The Supreme Gods however, whom are 9-ether, biblically called *Seraphim,* existed etherically prior to the Universal Event-Horizon. These are the melanin dominant Nubian black-skinned Gods spoken of by all Afrokhan tribes and cultures. These are the super-intelligent conscientious beings that Involutes the Universe from the Nuqta right through to the eventual evolutionary cycles. They manifest on earth (by way of Ptah, Asaru, Atum, Olodumare, Nkulu-Nkulu etc.) as the woolly haired blacks, which, in their purest of states cannot be physically or spiritually influenced by lesser entities.

The lesser gods, whom also existed etherically, biblically called *Cherubims,* are 6-ether entities or forces – the bi-product of 9-ether. These entities manifest on earth (by way of Khnum's manipulation of Nirvana forces) as the melanin recessive straight-haired black-skinned Hindus of Indonesia, of which evolution ultimately produced their ghosted version – the Caucasian race. With a situation as complicated as this is, (i.e., a 3-dimensional bottle, that occupies three different types of mind-sets), what are the implications of let's say, Involutionary beings existing within evolutionary cycles?

The Implications
    It is of no wonder that blacks of the western world and even many of those of the Afrokhan and Eastern worlds have fallen from their divinity. Black peoples have exponentially fallen periodically, over what seems like thousands of years, toward degeneration of cultural heritage, legacy and antiquity. We have taken on the Mental faculties of the Asiatic Hindu, and the European and Aryan races, which have taken us completely off the path of our spiritual covenant. The fittest shall

survive one might say. The Eastern and Aryan races are living within a cycle of evolution that is conducive for their type of be*ing*. The earth currently occupies an envelop that is supportive and beneficial to evolutionary species such as the anthropoidian evolutionary man, – the evolution of animals – the birds – the fishes – and plant life etc., but not completely supportive or beneficial to Nubians. The implications are obvious. All one has to do is look at the history of Afrokhans and blacks of the West Indies, when since they started allowing whites to enter into their domains. This is why Afrokhan culture has been a very strict and stringent system of living. We had to observe a very tight way of life, as this planet is such a hostile place for us. Just think… of all the species of humans and animals on the planet, with the exception of the sheep, which were genetically created, Afrokhans are the only beings with naturally occurring wooly hair. This says that there is something unique about us. Our home is in the heavens, in and beyond the stars, on into ether, for we existed before evolution. Our culture involves consistent communication and reconnection with the Ancestors, via specific spiritual forces and via a specific Consciousness envelop.

This is where Tehuti and the elder Gods step to the stage. They created a fourth dimensional bottle within the Earth Plane in order for Nubians, having been rooted with the 'Law of One' doctrine as a part of our heritage, to function according to our Universal potential. This bottle, also referred to as an artificial Christ-Consciousness grid, was created during Lemurian times, where the earth was roaming with fourth and fifth-dimensional beings, governed by the 'Law of One.' We have forgotten that such a doctrine and system of initiation thereof exists, and therefore, we have forgotten who we are. This fourth dimensional bottle or warp is connected to what is sometimes called the Halls of Amenta, where the entire history of the planet is mentally stored. Amenta is the collective term for the individual Akasha systems of earth's many species of lifeforms going back through time immemorial. The Afrokhan, having forgotten that this environment is of a lesser nature than that of her original habitat, must realign with her own ancestors, which are forever connected to the collective Akasha of earth's history. Our ancestors are the key to our remembering who and what we are, for we have disconnected ourselves from our corporeal Knower, and have allowed the faculty of a lesser mind-set to take over and govern our way of life. Thus we are suffering as a people, lost in the wilderness of an extremely hostile jungle, of which many of us have caught a fever!

<u>We have forgotten who we are!</u>

Our Ancestors, the ancient Kushites of Afrokha and Asia, reminds us of our connection to the Divine. The cosmogonies of the Ancient Ones tell us that we are a part of a celestial deity; we exist as miniscule corpuscles of this great be*ing,* of which we all serve particular individual functions. The most common of such doctrines today is the Kaballion. As an oral tradition, its contents were handed down to Moses (Thutmose) as a commendation received within the order of Tehuti, and as a sacred trust, on Mount Sinai. Moses then passed the information on to Joshua who delivered it to the Judges and, them to the Sanhedrin, until finally it was seized and elaborated upon by Tanaim and the later Kaballistic Rabbis. So folks, the question is this, which part of the Anatomy of God do we play?

~

Notes

[1] Nebu Ka Ma'at, *MMSN Vol.1,* p5
[2] Dr Malachi, *The Holy Tablets,* p693
[3] Ibid, p731
[4] Famine Steel
[5] Dr Malachi, *The Sacred Records of Tamare,* p114-118
[6] Marcus Chown, *The Universe Next Door,* p233

[7] Nebu Ka Ma'at, *The Legacy of the Black Gods in Time before Time.* This work outlines a significant distinction of who the real cyclopean deities are, as opposed to the common definitions of modern day interpreters of the Akasha.

[8] Dr Malachi, *The 9Ball – Part 1*

[9] Dr Malachi, *The Holy Tablets,* p3

Chapter 2
The Anatomy of God

"Man Know thy Self"

Written above the main entrances of the temples of ancient Khemet is the greatest of aphorisms – the admonition to know thy Self. In today's western terminology it may well be regarded as an urge to understand the anatomy of our physical body. However, the understanding of the human physical anatomy will only give us a starting point toward the understanding of the Anatomy of God, for the above aphorism is to be regarded as – being a minuscule part of God, knowing thy-Self is indeed knowing God.

The esoterical Jewish **Kaballion**, which is an *'Oral Tradition,'* (although not the original), still presents us with a good metaphorical representation of the Anatomy of God. It expresses creation and material existence originating from a source of 'limitless emanations' or 'limitless lights,' called the **'Ain-Soph-Aur.'** The Ain-Soph-Aur however, must be governed by the Godhead as the unseen undifferentiated **NTR,**[A] existing prior to the physical evolutionary creation. It is vitally necessary for us to note that prior to evolutionary creation, and, by whatever name we choose to call the Creator, there was indeed 'Existence,' Presenced by Awareness of 'Be*ing*' – of which the Creator has no name. The Khemetian cosmology tells us that, not only did the Creator create itself as Creator – and as the first act of creation, but it also created itself as the *things* that it created thereon. In terms of creating itself as Creator, the Kaballah represents this as

---

[A] Although NTR is the Khemetian term for the undifferentiated Be*ing*/ Creator, it is inserted here because the original doctrine of the Kaballah is Khemetic. Therefore, NTR, in all respect must represent the Godhead of all mysticism.

emanations of light through 10 spheres called the '**Sephiroths.**' These 10 spheres represent the underlying centres of our core energy – cosmological core energy as well as core energy for the physical body (as above so below). The original Nuqta or Black Dot initiates these spheres as the celestial Chakras, so to say.

Made in the Image of God

How is all of this information relative to us now, if indeed today's western religions on the face of them do not hold such doctrines as truths? Well, the Christian bible tells us that man is made in the image and after the likeness of God [Gen 1v26-27]. By *image* – it must imply that man looks exactly like God, as far as anatomy is concerned. By *likeness*, it must also imply that man has the same qualities and characteristics as God, but not in degree and magnitude.

'Made in the image of God,' also suggest that man be created within the imagination of God, since God created himself and the Universe through Mental visualisation – the reciprocal of meditation. The Khemetian mystery system reveals that the Universe and everything within it is Created and held within the Mind of '**Pa Tempta,**' meaning the Mind of The All. Therefore the Universe and everything within it is merely a Mental projection of the Universal Mind – created as emanations of the Ain-Soph-Aur (limitless lights). And, the ultimate physical manifestation of God/ NTR is called '**Kadmon,**' where Kadmon represents the Archetypal Body of the God, as recorded in the Akkadian language of Babylon and Assyria. Here, the Assyrian and Babylonian versions of the Sumerian epic of Creation, the 'Enuma Elish,' are written in the Akkadian language.

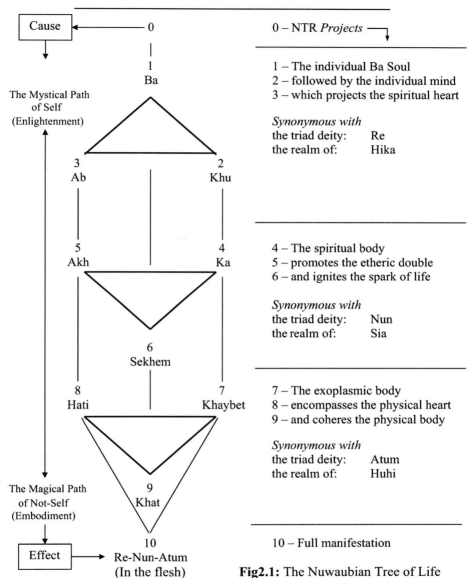

Fig2.1: The Nuwaubian Tree of Life

The Khemetian doctrine expresses this manifestation as '**Re-Nun-Atum**' – an esoterical triad enfoldment principle of the Creator through deities such as Atum, Asaru, Khnum and Ptah. According to the Akkadian tablets of Creation, Kadmon, who was later interpolated with the Khemetian Re-Nun-Atum doctrine into the bible as Adam, was given instructions by the angel **Nusqu**, also biblically called the angel **Gabriel**, to build a **Kabbah.** This structure is a materialised/ symbolic representation of the Tree of Life. This particular Kabbah, the original of its kind was destroyed by a flood,[A] but was later rebuilt by Ishmael and Abraham, when they were also instructed to do so by Gabriel. The word Kabbah, when coupled with the word Eloh [Aramaic Hebrew] or Allah [Ashuric Syriac Arabic], gives us the word Kaballah meaning: **Ka** – *Spirit,* **Ba** – *Soul* and **Allah** – *God,* or simply the 'Spirit and Soul of the Creator.' So the Nuwaubian Tree of Life as illustrated at fig2.1 is illustrative of the Anatomy of God encompassing and expressing 10 tears of Spirit and Soul-Energy in the form of light. It represents the spiritual unfolding and embodiment of this Great Creator/ NTR. Fig2.1 also illustrates the 9 Principles of the human being, where these levels of manifestation are the underlying faculties of the same that we take for granted in everyday life. Only those who are on the 'Mystical Path of Self' will attain Self-realisation and the consequent out growing of these limiting faculties.

The Mystical Path of Self

Take a silent/ still moment to observe the Kaballistic diagram at fig2.1. Allow yourself to become <u>Present</u> to the energy that is felt within the body's nervous system as you observe. Take a mental note (or notes) of the information that your Higher Self communicates to you, without prejudice of it being right or wrong. Remember… in the higher orders of awareness and be*ing* there are neither good nor bad, right or wrong feelings or emotions. Things just are… You may feel a certain level of resonance; or, a certain degree of acknowledgement that this diagram

---

[A] This flood could possibly be the biblical deluge of Noah.

relates to your self although you may not immediately be able to reiterate how. If you do not feel this way, don't worry. It means nothing. The diagram is meant for illustrative purposes only, though here it is intended to act as a metaphorical trigger to awaken your DNA to remind you of who you are.

Spirit, manifesting itself toward embodiment along its Magical Paths, created a system that would enable it to recall the memory of its experiences. This we call the Mental Plane, or the realm of **Hika**; or the realm of causality. Spirit understood that at some point it would experience amnesia and fall into a realm of ignorance and limitation, which was the ironic intention. However, Spirit proceeded as planned and produced a system of correspondence that enabled it to communicate with the Mental, from the lower planes of vibration. This system is the DNA. The DNA acts as a transceiver – it acts as an organic component that transmits and receives data from the Mental Reservoir.

As we step onto the path of meditative visualisation and spiritual enlightenment as (10-**Re-Nun-Atum**) 'Man in the Image of God,' we start off by intentionally reversing the ontological order of manifestation. However, one should do at least one grounding exercise before beginning such visualisation exercises (see Ch3). We proceed from (9-**Khat**) the physical form (our limited material consciousness) with a projection to attain 'Self-realisation,' or for lack of a better description, to attain a realm of 'God in the Image of Man.' This standpoint empowers us to remember that God is but the highest level of vibration and awareness of our very be*ing*, and thereby allows for the quickening of our spirit along this great path. By way of mediumistic communication with the forces of nature/ NTRU/ the Ancestors etc., we become familiar with (8-**Hati**) the physical heart and its synergizing connection to (7-**Khaybet**) the exoplasmic body/ form. The exoplasmic body is one layer/ form, above the physical form. It can sometimes be

43

seen by mediumistic spiritualists extruding from the body of one who is in meditative trance. This layer acts as the glue that tacks the physical form onto the etheric double. In retrospect, the spark of life (6-**Sekhem**), which is experienced through feeling and clairsentience, serves as a reminder of the reality that we once existed as sparks of light within the womb of infinite space – within the Universal Mind. This realisation aligns us with the Higher Self; that which blueprints the physical body – the etheric double (5-**Akh**). This vehicle is but of the lower levels of the Spiritual form (4-**Ka**), which transports our consciousness on into the spiritual heart of God (3-**Ab**). Here on, the master is able to see creation in complete reverse, from the Mind of God (2-**Khu**). This is the art of reversing the viewpoint of the Nuqta. The objective here is to try-on the Mask of God, which can only be achieved with total Unconditional Love for All of nature. Whatever we perceive God to be is exactly what we become within this space, the 'I-Am Presence.' The Khu reminds (re-mind) us that we create our reality as we go along. I.e., the experiences we had or have as life and living, we created. The master realises that nothing this side of evolutionary creation is consistent or true, for truth is forever changing. This Presence of be*ing* unites past-present-future into One reality; NOW. The individual Soul (1-**Ba**), now Complete within and of itself, with total recall of 'All that Is,' enters a realm where ANYTHING IS POSSIBLE. This, my dear reader, and here is the thing… is the ultimate goal for those practicing the sciences of mysticism. The Ba Soul, felt from the bosom of the Creator, gives us the opportunity to either transcend the creational matrix grids on into the real world, the world of the Gods, or return to the Earth Plane to carry on life as normal. Or at least, to carry on life within the world but not of it…

Mysticism

The Mystical Path toward Self-realisation can be further divided into two major distinct divisions – the path of Magic and the path of

Yoga.[1] This piece of truth is vitally important for anyone who truly seeks enlightenment. Often times we find that people who study and practice yoga whole heartedly, subconsciously opposed those who practice spiritual sciences such as astral projection or spherical breathing through the Merkaba etc. And of course visa versa. Yoga and Magic, the reflective and the exaltive methods respectively, are both different phases comprehended in the one term mysticism. Mysticism, as said by Israel Regardie, expresses the relation of the individual to a more comprehensive Consciousness either within or without *herself*. Going beyond her personal needs, she discovers her adjustment to larger, more harmonious ends.

Yoga

Yoga seeks to arrive at Reality by undermining the foundations of the ordinary waking Consciousness, so that upon the tranquil sea of mentality that follows upon the cessation of all thought, the inner eternal essence of spiritual splendour, of NTR, could shine to shed an irradiation of life, light and immortality. In short, yoga is to enhance the whole worth of man. All the practices and exercises in the many yoga systems are spiritually scientific, having as their one objective the complete abeyance of all thought at will. The Mind must be thoroughly emptied at will of all its contents.

A distinction has to be made here regarding the latter paragraph. Yoga in general terms has been accepted to be a Hindu system, and for that reason we must understand and know its origin. Or at least, we must recognise that the Ancient Egiptians had a system called **Smai**, which is 'Union Breath.' Smai-Yoga then, is the original yoga system practiced by the ancient Dravidian peoples; descendants of the blacks coming from as far back as Atlantis. We will look more into the Smai-Yoga system in volume 3 of MMSN.

Magic

Magic, on the other hand, is a mnemonic system of psychology in which the almost interminable ceremonial details, the circumambulations and conjurations are deliberately intended for the exaltation of the imagination and soul, with the utter transcending of the normal plane of thought. From academic sources Magic is defined as 'the art of applying natural causes to produce surprising effects.' Well, aren't our wake-a-day bodily functions a form of magic? Is it not magical that one can simply get up and walk across a room without even thinking of the mechanics behind such a fete? Every conceivable act in the whole span of life is a magical act!

Mysticism in Performing Arts

Erykah Badu, on her album *'Baduizm,'* produced a song called *'On and on'* (featured next page) which to me reflects the very fact that man is 'made in the image of God.' This album produced by Kedar, a relation to Dr Malachi, is an expression of Afrocentric Awareness and Presence in America.

During my writing of this volume, I took a two months break to write another book – **'Urban Cries'** Volume 1: *Communicating with God through Music and Performing Arts & the Implications of the Hip-Hop Culture.* I did this because volume 1 of MMSN proved to be a bit of a mind-full for the younger generation amongst us. I felt it necessary to produce a smaller and simpler book that young persons can pick up and follow without difficulty, and for it to act as an introduction to the MMSN Volumes. 'Urban Cries' Volume 1, therefore, is a 109 page book with the objective to introduce the 7Hermetic Axioms to the modern youth within the context of the modern Hip-Hop culture. It attempts to give the world a better representation of what the real Hip-Hop culture represents and also to inspire those of its movement to create grassroots organisations, thus turning their skills and talents into worldwide industries.

Oh my my my, I'm feeling high,
My money is gone, I'm all alone,
The world is turning
Oh what a day, what a day what a day!

Peace and blessings manifest with every lesson learned,
If your knowledge were your wealth then it will be well earned
If we were made in his image then call us by our names,
Most intellects do not believe in god but they fear us just the same

(Chorus)   oh on and on, and, on and on,
*   my fibre keeps moving like a rolling stone*
*   on and on, and, on and on,*
*   all night long till the break of dawn*
*   (repeat)*

I was born under water, with three dollars and six dimes,
Yeah you might laugh, cause you did not do your math
* Na qua 23… Qua 23… the world keeps tuning*
Oh what a day, what a day what a day!
The man that know something, knows that he knows nothing at all,
Does it seem colder in your summer time and hotter in your fall?
If we were made in his image then call us by our names
Most intellects do not believe in god but they fear us just the same

(Chorus)

I am feeling kinda hungry, coz my high is coming down,
Don't feed me yours, coz your food does not endure.
I think I need a cup of tea, the world keeps burning
Oh what a day, what a day what a day!

You're rushing to destruction coz you don't have nothing left
The Mothership can't save you so your ass is going to get left.
If we were made in his image then call us by our name
Most intellects do not believe in god but they fear us just the same.

(Chorus)

Erykah Badu

In mysticism, yoga and magic must be given their due credit. Magic, as distinct from phychism, witchcraft and other disciplines, involves exercises and techniques for developing the will and imagination and consequently having the ability to influence events super-naturally, using Conscience. Mysticism – Magic and Yoga – is the means therefore, to a new Universal Life, richer, greater and fuller of resource than ever before, as free as sunlight, as gracious as the unfolding of a rose. It is for man to have.

One part of mysticism that has always intrigued me is that of *'Astral Projection,'* or astral travelling. I had the privilege a few years ago to work with a gentleman called James, whom I acknowledged in volume 1 of MMSN. James as a child experienced at random astral projection, though at those times he did not actually understand what was going on. Or at least he weren't able to explain scientifically what he was doing or experiencing. He told me that sometimes he would, by complete chance, leave his body behind laying down somewhere, and consciously move throughout his house. He would sometimes talk to his brother and parents about what he were able to do, and surprise-surprise, they responded as if he was just imagining the whole thing. Needless to say James stopped talking about these events to his family. After getting a little more comfortable with his abilities, he would take his travels further, to the point of travelling throughout the planet to remote places and even meeting on the astral level with others having the same experiences. He also told me that sometimes he would take a journey inwards – that is to say he would travel into his body; he would adjust his focus in order to see a macrocosmic view of his organs. But on the contrary, as life went on, particularly as he sailed through his teenage life, James started to forget how to travel in this manner. He had gotten caught up in sports, music, and girls and so on. Not to say this was a bad thing, but the attraction toward other pursuits diminished his astral projection abilities. Later when he was about 20years old, I think, – one day his older brother brought home a book. And low and behold, it was a book specifically on astral travelling. His brother said, *"Isn't this the same thing that you use to talk about when you were younger?"* Well the two of them together read parts of the book and not unexpectedly James decided to re-establish his gifted abilities. This time however, he would do it knowing what he was doing – with intention. But, what exactly is astral travelling, and what are the conditions?

Astral Travelling

According to popular mysticism there are three fundamentals one must initially consider if she or he intends to practice astral travelling. But first, it must be noted here that astral travelling is not about secretly spying on people or peering into the future to find what is going to be the next winning lotto numbers. In fact one who is on the Mystical Path of Self, would no doubt have already disassociated her or him self from the cohesion of earthly pursuits. The idea by my understanding is to be able to transcend consciously through and beyond the constraints of the material world, to the point of experiencing the celestial body in totality, of which we are currently a conscious but minuscule component. According to Israel Regardie, the three prerequisites to be considered are; and he says:

> 'First: *that in the so-called Astral Light he may perceive an exact reflection of himself in all his several parts and qualities and attributions, an examination of that reflection tending to a species of self-knowledge.* Second: *the definition of the Astral Light from the magical point of view is an exceedingly broad one, including all subtle planes above or within the physical, and it is the objective of the magician to rise to the more fiery and lucid realms of the spiritual world.* Third: *before this particular portion of the invisible world can be transcended, it must be conquered and mastered in each of its aspects. All the denizens of that sphere must be made to submit to the magician, to his magical symbols and to*

obey unequivocally the reality of Royal Will, which these latter symbolise. [2]

Israel Regardie

As I paraphrase Regardie's work, he expresses the elements of magic as distinct from psychism. He says, 'Psychism may perhaps be defined as having for its objective the stimulation and preservation of the lower self at the expense or, in ignorance of the Higher Self. This as I agree with him, is clearly an abomination deserving of the severest censure. Therefore, any casual summary of Magic in the single word 'psychism' is utterly absurd, to say the least. On the subject of Magic, the magician must be in control of her entire nature, since no attempt is made to acquire powers for her own sake or for any base of nefarious purpose. Any power acquired must be subordinated to the Will, and kept in its own place and proper perspective. For the aspiring magician, every constituent element in her or his being must be developed to the topmost contrast of perfection. No one principle must be repressed, since each is an aspect of the Supreme Spirit, the Oversoul, and of The All.

Astral travelling is about spiritual freedom, to be in touch with the Higher Self, and indeed to be in touch with all other manifested parts of the Universe, for all that exists are connected through Spirit. Astral projection is however distinct from Merkaba ascension, which I will address in chapter 9, (there are many means to the same objective... or, should it be to the Subjective?). We sometimes experience astral projection when we sleep. We enter the dream world subconsciously; that is, we enter this realm not by our own volition but by way of the Higher Self. Anything seems to be possible in this world. There is a part of us that knows this reality – where anything we wish for can be manifested in the blinking of an eye. Astral ascension and realisation connects us to the Creator through stages of emanations of its *Aur,* light. The Anatomy of God, the Kaballistic system, the very nature of The All, is so below as it is above; it is so within as it is without. The Tree of Life, synonymous with the nervous system of the human being, is but a reflection of the tree of the Universe and its evolution. The nervous system manifests the emotional tendencies of the individuals' mind, just as the Tree of Life manifests the emotional tendencies of the Universal Mind – the Godhead.

The Tree of Life

'Pythagoras, returning form his eastern travels to Greece, taught the doctrine of the Metempsychosis, and the existence of a Supreme Being, by whom the universe was created, and by whose providence it is preserved; that the souls of mankind are emanations of that being. Socrates, the wisest of the ancient philosophers, seems to have believed that the soul existed before the body; and that death relieves it from those seeming contrarieties to which it is subject, by its union with our material part. Plato asserted, that God infused into matter a portion of his divine Spirit, which animates and moves it. Aristotle supposed the souls of mankind to be portions or emanations of the divine Spirit; which at death quits the body, and, like drops of water falling into the ocean, is absorbed into the divinity. [3]

Sir Godfrey Higgins

As stated in chapter 1, the ancients understood human life as minuscule components, living as a part of a larger celestial deity. In this cosmic body we, individuals and beasts and gods etc., are the minute cells and molecules, each having a separate function to perform in the social polity and welfare of that Oversoul. Each thereby having its own experiences, and, in reflecting the intentions of this Great Soul will at some future time realign with the Collective-Consciousness of the said Oversoul. This Kaballistic truth is admirably saying that as in the man of earth, there is an intelligence governing man's actions and thoughts, so there is likewise, figuratively speaking, in the Celestial Man a Soul

51

which is its central intelligence and its most important faculty. *'All that which exists upon the earth has a spiritual counterpart on high, and there exists nothing in this world which is not attached to something Above, and is not found in dependence of it.'* So wrote the doctors of the Kaballah; also found on the Emerald tablet of Tehuti (fig2.3).

The Tree of Life reflects the Anatomy of God, with the admonition for man to know Self. The Hon Elijah Muhammad taught me, or to the least was by who I first heard such truths, that, "The knowledge of Self is the knowledge of God" and of course vice versa. Therefore the knowledge of Self must encompass the Knowledge of 'All that Is.' Astral projection aids in the ability to communicate with the Higher Self, which bestows knowledge onto the lower self, though the highest of results are attained through True Meditation. More on the Hon Elijah Muhammad in Volume 3…

The Tree of Life system as originally taught by the Supreme Grand Hierophant Tehuti, in his Ha Kha teachings, reflects the grand unfolding of the mentally created Universe and the coming to fruition of the material world (see the Emerald tablet of fig2.3) as projected by the Godhead, NTR. The tree, composed usually of ten spheres, is better explained as having eleven, with three distinct triad creative Principles, all governed by sphere 0 – the Godhead (shown as the dotted circle of fig2.2), and a final sphere, number 10, representing the material manifestation as in the 'Re-Nun-Atum' of fig2.1. Thus we have 11 spheres, descending from 0 – 10. The three of the triad spheres are conveniently called: the *Father* or sphere one, the *Mother* or sphere two and, the *child* or sphere three. Or, it can be said to encompass a masculine and a feminine principle with a collaboration of the two, or a quiescent neutral aspect, the child principle. The triad is then repeated three times as the three great realms of Hika, Sia and Huhi (fig 2.1). The Hermetic philosophy of the same expresses this as 'Hermes Trismegistus,' meaning Hermes the Thrice Great.

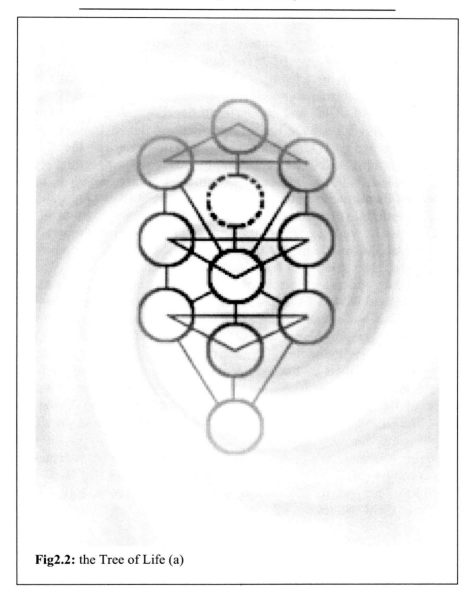

Fig2.2: the Tree of Life (a)

The Ain-Soph-Aur

To express its original context – the philosophy of the Kaballah, the 'Tree of Life' is one of Involution. The Universe, with all its galaxies and worlds and beings, was conceived to be the emanation from a primeval substance-principle, which some have called God, the Absolute, The All, Allah and so fourth. In the Kaballah, this one reality is named the *Ain Soph,* as in the Infinite. This substance, though indeed substance it isn't, is un-changeable, un-knowable to the Mind, illimitable, un-manifest and absolute. Beyond all intellectual comprehension in itself, inasmuch as a mental ability, which is but a segment of its all-inclusiveness could never grasp it, it is thus stated to be *Ain* – Nothing; yet existing – and limitless. The *Aur* – Light or lights, is the means by which a mentality, one of us, can get a glimpse or a reflection of the intentions of the *Ain Soph.* Moreover, we have the doctrine of the *Ain-Soph-Aur.* The zero rated sephirah,[A] though symbolised by the dotted circle of fig2.2, and is centred between the first and second triad, would have initially been situated above the first triad, as far as illustration is concerned. Here it demonstrates Consciousness, a subordinate aspect of the absolute, having the ability to descend into embodiment to experience its own doings, as one of us. The zero-sphere then is the Subjective, and can never within itself become objective. Consciousness objectively descends into the first sphere of the first triad, the first sephira, which is named Kether or *Keser,* the Crown. This is the Faculty of Asaru. This monad principle, though somewhat unknowable as is the *Ain Soph,* is the highest achievable aspect of Self realisation one can achieve, whilst maintaining Consciousness of the one and only fact that she or he is indeed Conscious. This sphere, the monad, whose number is one, births from itself the duad principle of Tehuti and Sekert, or, Wisdom and

---

[A] A sephira is a single sphere of light, whereas the sephiroth or sephiros as it is sometime called represents the entire 10/11-point Kaballah system. 22 lines of symmetry connect the individual sephiros, basically, although some illustrations show more or less lines of connection.

Understanding, or, sephira two and three. This is the Mental manifestation of the first triad of *Ain-Soph-Aur*.

Fig2.3: the Emerald Tablet of Tehuti

It is true without untruth, certain and most true, that which is below is like that which is on high, and that which is on high is like that which is below; by these things are made the miracles of one thing. And as all things are, and come from One, by the meditation of One, So all things are born from this unique thing by adaptation. The Sun is the father and the mother the moon. The wind carries it within its stomach. The earth is its nourisher and its receptacle. The father of The All, the Universal world, is here. Its force or power remains complete. Separate the earth from the fire, the subtle from the gross – gently with great industry. It climbs from the earth and descends from the sky, and receives the force from things inferior and from things superior. You will have by this way the glory of the world and all obscurity will free from you. It is the power strong with all power, for it will defeat every subtle thing and penetrate every solid thing. In this way the world was created. From it are born wonderful modifications, of which the way here is given. This is why I have been called Tehuti, having the three parts of the Universal philosophy. This, that I have called the solar work, is complete.

Sephira	Description	Faculty
Kether	The Crown	Asaru
Chokmah	Wisdom	Tehuti
Binah	Understanding	Sekert
Chesed	Mercy	Ma'at
Geburah	Power	Herukhuti
Tiphareth	Beauty & Harmony	Heru
Netzach	Victory	Het-Heru
Hod	Splendour	Sobek
Yesod	Fountain	Aset
Malkuth	The Kingdom	Geb

Table 4:
Faculties of each sephira

This diagram is a collaboration of the named sephiras taken from Israel Regardie with the named Kaballion deities taken from Ra Un Nefer Amen.

As above so below – as within so without (As experience so inperience)

So, as each individual is spiritually superimposed with a spiritual counterpart; so it is with her external world – a reflection of her inner world. The way in which the individual sees and experiences the world is but a reflection of what is rooted deep within. For instance, if you are someone who lacks self-confidence and is generally unsure of your value and worth, you will no doubt reflect this in your wake-a-day actions. And consequently, you would have created a vibrational aura that will attract people who will always seek to undermine your self-confidence and your self-esteem. Sometimes, or perhaps more than likely for some, our world-view is created and emanated from a collection of past life experiences, but is ultimately a manifestation of our *inperiences*. In other words, we can reverse the situation like this:

56

you might find yourself to dislike the company of people who lack self-confidence and self-esteem. This is because they remind you of either how you used to be when you were younger, or at best, they remind you subconsciously how you were in one of your past lives. This Kaballistic truth states that, the sole reason why one develops a dislike for someone else expressing a particular character, is based on the reality that they themselves were at some time exactly like that, and were probably also disliked by others for the same reason. So our worldly wake-a-day experiences are on one level a reflection of past experiences, and on another level, are reflections of our past inperiences. Our inperience is that which the creator deities, the shaping faculties of our being, intend.

The Tree of Life doctrine also encompasses two viewpoints of the Universal Anatomy. The first is the Tetragrammaton; the four primeval elements, also called the four primeval worlds. These worlds are metaphysical regions composed of Consciousness and matter, each having its own vehicle of embodiment. This viewpoint places the tree in each of the worlds thus having a total of forty plus four sephiros.

- The first world is called the **Olam Atsilus**, the Archetypal World. It is the '**Y**' or *Yod* of the Hebrew Tetragrammaton. This world occupies the highest Plane of spiritual Consciousness, the first appearance of Consciousness from the Ain Soph. This region maybe imagined also representing a human form, which, in the *Book of Splendour*, is named Kadmon, the heavenly man, containing within itself all souls, spirits and intelligences in every part of the cosmos. It is the Universal Soul, the Divine progenitor and parent of all others.
- As the process of physical manifestation proceed, Kadmon gradually projects itself further into matter, somewhat more dense, its unity being split up apparently, being mirrored in many facets, forming the second world. This is called the **Olam Briah**, the Creative World. It is the '**H**' or *Heh* of the Hebrew Tetragrammaton. In this world, the plan contained in the creative imagination of the Ain Soph is worked

57

upon further still. Here too, a complete Tree of Life is mirrored through reflection. (As above so below).

- From the Creative World, the tree is projected onto a third world, the **Olam Yetsirah**, the Formative World. It is the **'W'** or *Waw* of the Hebrew Tetragrammaton. Here the imaginative ideas of the Logos, the spiritual monadic sparks already clothed in the subtle Mental substances of the Creative World, are formed into definite coherent entities. These entities are the astral models that give rise to, or serve as the stable foundations of the physical world.
- The fourth world, the **Olam Assiah**, the Physical World, is the last of the four planes. It is the second **'H'** of the Hebrew Tetragrammaton. This is the crystallised projection of the Formative World and is the summarisation and concrete representation of all the higher worlds.

In this context, again, we see the justification of the Hermetic axiom, "As Above so Below." The Magi priests also remarks this principle as, "The visible is the manifestation of the invisible." However, the second viewpoint of the Universal Anatomy employs a single tree of which the four planes or worlds are placed onto it thuswise.

- The first is *Keser*, the Crown, occupying by itself the one plane, is the Archetypal World, the realm of the Logos.
- The second is *Chokmah* and *Binah*, the Supernal Father and Mother that constitute the Creative World, receiving and executing the Divine imagination.
- The third are the next 6 sephiros, concerning the Astral Plane or the Formative World.
- The fourth is *Malkuth*, the kingdom, and is the Physical World.

These two concepts provide a pivotal centre of the whole of magical philosophy. It is at one and the same time, a monotheism and polytheism in a single philosophic system. The whole Universe is permeated by One Life, the YHWH[A] of the Hebrew Torah, and that One Life in manifestation is represented by a host of Mighty Gods, Divine Beings, Cosmic Forces or intelligences – call them by what name you will! The spiritual state and diversity of the gods are tremendous, and, from them we are sprung, spiritual sparks thrown downwards from their Divine essence.

In my studies, and according to my own opinion, Ra Un Nefer Amen presents the simplest but yet comprehensive explanation of the Tree of Life with regards to systems of behaviour shaping. Coming from an Afro-Egiptian perspective, as opposed to a Jewish one, he wrote:

> *'Much of what has been written concerning the Tree of Life, has been presented in highly mystical and mythological language. On a less poetical note, it would be more useful to think of the Tree of Life as a filing system. It is based on the understanding that the shaping and organising forces of all events and things in the world can be organised in eleven categories. It states, fundamentally, that operating in all things are eleven sets of shaping forces.* [A]
>
> Ra Un Nefer Amen

On the same page further down he writes:

> *'The Tree of Life does not achieve its goal by merely acting as a list of Principles. The eleven Principles are arranged in a particular format that graphically aids in the explanation of the Principles, their functions, and their relationship to each other and to the world.* [5]

[A] The YHWH Tetragrammaton is the foundation of the Hebrew/ Babylonian Yahweh and Ya-Huwa Principles.

From this we can also deduce the said two fundamental shaping forces in the world, which are both divided into two parts also. See table 5 below. On initiation into the Ancient Egiptian Order, the aspirant will embark upon such truths through observation.

The Magical Path		The Mystical Path	
Technology & (Masculine)	Academic IQ (Feminine)	Magic & (Masculine)	Yoga (Feminine)

Table 5: shaping forces in the world

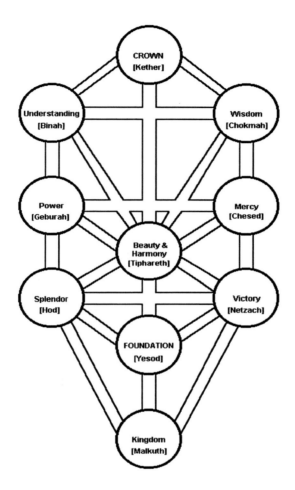

Fig2.4: the Tree of Life (b)

Initiation into the AEO

The purpose of the **Ancient Egiptian Order** (or AEO) today and of old is to make good people into better people, using the Mental technology of Nuwaubu also known as 'Sound Right Reasoning.' The same intent is true of the Ausar Auset Society, of which Ra Un Nefer Amen is associated. The initiation system of old took 100s, perhaps 1000s of years to develop, and was introduced into the ancient world to change the quality of the novice's soul on entering the sacred temple or lodge. It was to raise the Consciousness of the neophyte to a super-human level, and to make an eternal being out of her or him. Thus we have the rituals of Adonis and/ or Tammuz in the Near East, of Asaru in Khemet, of Orpheus in the Greek islands, of Dionysus in Hellas, which all depicts death and resurrection. This is so that one may symbolically experience a superhuman state and eternal life, says Dr Malachi as **Neter Aferti Atum Re**, the Supreme Grand Master and Deity of the AEO today. There are three distinct levels of aspiration as the student progresses in spiritual growth toward perfection. Neter Aferti Atum Re re-expressed these three levels as is written below.

*1. **Aspiring** devotees who are being instructed on a probationary status, and have not experienced inner vision. The important factor at this level is <u>awakening of the Spiritual Self</u>. That is, becoming conscious of the divine presence within one's self and the universe by not having faith but facts that there is a spiritual essence beyond ordinary human overstanding.*

*2. **Striving** devotees who have attained inner vision and have received a glimpse of cosmic consciousness. The important factor at this level is <u>purgation of the Self</u>. That is, purification of the mind and body through a spiritual discipline. The neophyte tries to totally surrender the '<u>I</u>' factor, 'personal' identity or ego to the divine inner Self, which is the Universal Self of All Creation.*

*3. **Established** devotees who have become identified with or united with the <u>Neteru</u> 'deities.' The important factor at this level is <u>opening of the higher intellect</u>. That is, experience and appreciation of the divine presence during reflection and meditation, union with the Divine Self, and the Divine marriage of the individual with the Universal. In order to have a better overstanding of what <u>istalgaan</u> 'initiation' is, we must look into the distinct past in order to discover its purpose and use.*

<u>The Initiative way of education</u>

Bodily discipline and Mind discipline are just as important as each other. The need for a true spiritual master cannot be overemphasised in the course of spiritual practice, and therefore we have this in Neter Aferti Atum Re, aka **Amunnubi Ruakh Ptah**, the incarnation of Tehuti in this day and time. It is impossible to promote true spiritual growth through written books and audio recordings in totality. In other words there comes a time when the Mind begins to create misconceptions and illusions about spirituality just as any area of ordinary worldly life. Therefore, a spiritual coach who is advanced in its practice should be sought out and approached with humility and honesty, and to ask questions in order to dispel subtle forms of ignorance and wrong knowledge.

The neophyte is initiated into Nuwaubu, a way of life, which she or he requires to learn and practice by studying, reflecting and meditating on the teachings. However, many people today do not find spirituality to be attractive because they feel they would loose out on life if they became seriously involved. Others see the prospects of spirituality as being too remote for their understanding or as just not necessary. On the flip side, a true spiritual master is not just someone who has excelled onto the Universal Presence of the Neteru and experiences the Anatomy of God, retrospectively speaking. The master is also well versed in all relevant scriptures as well as other day-to-day doctrines or systems of thought, plus having the wisdom to reach individuals and relate to them according to their current level of consciousness, perception and awareness. The master will have the ability to initiate the individual into higher levels of thinking without the person even realising what has taken place. As Dr Malachi has always said:

"I came giving you what you wanted so you would learn to want what I have come to give"

This is the exact stance that we, the students of the AEO, have also been taking as we take on the task of raising prospective souls into higher awareness. Sometimes the image of the media and from the traditional church, mosque or synagogue has promoted an image of occult, with mysterious and unnatural personalities as practitioners of bodily discipline, says Dr Malachi. The western world does not have a system of spiritual living, so therefore systems of bodily and Mental discipline are labelled as cults out of fear. The European race evidently fears the rise of the Afrokhan, should she develop a spiritual discipline in order to attain Self-empowerment. They fear the rise of the Cyclopean Intelligences.[6] As Farrakhan says, *"A Nation can rise no higher than its woman."* This means that spiritual growth and empowerment must be balanced throughout the different aspects of the society. Table 5 shows how the natural behaviour shaping forces in the world influence us. Here we have the Afrokhan woman who takes on personal development through systems of Yoga as well as through academic learning and attainment. This she tends to carry out more aggressively than the Afrokhan male. On the other hand the Afrokhan male tends to be more aggressive with technology and magical feats as means of personal development. The two compliment each other and are indeed necessary facets of a spiritually aspiring society. The mystical schools, though are well disciplined and possess detailed knowledge are themselves only stepping stones that help us reach the goal of true initiation – which is by way of the natural forces of nature – the Neteru – the Ancestors.

Initiation by the Ancestors

The Spirit of God, of Ra, NTR, enveloped as the Universal embodiment of Asaru, utilises the Mental Plane as Tehuti to maintain order and to bring forth knowledge and learning of creation, through the arts, sciences and through the language of our culture (hence the word cult). The masters of the many mystery schools only act as intermediaries between us and these higher Gods – the Cyclopean Intelligences.[7] They act as guides for those of us who are striving toward Self-realisation. That is, to have the faculty to realise what 'Is,' by our own Self. The first realisation is that nothing is invented by man-kind; he can only modify upon that, which already exists, which are impressions stored in the Halls of Amenta. Everything that is made is but a modification of a mental intent and is thus grown into physical manifestation. Such is the Anatomy of God – human-kind, the Anatomy of the Universe and the Anatomy of Existence. To think otherwise would be an egotistical thought. Conscious astral travelling is a practical journey, though consciously and without ascension the student can tune into the **Tuat** and **Amentet** realms of the Astral Plane also called the Astral Light. The more the Afrokhan becomes in tune with the mentality of the Astral Plane, with Tehuti, the more she or he will embrace Universal knowledge and experience True Love, Peace and Joy – order, Ma'at. The consort of the Mental Plane is order; therefore Tehuti and Ma'at must be in perfect consort and harmony. Tehuti is also in consort with Sekert (table 4). In fact he is in tune with all the deities in some way or another. Sekert in this context brings understanding to the Afrokhan Mind as the Tree of Life, the Anatomy of God, unfolds. The student, through the AEO must learn and develop the wisdom of knowing when to initiate her or him self into the faculties of Asaru and/ or Tehuti in combination with other creator principal deities such as Ma'at, Sekert, Aset, Sekhmet, Nut, Nebthet and Tefnut etc.

These truths are echoed throughout the many Afrokhan tribes within the initiation systems of them, of which the central mystery school was that of the Great Pyramid of Egipt's Old Kingdom. The Ancient Yoruba people of Nigeria speak of the Anatomy of Olodumare as the head of the cosmic as well as the earth-bounded existence of the Orisha – the Orisha or Orisha-nla being the many deities that sprang from Obatala, one sent by Olodumare. This is analogous to the Tree of Life Kaballistic system, where the Godhead is dismantled into many systems of Mental faculties. The Yoruba devotee must learn and understand the different Orishas and the Divine Principles that they represent. Therefore, the devotee will consequently know through wisdom which deity to call upon when help or assistance is required. Western religion has been deliberately used to replaced Afrokhan culture and science, thus we have a system that works against all Afrokhan peoples – a system that promotes calling on gods, deities and prophets who do not hold our best political interests at heart. Afrokhan culture is indeed scientific since it deals with relative truths and facts rooted in a reality. The deities, the Orisha or the Paut Neteru for instance, are simply corresponding metaphorical representations of actual spiritual forces. These forces, if clearly understood by the aspirant, can be utilised and manipulated to encourage a rich spiritual life whilst living on earth.

Spiritual aspiration is the most difficult task on earth but also it is the most rewarding. One of the challenges is to dispel the erroneous notions about what bodily discipline is and how it is to be overstood and practiced, if not to others, then at least to yourself. An initiate needs to develop enough strength to go beyond the popular culture in order to overcome the limitations of the said society. Having done this, one will begin to see the possibility of transcending her or his personal limitations. This beloved, is what true spiritual and aspiring desires is about. During the initiation process and thereafter, the neophyte and the instructor must have a balanced relationship with each other. The understanding must be that the student will be willing to experiment and to practice the teachings as they are directed with total truth and honesty. Truth means that you must strive ceaselessly and honestly means that you will not be willing to fool your self any longer. Spiritual aspiration means striving to develop a keen intellect, which will not allow even the slightest infractions of the teaching to go by without being acknowledged and redressed. The aspirant is to raise her awareness from out of the confines and limitations of Tuat onto the realms of Amentet, at least.

Tuat and Amentet

The Astral Plane or Astral Light is divided into two main regions according to the Khemetian Theurgists;[8] the lower called Tuat or the subconscious, and, the upper called Amentet or the Superconscious, circumscribes the entire astral reality. Respectively, the two regions are also known as the under-world and the upper-world, governed by Asaru and Tehuti. The pseudonymous theory of modern metaphysicists[A] suggests that 'in the upper strata of the Astral Light, two or more objects may occupy the same space and at the same time without interfering with each other or loosing their polity.' The theory also suggests that 'in that light, objects can change their appearance completely without suffering change of nature. The same *thing* can reveal itself in an infinite number of ways by its own volition.'

The upper region – the <u>Divine Astral Light</u>, is solar in nature and relates to the sun or to the stars, whereas the lower region – the <u>gross astral light,</u> is lunar in nature, reflective and purely automatic and relates to the moon and other dead lifeless celestial bodies. The Astral Light is therefore bi-sexual, inasmuch that the Divine region is masculine and creative with the gross region being feminine and destructive. This is not to be misunderstood as good and evil, but as the necessary

---

[A] These are occultists such as Madam Blavatsky

centripetal/ female and centrifugal/ male forces that balances all aspects of the cosmos. The Divine Astral Light, Amentet, also known as the Kingdom of Tehuti is guarded by the underworld God, Asaru. At the reckoning of each deceased soul in the underworld, Asaru would make the final judgement as to whether or not the individual should enter the gates of heaven – the Divine Astral Light. This is to say that at the moment of death, Anubu, the angel of rapture, will usher each soul into the underworld – the gross astral light, where her deeds would be weighed against her cultured life-lived standards of truth. If she passes the test, she will ascend. But if she didn't, then she may have to return to the Material Plane to re-sit certain lessons. This form of initiation is also relevant to the neophyte during life on earth. The probationary student will at some point meet the elders in a dream-like state, usually unexpectedly. She will be given by the masters, secret words or maxims, which she is to remember in some future time. When the time comes for initiation into the third or master-level, on the Physical Plane, questions will be asked pertaining to what was previously told in that dream state. If she remembers, then she will be allowed to enter the master-lodge, as an established devotee. The fact that she remembered meant the initiation into the second order had also taken place; she had received inner vision and a glimpse of Cosmic-Consciousness.

The Collective Unconscious

Initiation into the higher orders and, getting in tune with the Initiator Ancestors is indeed a huge stepping stone, for it is to enter into or to become One with the Astral Light – and the Collective Unconscious. It is to become established and in consort with the Divine Creative forces of the cosmos, as opposed to being caught up in the realms of the destructive lunar forces. On the Tree of Life, *Yesod*, the sphere of lunar, is placed immediately under *Tiphareth*, the sphere of the Solar, the Sun, thus reflecting the Creative forces from above (see fig2.4).[9] Throughout the concept of the Astral Light also, is echoed the concept of the Unconscious, a term not to be confused with the sub-conscious. The term implies a dynamic stream of thought, memory and tendency, which run below our normal wake-a-day consciousness, serving as the receptacle of instincts and race-memories. The latter, drawn from by primitive man, is the origin of inherited cultural habits, race-myths and legends and of course race-memories. It is a dynamic warp of long forgotten information and is why psychoanalysts have called it the Collective Unconscious. Every so-called primitive race of people,[A] in particular the many Afrokhan tribes, regardless of whether they had social intercourse and communication with each other, the myths and legends of them are essential identical. Therefore, there is indeed a correspondence between the Astral Light and the Collective Unconscious. Lack of awareness of the Collective Unconscious and its qualities is owed to the world of ills, conflicts, disharmony, religious divisions' etc., and must therefore be overridden by the magician and yoga practitioner. At the same time, however, the Collective Unconscious with its wealth of animative material, its fertility of impressive ideas and suggestions may be for some people the source of poetic and artistic inspiration.

Carl G. Jung

The psychologist Carl Jung being one of the first in the modern world to put forth the idea of the "Collective Unconscious,"[10] says the basic concept of it is that *"At the deepest levels of Mind, all humans share the same basic reality structure."* The shared Mind is now known as the Collective Unconscious. And, indeed it is from this shared Mind that springs the archetypes of our many personalities. In the ancient mythologies and folklore, these archetypes took the form of gods and goddesses and also *monsters* that demand our reverence and worship. We experience these archetypes as feelings, as emotions and as nervous reactions. The spiritual science of Nuwaubu however, which has its

---

[A] By Primitive, we are also talking about the seven root races of Atlantis and Lemuria.

roots in the Ha Kha Doctrine, and is to be explored in volume 3, will teach us how to reconnect at *will* to this Collective Unconscious.

> *'Anyone who wants to know the human psyche will learn next to nothing from experimental psychology. He would be better advised to abandon exact science, put away his scholar's gown, bid farewell to his study, and wander with human heart throughout the world. There in the horrors of prisons, lunatic asylums and hospitals, in drab suburban pubs, in brothels and gambling-halls, in the salons of the elegant, the Stock Exchanges, socialist meetings, churches, revivalist gatherings and ecstatic sects, through love and hate, through the experience of passion in every form in his own body, he would reap richer stores of knowledge than text-books a foot thick could give him, and he will know how to doctor the sick with a real knowledge of the human soul.'*
>
> Carl Jung

Carl Gustav Jung was born July 26, 1875, in the small Swiss village of Kessewil. His father was Paul Jung, a country parson, and his mother was Emilie Preiswerk Jung. He was surrounded by a fairly well educated extended family, including quite a few clergymen and some eccentrics as well. Although his first career choice was Archaeology, he went on to study medicine at the University of Basel. While working under the famous neurologist Krafft-Ebing, he settled on psychiatry as his career. After graduating, he took a position at the Burghoeltzli Mental Hospital in Zurich under Eugene Bleuler, an expert on schizophrenia.[A] He also taught classes at the University of Zurich, had a private practice, and invented word association at this time! Long an admirer of Freud, he met him in Vienna in 1907. The story goes that after they met, Freud cancelled all his appointments for the day, and they talked for 13 hours straight, such was the impact of the meeting of

---

[A] Eugene Bleuler also coined the term schizophrenia.

these two great minds! Freud eventually came to see Jung as the crown prince of psychoanalysis and his heir apparent. But Jung had never been entirely sold on Freud's theory. Their relationship began to cool in 1909, during a trip to America. They were entertaining themselves by analysing each other's dreams (more fun, apparently, than shuffleboard), when Freud seemed to show an excess of resistance to Jung's efforts at analysis. Freud finally said that they'd have to stop because he was afraid he would lose his authority! Jung felt rather insulted. World War I was a painful period of self-examination for Jung. It was, however, also the beginning of one of the most interesting theories of personality the world has ever seen. After the war, Jung travelled widely, visiting, for example, tribal people in Africa, America, and India. He retired in 1946, and began to retreat from public attention after his wife died in 1955. He died on June 6, 1961, in Zurich.

Jung's theory divides the psyche into three parts. The first is the **ego**, which Jung identifies with the conscious Mind. The second, closely related is the **personal unconscious**, which includes anything, which is not presently conscious, but can be. The personal unconscious is like most people's understanding of the unconscious in that it includes both memories that are easily brought to mind and those that have been suppressed for some reason. But it does not include the instincts that Freud would have it include. But then, Jung adds the part of the psyche that makes his theory stand out from all others: the third, the Collective Unconscious. You could call it your 'psychic inheritance.' It is the reservoir of our experiences as a species, a kind of knowledge we are all born with. And yet we can never be directly conscious of it. It influences all of our experiences and behaviours, most especially the emotional ones, but we only know about it indirectly, by looking at those influences. There are some experiences that show the effects of the Collective Unconscious more clearly than others: The experiences of love at first sight, of deja vu (the feeling that you've been here before), and the immediate recognition of certain symbols and the meanings of certain myths, could all be understood as the sudden conjunction of our outer reality and the inner reality of the Collective Unconscious. Grander examples are the creative experiences shared by artists and musicians all over the world and in all times, or the spiritual experiences of mystics of all religions, or the parallels in dreams, fantasies, mythologies, fairy tales, and literature. A nice example that has been greatly discussed recently is the near-death experience or NDE. It seems that many people, of many different cultural backgrounds, find that they have very similar recollections when they are brought back from a close encounter with death. They speak of leaving their bodies, seeing their bodies and the events surrounding them clearly, of being pulled through a long tunnel towards a bright light, of seeing deceased relatives or cultural figures waiting for them, and of their disappointment at having to leave this happy scene to return to their bodies. (Perhaps we are all 'built' to experience death in this fashion.)

Sigmund Freud

Freud didn't exactly invent the idea of the conscious versus unconscious Mind, but he certainly was responsible for making it popular. The conscious Mind is what you are aware of at any particular moment, your present perceptions, memories, thoughts, fantasies, feelings, and what have you. Working closely with the conscious Mind is what Freud called the **preconscious**, what we might today call 'available memory:' anything that can easily be made conscious, the memories you are not at the moment thinking about but can readily bring to mind. Now, no one has a problem with these two layers of Mind. But Freud suggested that these are the smallest parts! The largest part by far is the unconscious. It includes all the things that are not easily available to our awareness, including many things that have their origins there, such as our drives or instincts, and things that are put there because we can't bear to look at them, such as the memories and emotions associated with trauma. According to Freud, the unconscious is the source of our motivations, whether they are simple desires for food or sex, neurotic compulsions, or the motives of an artist or scientist. And yet, we are often driven to deny or resist becoming conscious of these motives, and they are often available to us only in disguised form. We will see this more clearly in volume 3.

'It is a mistake to believe that a science consists in nothing but conclusively proved propositions, and it is unjust to demand that it should. It is a demand only made by those who feel a craving for authority in some form and a need to replace the religious catechism by something else, even if it were a scientific one. Science in its catechism has but few apodictic precepts; it consists mainly of statements, which it has developed to varying degrees of probability. The capacity to be content with these approximations to certainty and the ability to carry on constructive work despite the lack of final confirmation are actually a mark of the scientific habit of mind.'

Freud

Freud was very good at his research, concentrating on neuro-physiology, even inventing a special cell-staining technique. But only a limited number of positions were available, and there were others ahead of him. Freud's books and lectures brought him both fame and ostracism from the mainstream of the medical community. He drew around him a number of very bright sympathizers who became the core of the psychoanalytic movement. Unfortunately, Freud had a penchant for rejecting people who did not totally agree with him. Some separated from him on friendly terms; others did not, and went on to found competing schools of thought. Freud immigrated to England just before World War II when Vienna became an increasing dangerous place for Jews, especially ones as famous as he was. Not long afterward, he died of the cancer of the mouth and jaw that he had suffered from for the last 20 years of his life.

Afrokhan spirituality is indeed a vast subject and is not to be confused with Western astrology and astronomy, nor should it be confused with the concepts of Western psychoanalysis. In fact, one of the principles of studying the Anatomy of God and the Universe according to the Ancient Theurgists was the science of Solar Biology, postulated today through the AEO and Nuwaubu.

Solar Biology Vs Lunar Astrology

The mystics of the ancient world, such as the Essenes and the Livitical and Magi priests practiced this unique spiritual science. These are just three of the mystic brotherhoods that sprang from the Tat brotherhood of Akhenaton (Amenhotep 1V), of Dynastic Egipt, which in turn emerged from the Ha Kha Doctrine of Tehuti. Note that Tat however, is one of the sons of Tehuti. The Essenes in particular were very strict in their observation of daily prayers, foretelling the future and being well learnt in the scriptures. They were particularly skilled in the logging of the motion of the stars. These devout men kept themselves isolated in closed groups and lived for and by each other. One group resided in the Jordan Mountains, known today as the Qumran Mountains where they received many teachings from Egiptian elders. The biblical 'John the Baptist' is an interpolation grafted from *Yuhanna*, a devout scholar of the Jordan group,[A] who sought to convert the Pharisees and Sadducees due to their transgressions from the original culture of Old Jerusalem.

[A] The Essenes moved to mount Zion, Jordan, and set up the New Jerusalem after their disgust of the Pharisees and Sadducees who became as corrupt as the Sanhedrin and false Kohane priests – of the Old Jerusalem.

Star signs?

The science of solar biology was to log the birth of individuals according to the positioning of the stars. But the system is unlike astrology of the Western world today. The Essenes understood that each individual is composed of 33 1/3% of their mother's, 33 1/3% of their father's and the remaining 33 1/3% of their own soul, and, DNA material.[11] So that means each individual is not just of the star sign that they are born under but in actual fact a combination of three. For this reason the Essenes believed in selective births to bring forth specific characters. The individual star-signs of the zodiac represented a particular quality and characteristic and were therefore presented in an anthropomorphic manner. For instance, in today's astrological system we have the depiction of animals – which is to represent specific archetypal characteristics found in humans.

The idea of developing a science to log star movements came with the fact that the Essenes, a branch of the Tat brotherhood, which in turn stemmed from the order of Tehuti, knew that the Supreme Elders had come from the stars. The root of the word Essenes comes from the same root as *Seir*, where we get Mount Seir – also Usir, Ausar, Asaru and Osiris, which are also reflective of the word Sirus or Sirius. The gods, the Neteru etc., had come to earth from the tri-star system of Sirius. The Essenes therefore acknowledged the great deity Osiris. They also acknowledged the deities **Atum** (or Atum Re), **Atun** (or Aten, or Aton) and **Amun,** (or Amen Re, or Amon Ra), and one of the names of their domain was called Ammuna. The Essenes were spiritual masters, but in some respect they were also students of the supreme 24 Elders of ancient Khemet who were from above.

The Biology of the Stars

Solar biology by definition is, *solar*, which is the study of the Sun and, *biology*, which is study of two ologies, the circulatory and respiratory systems of the body, as taught by Neter Aferti Atum Re of the AEO. So this science is the study of how the solar energies from the Sun affect the human species as well as all other aspects of nature. It also addresses how the stars are but relay stations, of the energy that emanates from the sephiroths within the Anatomy of the Universe, the Anatomy of God. The microcosmic god-body, the human being, is composed of billions of nerve cells called neurons. These cells are but relay stations of energy in the form of synaptic electro-chemical neurotransmitters, and, are analogous and comparative to the Universal Anatomy, where the stars act as the nerve cells of God. The stars transmit the e-motions of God (energy in motion), just as the neurons transmit the e-motions of man.

Fig2.5: the zodiac disc

Astrology on the other hand is moreover a pseudo Christian Science that attempts to identify the characteristics and personalities of people according to what star-sign they are born under. And, astrology today is better called <u>Lunar Astrology</u> as opposed to <u>Solar Biology</u>. This is because western astrology is not primarily based upon the motions of the Sun; it is based on the moon which is a dead lifeless body that does not absorb, nor does it give off energy. The moon only reflects the energy of the sun, just as the Caucasian only reflects the energy of the Afrokhan. Most of the information that is propagated today regarding astrology and star-sign readings etc. is presented by Caucasians and Mulattos. These teachings are therefore definitely not for the melanated Afrokhan who aught to follow a system of Solar Biology, since she is created of the Divine Astral Light – of 9-ether and Involution. Astrology is a European 6-ether pseudo-science, and is also based round a sex-spirit force called Leviathan, where propagation of the culture and society is driven by sex, the animalistic way of cohesion and physical duplication – never mind it just being about logging births and monitoring characteristics. Since the female aspect of the Astral Light, the gross astral, is tainted in one sense, with matter, it *is* indeed matter, and therefore is destructive by nature to the Afrokhan who is of the Divine Astral Light. The science of Solar Biology also indoctrinates the science of lovemaking – not just the physical aspects of intercourse but the celestial and Divine implications also.

Notes

[1] Israel Regardie, *The Tree of Life,* p36-37 (Samuel Weiser, INC, USA, 1972, ISBN: 0-87728-149-1)

[2] Ibid, p36-37

[3] Sir Godfrey Higgins, *the Anacalypsis,* p41 *(A & B Books Publishers, New York, 1863, ISBN: 1-881316-16-5)*

[4] Ra Un Nefer Amun, *T.O.L.M.*, p23 (Kamit Publishers, Inc, USA, 1996, ISBN: 1-877662-13-5)
[5] Ibid, p23
[6] Nebu Ka Ma'at, *The Legacy of the Black Gods in Time before time*, Introduction (Tamare House Publishers)
[7] Ibid, Introduction
[8] Israel Regardie – *The Tree of Life* – p60-72
[9] Ibid, p60-72
[10] Ibid, p60-72
[11] Dr Malachi, *Coming Forth by Day*, pXIX

Chapter 3
The Science of Love in the Making

Impulsive Behaviour

The material world as we perceive it is but a manifestation of *energy* that is expressed as different forms of magnetic, radioactive and electrical currents – which are the resultants of the tearing energy coming from the Ain Soph. That, which is perceived as the gross physical body of the Oriental, the Asian and the Caucasian, is of the gross astral light, and is but a collection of electrical and radioactive energies having a physical experience. The Afrokhan's gross physical body is of the Divine Astral Light, and, materialises as a collection of electrical and magnetic forces. We experience electrochemical synaptic impulses within the nervous system, which we translate as e-motions of joy and pain, love and hate etc. And ultimately we experience 'love making,' as the highest and most powerful form of physical e-motion.

Impulsive behaviour simply means to act on impulse; or, to act on sudden urges. It also means to act or react to our emotions, or to have impetuous emotional responses without the intervention of logical thoughts. This is the postulated impression of the European system, as it propagates its interpretation of what love and sexuality entails through the media etc. However, the purpose of this chapter: 'The Science of Love in the Making,' is to give the reader an understanding of why and how we fall in and out of love, and, why we make Love, and to understand the magical sciences of ritualistic intercourse and its positive and negative implications. We must grow to understand the power of intercourse as well as the negative impacts that can be inflicted upon the physical body if we misuse it. Intercourse can indeed be a wonderful experience, especially when it is done with someone we truly love.

However, most of us tend to have sexual intercourse just for the sheer enjoyment of it. This is purely a mechanical feat. It is like a two-handled slot machine with two operators trying to get a jackpot at the same time... then it's all over – and that's it... Surely this cannot be what sex is all about!

Sexual Energy

Sexual energy – or the energy that is transferred during the act of intercourse is the highest form of energy that the human body can impart or absorb. In order for us to understand these energy transferences it is imperative that we have an understanding of energy in general. Everything within our Universe is based upon energy, and as a microcosm of the cosmos, human beings are an amalgamation of energy also. All physical matter is a coagulation of units of force expressed as energy, and thus energy is required for the maintenance of all physical manifestations – all of which are controlled and directed by the Universal Mind; the Subjective Conscience of the Self. Energy and Spirit are one and the same, and matter, is a physical manifestation of Spirit – or Spirit in its lowest form of vibration.

Humans are created and are thus born with a certain amount of energy, called *Chi* energy or *Sekhem* or *Prana*.[A] This original substantial energy cannot be replaced once it has been used up, but it can be replenished by way of our diet, and our breathing, but is also dependent on a sound state of mind. The amount of energy or quality of energy we ingest or expel is largely determined by our mental state of being. We think our selves into whom and what we become, which is then enhanced by the foods we eat and the quality of air we breathe. This also means we think our selves into our own demise due to the lack of awareness of whom and what we are – due to the lack of Conscience

---

[A] The Orientals know this vital life force as Chi, as Sekhem to the ancient Khemetians, and as Prana to the Hindus.

and Divine Astral Awareness. We create our 'somatic body'[A] based upon the conditioning of the latter. We are conditioned to believe that we can only live for a certain amount of years, and so this subconsciously programs the brain to create a somatic body with a limited life span. Sexual energy, if understood and used correctly is one of many stepping-stones toward immorality. This is because of the unlimited amount of spiritual energy that can be attained by way of intercourse. There is an old saying: 'The making of man and woman, is like the making of heaven and earth.' Humans have long forgotten this aphorism. It is an axiom that embodies the truth that heaven and earth (i.e., stars and planets) can live for aeons upon aeons of time. In ancient Afrokhan cultures this axiom was clearly understood and the peoples thereby lead a way of life that was focused on developing their ability to harness and store Chi energy to sustain their lives. One of the methods was to master the use of Sexual Energy and Power.

The purpose of intercourse is to enable the participants to reach higher states of awareness and Consciousness. It should not be intended just for the goal to reach ejaculation or to have an ecstatic orgasm! In fact, ejaculation and orgasm are two completely different biological functions. In the male, ejaculation is but a physiological function that is hardwired into the brain for the sole purpose of procreation when the penis is stimulated through intercourse or otherwise. Ejaculation through intercourse should therefore only happen if the intention of both parties is to have a child – to procreate in correspondence with the Divine order. The amount of Sekhem or Chi energy that is used up during every ejaculation is equivalent to an unfit male doing a 20-mile run within a 5-10min slot. This is devastating to the body. Hence,

---

[A] The somatic body is created and grown by the mental programming of the soma cells, where these cells are constantly being reproduced, as opposed to our germ cells that never die. Somatic programming has become one of the fundamental means of systematic mind control, because these cells can be conditioned to mentally produce a body that will be in line with the enforced mental state.

professional athletes are always being advised by their coach to refrain from sexual activities for at least three days before they perform. Too much ejaculation is also one of the causes of prostate cancer in the male because of the excessive amount of activities within the prostate area.

> *'Abstaining from ejaculation for 90 days can develop sexual potency, as it takes 90 days to fully develop sperm. Unused fully developed sperm is then dissipated and spread throughout the body as an energy source. Remember... each time the male ejaculates he is using up his life essence – Chi – Sekhem. A very Yang-male, with fully developed sperm can ejaculate up to 777,777,777 sperm in one go.'* [1]

Paraphrased from Dr Malachi

> *"On the average the male may ejaculate up to 5,000 times within his lifetime or ejaculate 5 gallons of sperm in total."* [2]

Wayne Chandler

Sexual Mantras

A mantra is a vocally produced tone or series of tones in the form of a chant or chants, which resonate within the body to invoke specific energies. During the act of intercourse we may fall into an automatic mantra without realising it. The moans or groans that we experience are the result of our neurological system corresponding with the brain – informing it that climax is on the way. The moans are automatically produced as forms of mantras to incite our spiritual centres to open up thereby allowing the Divine aspect of the entity to be incarnated to enter. If moans or groans are not produced, you may find yourself automatically breathing deeply. Breathing deeply is a very convenient and powerful way of aligning all of our spiritual centres – such as the chakras. Breathing deeply also powerfully helps to revitalise the body in totality. Mantras and chants, when done intentionally and consciously should be performed with specific breath taking exercises. Sexual intercourse should therefore be treated as a sacred ritual.

During coitus, or just before ejaculation, the <u>spirit of the semen</u> follows the path of the **Khundalini**,[A] by rising up along the spinal column passing all major Chakra points until it reaches the medulla oblongata. Here, the 'spark of life' occurs – the 'Big Bang' of Sekhem/ Chi – the entity to be incarnated enters via the pineal gland, then marries with the semen at the junction of the brain stem and the spinal column. Here, the spirit of the semen is collaborated with the spirit of the incarnated being, Consciousness. The spiritual entity then travels back down the spinal column in a rush, marries with the actual semen, the liquid form, which now becomes sperm and ejaculates through the phallus on its way to seek fertilisation of the female ovum.

So the act of coitus, coupled with correct conscious breathing, also coupled with automatic mantras is but a spiritual science performed on the physical level, but with psycho-spiritual correspondences. This connects us to higher vibratory planes of existence and experience. At this level of spiritual initiation one can choose to bring a new life into the world by way of ejaculation, or may otherwise choose to simply enjoy the experience and ending with full rejuvenation of the body, without actual ejaculation. The raising of the Khundalini during intercourse is extremely powerful, if we understand how to harness and use the available energy. Each Chakra along the spinal column represents one of the 7/9 planes of existence and experience. The 7 major chakras are shown below this paragraph, table 6. Generally, the Khundalini energy lays dormant within the Root Chakra, as most of earth's humans are only consciously in tune with the plane of physical manifestation. As the Khundalini energy rises, whether through meditation, chanting, breathing or coitus, one becomes consciously

---

[A] The word Khundalini is sometimes translated as the sleeping serpent, where the serpent is symbolic of healing and transformation.

attuned to the corresponding planes. Understand that there are specific techniques of meditation, chants, breaths and intercourse that enable us to tune in and experience these higher states of awareness. In volume 1, I re-presented the doctrine of creating the **Merkaba** as taught by **Drunvalo Melchizadeck**. The Merkaba is a time/ space vehicle that allows one to phase out of the 3rd dimension and tune into the 4th dimension taking their body with them. This magical exercise is essentially done by manipulating the Khundalini to be raised to a specific point along the spinal column, by way of 17 breathing steps coupled with visualisation techniques. In Ch9 we will redefine the Merkaba and the benefits of utilising it.

Table 6: the 7Chakras and corresponding Planes

Chakra	Plane of manifestation
Crown Chakra	Bosom of God
Brow Chakra	Plane of Divine Reality
Throat Chakra	Plane of Divine Truth
Heart Chakra	Plane of Mind
Solar Plexus Chakra	Plane of Spiritual Animation
Spleenic Chakra	Plane of Spiritual Force
Root Chakra	Plane of Physical Manifestation of God

Love in Creational myths

The Divinity of Love has to be at the root of the conception of The All and of its Creation, projected by the undifferentiated stuff. Without Divine Love, manifestation will not happen, because Divine Love is the basis of Substantial Integrity. Divine Love is the ultimate healer also, projected by the Divine Astral Light. The raising of the Khundalini brings us back in tune with the Creator, Conscience and Love, which by default afford us with youthfulness and vitality in the moment. This means that one who is on the Mystical Path ought to live life in meditation – meaning we must conscientiously travel, talk, eat, and sleep etc., in meditation. We often hear the 'truth' that God created the world out of Love. This type of Love is not to be confused with desires to have a *thing* or to have an *experience*. This is Love beyond Mental description – a *state* that is achieved once we escape the boundaries of the matrix grids – a *state* coupled with Divine Peace and Joy. This *state* of be*ing* rewards us with the ultimate gift of unlimited creativity and infinite potential. It is the *state* of being '<u>Present in the Now</u>.' I must explain however that although I use the word *'state,'* it is an irony because within that level of awareness there are no states. States are like conditions that we perceive mentally or by way of our senses, and are therefore limiting. The word <u>Presence</u> is better suited for such awareness.

<u>Yin and Yang</u>

The source of our yin and yang aspects is created directly out of Love. In the 3 dimensional world of manifestation, they represent our duality concepts of male and female, masculine and feminine or positive and negative, centrifugal and centripetal forces etc., all of which are objective. The source of Love is therefore Subjective and must also be perfectly and completely united. The Subjective Mind unites all of Creation as one Created phenomenon; as one complete experience. Our perception of the objective manifestation of the latter gives rise to the illusion of space/ time/ separation etc.

As we manifest into the world of duality and of low vibratory rates, we loose our perception (due to amnesia, from the shock and trauma at birth) of the inter-connectedness of all *things.* We also forget that we have a higher aspect to our be*ing*, referred to as our twin flame or twin Soul. This higher aspect usually resides in the 4th dimension although it can be experiencing ever higher dimensions simultaneously. However, the DNA is encoded in such a way that we periodically remember that there is something missing from our lives. The Astral

Light triggers us involuntarily through DNA excitement since it holds all information and memory of our entire existence. This memory jogger may also be triggered, by watching a movie like Star Trek or Babylon 5, or by listening to a spiritual sermon, or even by reading esoterical books such as this one. But due to our own ignorance that constrains us we tend to seek out this twin soul in our so-called love relationships. We set out on an earthly mission to find our soul mate. And assuming that we have found her/ him, ultimately the act of coitus or 'love making' gives us the experience of uniting with our 'soul mate' on a higher level. This is not to say that this is wrong, but to understand that intercourse, is a method that two people <u>standing in love</u> together can use as a vehicle to help each other connect with their own twin soul or to the Higher Self – not with each other! This is the illusion of 3rd dimension and egoic conditioning. The ego-self has a tendency to obscure us from connecting to the Higher Self, so it tricks us into believing that we can find true Love, Peace and Joy in another than God. Yes, we do experience these 3 paradigms within our more serious relationships, but only as reflections of the real deal... in fact, that is the very nature of the ego – to give us reflections of Reality, which we tend to believe and call truth. The ego is therefore lunar or lunatic in nature.

The ancient Khemetic mystery system taught its neophytes about the duality concepts of 3rd dimensional living. This was expressed by way of the attributes of NTR as Shu and Tefnut. In this context, Shu represents the yang (masculine) and Tefnut represents the yin (feminine). But Shu also expresses the yin within his yang nature, and likewise Tefnut expresses the yang within her yin nature. So, even though they are separated by way of Duality Consciousness, both are still complete within and of themselves – by way of their intimate connection with their own twin flame or soul – with God. Ancient myths and legends are often sexually explicit in their narration of bi-sexual creative forces, such as the accounts of Aphrodite and Venus.

Aphrodite and Venus

The planet Venus, the emblem of love and emotion, is the planet attributed by the magical philosophers to the 7th Sephirah on the Tree of Life, the *Netzach*. Likewise the colour green, which, traditionally, belongs to Aphrodite, as pertaining to that Sephirah are peculiarly connected with growth, harvest and agriculture. During the Neolithic times, (the so-called later stone-age periods,) the notion of a Goddess or of a woman as ruler of an entire tribe, people or nation was commonplace. This is especially so amongst the Sumerian and later the Babylonian, Anatolian and Canaan cultures of that time era and indeed prior. There is a common theme or concept of a worshipped female deity, whom is always portrayed with a young husband or lover. Some folklore presents their goddess as having sexual relations with her son or younger brother (obviously symbolic). We get reflections of this concept within the Greek legends of Aphrodite and Adonis, and were even known as Cybele and Attis in pre-Christian Rome. Charles Seltman wrote in 1952 of a highly developed culture of Crete, whose beginnings predate biblical times by many centuries. He states that, upon Crete, matriarchy had been the way of life. He discussed the sexual freedom of women, matrilineal descent and the role of a *King*, pointing out the high status of women in and around the land in which the Goddess appears to have been the very core of existence. Men became *King* only by way of a formal marriage, and, his successor would be the man who married his daughter, not his son. In other words the women would choose who would become king.

In the upper Palaeolithic societies, (the so-called early stone age periods), in which the mother may have been regarded as the sole parent of the family, ancestor worship was apparently the basis of sacred ritual, and, the means for ancestral reverence were generally through matrilineal agents. This is because the concept of a Creator in the clan's image was female. Images of goddesses of these Palaeolithic times, as far back as 25,000BCE, were called Venus figures, made of stones, bones and clay. The legendary Greek Goddess Aphrodite is also known as Venus in early Rome, as Astarte in Phoenicia, and as Ishtar in Babylonia.[3] She is said to be either the daughter of Zeus, or, she sprung from the foam of the seas. She is also said to be the mother of Eros, the Greek boy-god of love, identified with the Roman Cupid. Now, the whole malarkey surrounding Aphrodite and Venus is the idea that these pseudo Goddesses symbolise subliminal sexual aphrodisiacs. The Goddess is also portrayed as the notoriously unfaithful wife of Hephaestus, the God of fire. And what you may ask, does all of this have to do with True Love? Nothing. The majority of myths and folklore that we find concerning Love in Creation is either Hindi and Oriental, or Greek and Roman. Afrokhan cosmologies tend to deal more with balancing Principles or, union of yin and yang forces etc., as opposed to aphrodisiac-based stories. One Hindu commentary talks of how the Creator Brahma was in a lovers embrace with his consort for what seemed like eternity before eventually ejaculating thus producing the first human beings.

<u>Love & Sex in the Sumerian epics</u>
    I quote from the book of Genesis just as a reminder of where we find the apparently first acts of love and sex; or is it?

> *"And the eyes of them both were opened, and they knew that they were naked; and they sewed fig leaves together, and made themselves aprons."*

Gen 3v8

And then in chapter 4 we have:

> *"And Adam knew his wife; and she conceived, and bare Cain, and said, I have gotten a man from the Lord."*

Gen 4v1

In his book *'The Twelfth Planet,'* Sitchin elaborates on these quotes and writes:

> *'They were, we are to understand, at some lesser stage of human development than that of fully developed humans: Not only were they naked, they were unaware of the implications of such nakedness.*
>
> *Further examination of the biblical tale suggests that its theme is Man's acquisition of some sexual powers. The "knowing" that was held back from Man was not some scientific information but something with the male and female sex; for no sooner had Man and his mate acquired the "knowing" than "they knew they were naked" and covered their sex organs.* [4]

Zecharia Sitchin

Throughout the Old Testament the term *'to know,'* is used to denote sexual intercourse, mostly between a man and his spouse for the purpose of having children. The quote informs the reader of the first act of sexual intercourse between the so-called Adam and Eve, the first man and woman. Not to put too fine a point on the fact that the consummation was not preceded by a formal agreement or wedding ceremony! Sitchin also extensively writes about the fact that the Genesis account is but a summary of ancient Babylonian and Sumerian texts, of which he spares no unturned stones in his book, *'Genesis Revisited.'* He says, *"the Mesopotamian texts speak freely and eloquently of sex and lovemaking among the gods"* – that is, the Anunnaqi. There are texts that describe in detail, intimacy and tenderness among the gods. Some texts describe violent lovemaking also, such as, the raping of Ninlil by the god Enlil. Other texts describe how the gods frequently divulged in sexual activities with their unofficial concubines, with their sisters and daughters, and even with their grand daughters. The god Enqi was well known for such activities, and could hardly turn against mankind for acting in ways that he himself did. Thus we have the opening of Gen Ch6:

> *"And it came to pass, when men began to multiply upon the face of the earth, and daughters were born unto them, that the sons of God saw the daughters of men that they were fair; and they took them wives of all which they chose."*
>
> Gen 6v1-2

Notice it uses the word *'took,'* implying sex by force. And verse 4 takes it a step further by stating that another group of 'sons of God' married the daughters of man – by using the phrase, *'came in unto'* the earth in those days; and also after that, when the sons of God came in unto the daughters of men, and they bare children to them, the same became mighty men which were of old, men of renown."

> Gen 6v4

The Sumerian tales, not only speaks of poor sexual morals, but also tell of new guidelines for sexual intercourse amongst mankind. After setting a bad impression of sexual conduct, the gods, the Anunnaqi, established wedding ceremonies and taught mankind the meaning of compatibility, commitment and loyalty in marital relationships.[5] In particular, the gods taught the earthlings about genetic compatibility, as we shall explore shortly – according to our own times though.

Egiptian Viagra

But, "What about natural Aphrodisiacs?" Well, the following may certainly explain a lot about rabbits: *'Lettuce is an ancient Viagra, which can boost your sexual performance,'* scientists revealed recently. They say that it produces chemicals that were used by the *'Egyptians'* as an aphrodisiac. Botanist Giorgio Samorini made the discovery when he solved a riddle that foiled experts for decades. **Min**, the ancient

90

Khemetian god of sexuality, is often depicted in bas-reliefs with a vegetable – and nobody knew what or why. But Samorini identified the plant as a bitter-leafed lettuce known as Lactuca serriola. This initially confused him because, since Roman times, the sap produced by lettuce has been thought to dampen sexual desire. Emperor Nero is said to have eaten it to rid him of erotic dreams and Pliny the Elder wrote that lettuce can 'cool sexual appetite as well as a feverish body.' The Italian botanist carried out tests on the vegetable, which revealed that in small amounts the sap does, indeed, have a sedative effect. But in larger doses the substance – which includes a cocaine-like chemical – acts as a sexual stimulant. *'About 1g induces calming and pain killing effects,'* said Mr Samorini, editor of the botanical journal Eleusis. *'At the highest doses, 2g to 3g, the stimulating effects prevail.'* He added: *'This finally solves an ethno-botanical riddle and explains the association with Min and lettuce.'* Many would agree that as informative as all this may appear, in today's societies, relationship compatibility has to be at the forefront of all discussions regarding marital relationships, let alone sexual relationships.

Compatibility and Relationships

Because the subject of compatibility is a very sensitive one, it tends to confront people, should they be asked: *"Are you truly compatible with and for your partner?"* It sort of makes the hair on the back of our neck stand up, as we cringe due to the figmentive flash of the reality that maybe we are not in a fully compatible scenario. Most people fall into love relationships for the wrong reasons, though many of them may last many years. The same applies for people who choose to go into business with another; compatibility is very important, in so far as having common goals and agendas – not to mention trust. But first things first, that is, make sure you get into a relationship for the right reasons. I'm using the word 'right' loosely as a relative term. I mean 'right,' relative to the larger purpose you hold in your life. As stated, most people enter relationships for the wrong reasons – to fill gaps, end loneliness, and bring themselves love or to have someone to love – and these are some of the better reasons. Others do so to salve their ego, end their depressions, improve their sex life, recover from a previous relationship, or, believe it or not, to relieve boredom. None of these reasons will work in the long run, and unless something dramatic changes along the way, neither will the relationship.

We ought to take a journey back down memory lane into our past relationships and get Present to why we actually got involved with those persons. Is it just because we fell in love? Most of us will find it difficult to remember the exact reason why we actually started a particular relationship. We tend to only remember what we decided about the relationship and not what actually happened. What we decided is based on an emotional interpretation of what actually happened. For most people, love is a response to a need for fulfilment. So it is very easy to fall in love… but extremely difficult to think in terms of the longevity of the prospective relationship. Too many warning flashes and signposts pop up and smack us in the face. The first analysis ought to be one of compatibility, and, the second, one of relativity. And, this also depends on what our bigger goals in life are.

Now, in creating that which is *"here"* and that which is *"there,"* God made it possible for God to know itself. So God created *relativity* – the greatest gift that God could give itself. Thus, *relationship* is the greatest gift God could ever give to you. From the No-*thing* sprang the Every-*thing*. First there was the first *thing*, then, there was the second. The period that is taken to travel from the *thing* over *"here,"* to the *thing* over *"there,"* became measurable, thus we have the creation of *time* and two *relative* points, hence relationship. God knew that for love to exist – and to know itself as Pure Love – its exact opposite had to exist as well, and this we call fear. Everything that Love is not we experience through fear. There is no "hate" in reality, only fear of not having Love, and the discomfort of this fear creates the illusion of hate. In the moment that fear existed, love could exist as a thing that could be experienced. Just as humans have chosen to personify Pure Love as the character God, so have we chosen to objectively personify fear as the character called the devil. And therefore we have great mythologies and folklore that teach of this creation of duality – with episodes of conflicts between good gods and bad gods, the forces of light and dark etc. In our relationships we all talk about how we feel love for, or, feel love from our partner. But is this a reality, or is it a misinterpretation of emotional responses to biological stimuli?

<u>The feeling of Love</u>

So why exactly do we fall in love? The soul of our very be*ing* yearns for a feeling, one only attained through physical life and living. The soul does not seek knowledge of what Love is for it already has that knowledge, since the Universal Soul through Spirit, is indeed created out of Unconditional Love. So the soul in its earthly embodiment seeks to experience through feeling; sensation, and therefore e-motion, what Love is. Your soul's ultimate desire is to feel and experience the highest feeling of love ever possible. That is its purpose. Knowledge of love is conceptual, but the feeling is experimental says Neale Donald Walsch, in his book *'Conversations with God.'*

The highest feeling is attained with complete union with 'All that Is.' It is the great return to Divine Truth and Divine Reality that the soul seeks. This beloved, is the Presence of Perfect Love. Love is not emotional nor is it the absence of emotions. It is rather like the colour Black, which is the collective of all colours. Love is therefore the collective of all emotions – care, hatred, anger, lust, concern, covetousness etc. Thus for the soul to experience Perfect Love it must first experience <u>every</u> human feeling; sensation. Ask yourself these questions... "How can I have compassion for that which I don't understand?" "How can I forgive in another that which I have never experienced in myself?" "How can I be right if I don't know what wrong is?" However, and this is the key… out of every decision the soul makes i.e., to go left or right, up or down and so on, its task is to select the best of the two possibilities, and, never condemn that which is not grand. This is a big task, and can possibly take many lifetimes to master.

> *"Condemnation without investigation is the height of ignorance."*
>
> Albert Einstein

We are quick to judge our feelings about situations as "bad," as "wrong," or "not enough," rather than to bless what we have as a Divine lesson. Sometimes we do worst than condemn our own feelings, and, seek to do harm toward that which we say we did not choose. We seek to destroy it, or at least to prove it wrong. If there is a *person, place* or *thing* with which you do not agree with or, does not agree with you, you deploy an attack. If there is a religion that doesn't believe in what you believe, you oppose it. And, if there is even a thought from another that contradicts or challenges yours, you ridicule it. This creates very serious errors within your soul, for it causes a bias toward only one half of the created Universe. And so how can we even begin to understand our own half if we completely reject the other half. These are the exact implications of sensed incompatibility in our love relationships. 'The Science of Love in the Making' has therefore gone completely out the window. Pun.

How can we have a truly loving relationship with another if we are not mentally strong enough to deal with opposition? To deal with opposition is simple, but definitely not easy. The first thing is to realise that there is no opposition in reality – situations just are. For every action, personal characteristic, place, event or thing, that occurs in the manifested world, there is an equally opposite one. Or, according to the Kaballah, for any *thing* (universes, gods, men and beasts) to be manifested in the lower realms of the Astral Light, there must be two possibilities in order for it to occur and exist. The extremeness of the two possibilities creates the illusion that they are in opposition. Lack of awareness of these basic spiritual Principles can cause serious disturbances within our soul, which on the face of our daily behaviour creates enmity between our self and our loved ones. We have forgotten what it is like to be loved without condition. We do not remember the experience of the Unconditional Love of God. And so we try to imagine what the Love of God must be like, based on what we see of love in the world, thus we mimic televised love relationships.

An associate of mine once said in jest, *"Love is a concept created by Walt Disney to give people hope."* And indeed, it is the human being that has created the concept of love, surrounding a fear-based reality, rooted in the idea of a fearful, vengeful God. We have projected the role of parenthood unto God. We remember how our own parents would scold us for being disobedient etc., and thus come up with a God who judges, rewards and punishes, based on how good He <u>feels</u> about what we have been up to. Having thus created an entire system of thought about God based on human experience rather than spiritual realities, we also created an entire reality around love. Every action taken by human beings is based in love or fear, not just those actions in our love relationships. Decisions affecting business, industry, politics, religion, education, war, social structures and so forth are all rooted in love and fear. It seems that the fear-based decision wins more often than not, why is this? We have been taught to live in fear. The Western system does not propagate love in all aspects of its societies. We have been taught about the 'survival of the fittest, the victory of the strongest and, the success of the cleverest.' Precious little is said about the glory of the most loving.

Compatibility in relationships in ancient times was on a more scientific level, particularly in Royal and Monarchy systems. In other words, the priests, on the genetic level, screened Royal couples to determine whether or not they would be compatible to have children, since ultimately this is what marriage is all about. This was an actual science, known today as eugenics.

Choosing a mate or partner

Eugenics by definition is, *'the study of methods to improve the mental and physical characteristics of the human race by choosing who may or may not be compatible to marry.'* Today however, many couples do carry out blood tests before marrying, but only to screen for diseases or impurities, never really for procreative compatibility. I married the mother of my twin boys, Sahleem and Sahlee, when I was 25years old; the marriage lasted less than one year... "What happened?" I hear you ask. To put it plain and simple, and without going into why I chose to marry, other than the obvious reason – falling in love, we were not compatible. Nature also had something else in store I was unaware of. We both had a particular trait of sickle cells, a condition found amongst Caribbean and Afrokhan peoples. This is to say we were both carriers of the traits of the disease sickle cell anaemia, but did not actually suffer the disease our selves. This meant that our children stood a very high chance of being born with the actual disease, and that is exactly what happened. In my wife's world at the time, the idea of having to deal with the potential suffering of two babies at once was a lot to bear and take on. This put a huge strain on everything and thus our intentions of marriage and staying married faded drastically. There were other incompatibilities present also, which are not necessary to be expressed here. But, had I carried out a screening of my own blood and DNA, we probably would not have married, let alone had children, because marriage is indeed about children and the propagation of the human specie in the image and after the likeness of God.

The principle that we are working on here is Choice...

'Choice is the ability to recognise alternatives and possible consequences, thereby enabling the selection of that which is most desirable, admirable, and honourable – the ability to act in response to the recognised alternatives.'[6]

Iyanla Vanzant

However, here is a traditional Jewish fable about decision-making: There was a young boy who was having a dream about a motor accident that took place. The car, driven by his father, with his mother in the front passenger seat and him in the back, went out of control and tumbled over a bridge and into a lake. Now here is the dilemma. The boy is able to save himself as he is a good swimmer, but can also only save one of his parents. What should he do…?

Wake up!!!

The lesson here is: just because we are presented with a dilemma to make a choice between two things, doesn't mean that we actually have to make a choice. Sometimes the best selection is to not choose at all, and allow whatever is to be, to be. Decision-making in starting a relationship or, whilst already in a relationship, regardless of the nature of it, brings forth responsibility. The moment we decide to go 'East,' instead of 'West,' responsibility sets in. That is, we have to take responsibility for our decisions and the outcomes of them. We have to accept that we automatically create the implications and the impacts of our actions through our choosing of what to do, and of what not to do. The consequences of our decisions or our failure to choose, teaches us how to live in harmony with our Self and with others. God, the Self, the Conscience, the energy of the Divine Astral Light, always guides and protects us. It is however, up to us to listen intimately to what the Higher Self is saying. It speaks to us as feelings. It speaks to us as the need to understand and to grow, and to develop into a super conscious be*ing*. Sometimes the pace of life and nervous habits forces us to make quick decisions without listening to the suggestions of the Higher Self, God, – perfectly understandable. But, awareness of this helps. Just being aware of the Presence of the Divine Self and its guiding obligations strengthens us in our choosing.

When choosing a mate or partner, weigh all the possible alternatives, and evaluate all the possible consequences, then choose freely, for you will be responsible for the outcome – not your partner. Your partner will be likewise responsible for her or his decision-making on entering the relationship. I have experienced a number of relationships since my divorce, and indeed, quite a few before I was ever married. My love relationships provided me with the greatest lessons in life. As Iyanla Vanzant would say, *"Meantime relationships provided us with lessons that help us understand who we are, and prepares us for the ultimate experience."* Quick decision-making, which I have been well known for, without the intervention of inner thoughts, quickly teaches what works and what doesn't work in our lives. On the other hand, clearly focused choices, grounded in self-awareness and trust in the Divine Astral Light, God, reveals to you the Divine Truth and the Divine Reality of your inner knowing. All choices, whether forced or focused, resistant or courageous, will take you to a level of understanding that will ultimately affect the way you view life. And, will influence the way you choose your mate or partner. Having the willingness to make choices promotes a willingness to grow and develop. When we consciously and constantly choose growth over stagnation and fear, the Divine Astral Light of the Universe supports us in the decision, by bringing us the lesson gently and lovingly. Stagnation and fear on the other hand goes against the most fundamental principle of the Universe, and that is change, which is to grow. This way we learn lessons that are not presented by the Divine Astral Light, but rather presented by the gross astral light, the hard way!

Some say we live in a world dominated by *sin*, forces of evil that work against the betterment of humanity; forces that do not love nor understand love. But the word *sin* is also an acronym for, 'self inflicted nonsense.' In reality no one individual can inflict sin upon you. And similarly, no one individual can do anything for you or against you; you create your reality as you progress through life, by the decisions you make. The matrix mentality is what we are dominated by; and it has created for us *an 'Emotional Alcatraz,'* says David Icke. The matrix mentality is based around our not expressing our selves truthfully, as we are too worried and concerned about how others will <u>feel</u>. Just think of the amount of people around you, who you care about, who you allow to suppress what you want to do with your life because you are concerned by the way it will make them <u>feel</u>. So it is clear to see that the 'feeling of love,' 'choosing a mate or partner' and, being brutally honest with everyone about your intentions, can create an emotional prison. Surely the Creator did not intend for us to create our own spiritual demise in this or any manner; no, it is us who, through so called free will, and through the desire to rule ourselves, have caused our own pain and suffering, just because of a concept called feeling, having 'love and fear' at its polar opposites. See fig9.1.

Making the wrong decision in selecting a wife or husband can turn the marriage and the relationship into a prison sentence, and a family home into a prison cell, where no one, including the children, are able to express themselves freely. Please, don't get me wrong. I am not saying to mistreat people just because you feel like it, or to make peoples' lives miserable just for the sheer sake of it. No, no. I mean to express what you are, say what you think, live your uniqueness, without suppressing yourself because those around will not understand the real you. It means to stop living what *they* think you should be; and start being the way that you really *are*. If they can't handle that, that's their problem and they should find someone else who would suit them better. And if they can't, and insist that you suppress the real you to suit them, then they are unaware unpaid gatekeepers of the emotional Alcatraz. Usually we encounter these types of issues and problems where misinterpretations of conversation occur. We express ourselves generally with the intention to be heard and understood, but not always with care and love. In our minds, As long as we are heard and understood, who cares how the listener feels. This is not good practice.

Communicating with Love

The art of conversation, powerful communication, and charisma, create great interpersonal and relationship skills. But how about approaching your loved ones, your friends, and even strangers for that matter, with Unconditional Love? Obviously not love as in the desire to be with any and every body, but to approach with compassion, care and concern. It is to approach people as if you are God in the flesh. Yes, why not use God as your yardstick? Is this not what modern religion is all about? Aren't the Muslims using Muhammad and Allah as their yardstick? Aren't the Christians using Christ Jesus and God/ Theos as their yardstick? And, aren't the Jews using Abraham and Yahweh as their yardstick? In my understanding, that is exactly so. Whatever concept you choose to accept as the Creator of the Universe, ought to be your mentor. This may take some practice if you are not already that way inclined. You may choose to initiate yourself into higher levels of awareness, and indeed higher levels of communication with others. The Ancestors will congratulate and welcome you, but you still have to remember that 95% of the population of your environment are to the least, on a spiritually aspiring path, let alone the same path as yourself. So you have to develop with keenness, a way or ways, to have conversations with people who are on different levels; with people who are of different cultures and who have different past experiences and, different ideals. And, to have the ability to communicate powerfully, in ways that they are "touched," and or "moved," and or "inspired."[A] As

---

[A] This principle I picked up from the Landmark Forum in Action seminar series.

you can see, 'The Science of Love in the Making' is not just about sexual intercourse at all – that is only a very tiny part of the subject. Love as a subject is vast, in fact it is infinite inasmuch that everything infinitum were created out of Love. We therefore experience Love in an infinitum of ways along the great Mystical and Magical Paths.

> *"We are not humans on a spiritual journey. We are spiritual beings on a human journey."*

Says Stephen R. Covey, author of the best selling book, *'The 7 habits of highly effective people'*. And Charles Swindoll says:

> *"We are all faced with a series of great opportunities brilliantly disguised as impossible situations."*

Relationships are everything; they are indeed disguised as opportunities for us to aspire spirit-ward. Relationships exist as communication between planets and stars, water and air, heat and cold, thought and energy, and constantly create and change the world around us. Relationships are literally what make creation possible and human relationships are an expression of this truth. Through communicating and relating is the way we learn and grow. But, if blueprint rules are laid down that dictate how a relationship should be, or the direction that it should go, then, we are immediately building barriers to all other potential experience and, therefore, greater understanding. The flow of life leads us into what we need to experience and with whom, in order to get to the next level, and this flow comes from within ourselves. Once we lay down the way it must be, *or else,* whether for ourselves or to impose upon others, we are challenging that flow, which may have other unforeseen plans for us. And, in situations like this, we may as well forget about sex magic and the unlimited possibilities therein.

Sex Magic

Many once thought that sex magic was an unsavoury and evil act, relegated to the 'left hand path' or the 'black magic' side of a number of mystical traditions. Modern thinking however concludes that this is not at all true. The idea that sex magic is evil came from the antiquated and malignant idea that women were, in and of themselves, somehow impure. Hence, any connection with women was sometimes considered to be 'taken with extreme caution.' Today we are capable of recognising that this is absurd.

Sex magic is a beautiful sacrament; a sacred ritual performed with a lover. Through this connection you and your partner can achieve communion with the Collective Unconscious, with the Divine Astral Light and the Cosmic Consciousness of the Universe. *"When a man and a woman come together in this sacred ritual, they are, at that time, the true image of the living God, male-female, mother-father, Pangenetor-Pangenetrix,"* says Jason Newcomb on the subject of sex magic. He also says that sex magic can be performed by any other combination of partners, male-male, female-female, or even by oneself – with varied results of course. Sex magic is not complicated at all; it is relatively simple to understand. We must first recognise that within our genital fluids there is Universal Power to create life, and, with that understanding comes the knowing of the power to assist and make things happen in life. Whether to acquire wealth, peace with others, health improvement, or any other self-empowering experience, the required driving force is available through the power of orgasm. The moment of orgasm is one of pure cosmic power, which can either be directed to create life or directed to enhance life in whichever way we desire. Orgasm simply results in creation – but creation of what? You conscientiously choose.

In the coitus act, we are practically connecting the Mental Plane and the Material Plane as one single experience, with our emotional body/ soul acting as the path of communion. So through our emotions we can manifest that which we mentally desire. There is unlimited possibilities and potential available through this sacred act. Yes really. Any purpose or objective can be adapted to a sex magic context. However, this science should only be used if you have mastered the basics of mysticism. The Hermetic Order of the Golden Dawn and the Rosicrucian Order, as well as the New Hermetic systems bare witness to this science. Moreover, in volume 3 we will explore the Spiritual Sciences of Nuwaubu as taught by the Ancient Egiptian Order.

In practice of sex magic, both participants must agree on a purpose or objective before the act commences. A talisman or amulet may also be useful in conjunction with the rite. And, all persons involved in the operation ought to share the same goal. This is very important. You and your partner should bathe consciously (together or separately), purifying the body with the element *water*, thus preparing the mind for the upcoming *fire*. Before beginning, some grounding or centring exercise should be carried out in preparation. I have included a very easy and simple grounding exercise below that can help to create an altered state[7] in preparation for the ritual. It is not intended for sex magic only; it can be used just as a tool for preparing for the day ahead or just for sheer relaxing. However, after performing the exercise in this case, sexual stimulation can now begin. For the moment, the actual intention of the operation may be forgotten or ignored, in order to focus on igniting the fires of passion. The stimulation procedure should be complete and passionate... Once both are ready, begin intercourse. At this stage, concentration must be turned back to the purpose of the rite, and remain focused throughout the entire operation. Direct your passion ecstatically toward the purpose of the operation, connect with your partner (on less you are alone) on all levels of passion, and direct your *will*. The passion must be extended for as long as possible, no less than half an hour. Continue until it seems like orgasm is completely unavoidable. However, do not loose focus due to the actual orgasm. Instead, continue to focus on the purpose, and direct it through the ecstatic connection with your partner.

Grounding and Centering Exercise

1. Sit or lie down in a quiet place where you will not be disturbed for at least 20minutes.
2. Take a few deep breaths and allow yourself to get into a comfortable position.
3. Close your eyes and take a few-more long, slow deep breaths, totally settling into the position you have taken.
4. Notice the sensations in your body and readjust if necessary
5. Starting with your feet, progressively relax your entire body up to the crown of your head by feeling and visualizing a slow calming wave of energy moving soothingly up your body. You may mentally say, "My toes are relaxing, my feet are relaxing, my ankles are relaxing, etc."
6. When you have reached the crown of your head, you will be thoroughly relaxed. Feel the sensations of your body and relax any parts that have become tense again.
7. Mentally say to yourself that you are about to countdown from 20 to 1, and that, when you reach 1, you will be in a deep state of relaxation and focus.
8. Slowly begin counting backward from 20, mentally saying "20, and deeper, and deeper, I am relaxing deeper, 19, so much deeper, and 18, and deeper, and deeper, etc.," until you reach 1. When you reach 1 you will be in the altered state.
9. You may stay here for as long as you wish or go even deeper.
10. When you are ready to return to normal awareness, simply count upwards from 1 to 5, telling yourself mentally that you will awaken refreshed and relaxed.

It may be useful to chant some sort of mantra to keep you directed. Orgasm should be simultaneous with your partner, noting that the male can achieve a spiritual orgasm without actually ejaculating semen. Climaxing together indicates the intimate connection and the singularity of the act. At the very moment of orgasm the *will* must be entirely focused on the purpose of the operation, although Consciousness may be temporarily lost in ecstasy.

As long as you and your mate are fully 'Present' to the science of the act, the sexual fluids can be gathered, for the final part of the ritual. This is according to Jason Newcomb; he says: *"A portion of the fluids must be placed on the talisman or amulet if there is one, and the rest must be consumed. This is absolutely important and must not be omitted from the ritual."* The fluids, being the charged products of the operation, complete a true Eucharist. The combined fluids of the man and woman are a perfect substance, 'not living not dead, neither liquid nor solid, neither hot nor cold, neither male nor female.' It is one substance containing all possibilities. This is the Elixir of life. It is said that, 'Once a person starts using sex magic, all sexual acts must be consecrated toward magic, or negative forces may be attracted due to the unbalanced forces of undirected sexual energy.' However, a true Kaballist will be intentionally balanced as a rule of thumb.

Love and Relationship Archetypes

The contents of the Collective Unconscious are called archetypes. Jung also called them dominants, the imagos,[A] the mythological or primordial images, and a few other names. But 'Archetypes,' seem to have won out over these. An archetype is an unlearned tendency to experience things in a certain way. The archetype has no form of its own, but it acts as the 'organizing principle' on the things we see or do. It works the way that instincts work in Freud's theory: At first, the baby

---

[A] An imago is an optical representation of a *thing*.

just wants something to eat, without knowing what it wants. It has a rather indefinite yearning, which nevertheless, can be satisfied by some things and not by others. Later, with experience, the child begins to yearn for something more specific when it is hungry – a bottle, a cookie, a chicken leg, or a slice of pizza. The archetype is like a Black Hole in space: You only know it is there by how it draws matter and light to itself.

<u>Daddy's girl and Mummy's boy</u>

There are clichés that say men usually try to find a girlfriend or wife modelled after their mother. And likewise, women try to seek out a boyfriend or husband modelled after their father. But then, when we study and analyse the theories of Freud and Jung, we discover that most of us seek out a partner based on our archetypical ideas of what our partners should be like. By this I mean: each and every one of us has an archetypical blueprint of motherhood, fatherhood, wifehood, husbandhood, childhood and so on. We carry around with us deep within our psyche, the very qualities of these roles, with the misinterpretation of them being what we are to be seeking out. So we say to our selves *"I would like to find someone who is like this... and like that..."* And, it very seldom seems to occur to us that these impressions are what we are to become and not necessarily what we ought to be looking for. Our inner being, our Conscience is telling us desperately, they way we ought to be in order to learn certain lessons.

In volume 1, I wrote about the 'BE DO HAVE' philosophy, which I learnt from Robert T. Kiyosaki, author of the best selling *'Rich dad Poor dad'* series of books. We all want to *have* "this" and "that," and then "more." But, we miss the part that involves <u>*becoming,*</u> in order to <u>*do*</u> that which is necessary so that we may then <u>*have*</u> what we desire. It is a very simple Mental-Technology procedure. Conscience speaks to us by way of the thoughts we have of the perfect lover. It speaks to us as thoughts of what a good parent entails, as thoughts of how our children should behave and indeed of how our friends are to treat us. But these thoughts are not to be taken as our expectations of others but rather as what are deepest potentials are, and therefore it is for us to manifest these archetypes as an example for others. Instead, we pursue to effect change in others to suit our egos, thereby denying them the right to express themselves as how they really are and, on the contrary suppress our own potential in the process. This may sound monotonous to you as i rephrase this lesson in different ways. But I assure you that when these truths are put into practice, you will be exposed to unlimited power and self-expression.

You must understand that the archetypes are not biological things, like Freud's instincts. They are rather like spiritual demands. For instance, if you dreamt about long things last night, Freud might suggest these things represent the phallus and ultimately sex. But Jung might have a very different interpretation. Even dreaming quite sufficiently about a penis might not have the slightest thing to do with some unfulfilled sexual desire. It is curious that in some ancient societies, phallic symbols do not usually refer to sex at all. They usually symbolise spiritual power (see sex magic above). These symbols would be displayed on occasions when the Ancestors are being called upon to increase the yield of corn or fish or to heal someone. The connection between the penis and strength, between semen and seed, between fertilisation and fertility are understood by most Afrokhan cultures.

The Shadow and Persona

Jung, in his system also talks about sex and life instincts in general. He says that these are a part of an archetype called 'the shadow.' It is derived from our 2 dimensional animalistic past. This is talking about evolutionary Aryan man of course, on which he did his research, not the Involutionary Cyclopean Afrokhan. Our psyche is drastically structured different from that of the Caucasian. Nuwaubu teaches us of these long forgotten secrets. None the less, he says the shadow is derived from man-kind's animal past, when his concerns were limited to survival and reproduction, and was not yet Self-conscious. It is the 'dark side' of the ego, and the evil that man-kind are capable of is stored there. Actually, it is my belief that this aspect of mind that Jung speaks of is actually fundamentally inactive. That is, it is essentially neither good nor bad, just like animals. An animal is both capable of caring for and tending its young as well as being vicious when hunting for food to feed its young. But, the animal does not actually choose to do either; it simply does what it does through instinct. It is therefore innocent and is not aware of its Self, or what we would call morality. But from our human-world, the animal world looks rather brutal, inhuman and cruel. And therefore, the shadow aspects of ourselves, the survival aspects, we tend to hide away and pretend it doesn't exist. Symbols of this shadow include the serpent or the dragon, which quite interestingly guards the gates that lead us to our Collective Unconscious. So, next time you dream of wrestling with a demon, it may be yourself that you are wrestling with.

We cover up who we really are by what is called the '**Persona**.' The word is obviously associated with the words person and personality and comes from the Latin word *persona,* meaning a 'player's mask' – a player in the game of life in this case. So the *person* or *personality* is the mask we put on before we show ourselves to the outside world, and is definitely what we portray when we are seeking out a sexual partner, a business partner or a long-term relationship. At its best, (on the face of it,) it is just a good impression. It's the impression we all wish to fulfil that society dictates for us to become and not to express whom we really are. But, of course, it can also be the false impressions we use to manipulate peoples' opinions and behaviours. And at worst, it can be mistaken by others and sometimes even by our selves to be our true nature. Sometimes we really believe we are what we pretend to be.

A part of our persona is the role of male and female, or, of boyfriend and girlfriend we must play in our relationships. For most

108

people that role is determined by their physical gender. But Jung, like Freud and others, felt that we are really bisexual in nature. Dr. Malachi had also taught this. He said in paraphrase:

> *'When we begin our lives as foetuses, we have undifferentiated sex organs that only gradually, under the influence of hormones, become male or female. Likewise when we begin our social life as infants, we are neither male nor female in the social sense. Almost immediately – as soon as those pink or blue t-shirts go on – we become under the influence of society, which gradually shapes us as men and women.'*
>
> Paraphrased from Dr. Malachi

Jung says that they are no known number of archetypes that one can remember and document. They overlap and easily melt into each other as of when needed. Other persona archetypes talk of the hermaphrodite, one who is both male and female in gender, and represents the union of opposites, the merging of Yin and Yang. In some religious arts, Jesus for instance is portrayed as a rather feminine or *Yin* man. And likewise in China, *Kuan Yin* began as a male saint (the Budhisattva Avalokiteshwara), but was portrayed in a much feminine manner that he is more often thought of as the female goddess of compassion. And again we have Akhenaton aka Amenhotep 1V, being portrayed as a tall man with breasts and wide hips.

Love in Afrokhan Culture and religion

As an introduction to Love in Afrokhan culture and religion – below is a concept that I found on the Internet to be quite interesting and inspiring. It also prompted me to mention '**Friendship Day,**' which is the Nuwaubian alternative to Valentine's Day. For the Nuwaubians of the AEO and a field, this is a day of recognising and acknowledging friends and other relations. It is very much like the below conception of 'Black Love Day.' It is beautiful indeed.

Black Love Day, A Valentine's Alternative

Nya Akoma - (pronounced Knee ah Ah-coma) is the slogan and greeting used on BLD, meaning, "Get a heart! Be patient!"

Traditionally, February 14th is a day when men & women all over declare the day, a day for lovers & love. A day in which it's not uncommon to get a card, candy, flowers and for some lucky women, an engagement ring. A premature version of Valentine's Day, Black Love Day (BLD) held a day before on the 13th, is a commemorative, holiday or "wholly" day of observance, celebration, reconciliation, forgiveness, atonement and demonstration of love within & for the Black community.

The concept behind Black Love Day was established in 1993, by Ms. Ayo Kendi. Feeling the strong need & desire for more expressions of "black love" among those in the community, Ms. Kendi quickly organized the first Black Love Day public observance in Northeast, Washington, DC. Her idea, vision & efforts were widely accepted by the public and the media in its inaugural celebration. With this success, the following year, BLD became an official day of recognition, observance and celebration by Mayoral Proclamation in DC.

Black Love Day is meant to serve as an alternative to Valentine's Day. BLD is meant to be a celebration of all Black relationships…from self-love first to love for the family to love for the community & the race to finally love for The Creator. Instead of the trademark colors of red & pink for Valentine's Day, people should wear or display the color purple for spirituality or black which is the blend of all of the colors.

Just as how Kwanzaa is growing & being observed more by blacks, Black Love Day is being recognized & accepted by more in the community every year. To many, it's a refreshing break from the commercialism of the traditional "love in the month of February" celebration.

The objectives of Black Love Day are as follows:

1. To establish a day to focus on love in order to rejuvenate all of our relationships.

2. To demonstrate love in action and service by performing at least five (5) specific loving acts - Love for the Creator, love for self, love for the family, love for the community, and love for the Black race.

3. To create new traditions that is based on our African and African-American culture to provide an alternative to Valentine's Day.

So if Black Love Day is all about "love" like Valentine's Day, why celebrate it? BLD offers more than romance and tokens of affection as on Valentine's Day. On BLD, love is demonstrated through service, celebration, rituals of forgiveness and public reconciliation. Participants of Black Love Day are expected to involve themselves in the performance of 5 specific acts of love within the 24 hours of February 13th.

Black Love Day Pledge:

To show love for The Creator
To love myself first and to erase all traces of self-hatred for when I love myself, I therefore can love others.
To develop moral principles to stand for
To forgive myself for past acts of unloving behavior and move on
To show love for my family
To show love for my community
To show love for the race
To show love for myself, the community, and the race
To commit to the "Nguzo Saba" (The 7 Principles of Blackness) and to practice these principles on a daily and year-long basis not just during Kwanzaa: Umoja - Unity; Kujichagalia - Self Determination; Ujima - Collective Work and Responsibility; Ujamaa - Cooperative Economic; Nia - Purpose; Kuumba- Creativity; Imani - Faith.

I appreciated this so much I just had to include it here. The system of Umoja is based around the Afrokhan Principles of togetherness. And for this to be achieved in the 21st century, we will all have to stand in Love with each other all over again – and gain and again!

The Philosophy of Love

George James in the 1950s undoubtedly proved that Greek philosophy is stolen Egiptian or Khemetian philosophy. In fact the very word philosophy is not even of Greek origin. It is Khemetian, from the words *Philo* meaning 'he who loves', and, *Sophon* meaning science, (also *Sophos* and *Sophia* meaning wisdom). Therefore the etymology of the word *philosopher* means 'he who loves science and wisdom.' And, history tells us that the ancient Neolithic Egiptians originated all the well-known sciences that are often attributed to the Greeks. This will be further elaborated upon in Ch7 – the Anacalypsis Revisited. The term *philosopher* is also referring to a modern-day metaphysician – one who is calm, rational and temperate in her response to changes in nature and of life.

In the Afrokhan Khemetian culture, the pursuit for love was based on the love to know Self. The philosopher would strive with Unconditional Love, attention and devotion to understand and know her Self, as a microcosm of the macrocosm of the Universe. This to the adept was what Unconditional Love was all about. The philosophy, the love of wisdom, impressed the importance through application that the return to The All, is to be in the exact same format of which we differentiated as individual souls, and that is through Unconditional Love. It was never about giving or receiving Unconditional Love from others. The doctrine determined that the only *thing* that is worthy of such Love is the Creator, NTR. Human love relationships only give us an idea of what the love of the Creator is like. The philosophy of love meant that the student would pursue Truth with love and commitment and, with the intention to study and internalise found truths into a functional mental tool for her Self-empowerment. The seeking of love was a system of soul training says James in his book *'Stolen legacy.'* It is the path that raised the neophyte from human and mortal levels toward the level of virtue and God. James also described this system as the basis and purpose of the Egiptian Initiation System into the mystery schools, which was the first so-called salvation for man. It ought to be noted here also that the famed Greek philosophers were only initiated into the lower of the lesser mystery schools. They were not mentally trained to even deal with the fullness of the lesser mysteries let alone the greater mysteries. Therefore we can see why today's society, apparently rooted in Greek philosophy and scholastic thought, is lacking love and care on a planetary epidemic scale. If we are to re-establish care and love into the world, the powers that be, the preachers, rabbis and imams, the teachers and lectures, the scientists, physicians and parapsychologists, will all have to acknowledge the Afrokhan philosophy of Love, at least.

Throughout Afrokha and the Black cultures across the globe, we find these exact rites regarding Unconditional Love. It is at the foundation of every single Black culture, for its people to exhibit love toward nature and to the Universe as though their organs depended on it. This wasn't just a metaphor it was a reality. The practice of love in this manner was an Afrokhan sacred science, which included sex magic as a vehicle to materialise certain desires, as well as perhaps to bring back a particular ancestor. Whatever one desired can be achieved through Love.

In the Khemetian mystery system the 'Right Eye of Horus' training system, based on left-brain technology and its analytical abilities was mathematical and geometric. The geometric system was so advanced that the masters kept the higher levels of the information secret, meaning they treated it as sacred. Hence we have the doctrine of Sacred Geometry. The science attempts to explain the creation as well as the entropy of the Universe through mathematical postulations. This is because some people are wired such that they have to be mathematically convinced of certain truths, where others <u>know</u> through their intimate connection, with Divine Truth and Divine Reality.

~

Notes

[1] Dr Malachi, (a) *The True Story of the Beginning,* p8-10 (b) *The Holy Tablets,* p717

[2] Wayne B. Chandler, *Sexual Energy* (Audio Cassette)

[3] Dr Malachi, *The Fallacy of Easter, (Scroll #105),* p14-15

[4] Zecharia Sitchin, *The Twelfth Planet,* p364

[5] Dr Malachi, *The Marriage Ceremony, (Scroll #53),* p39

[6] Iyanla Vanzant, *One Day My Soul Just Opened Up,* p101

[7] Jason Augustus Newcomb, *the new hermetics,* p73

Chapter 4
Sacred Geometry

The Nature of the Universe

The Afrokhan worldview of the creation, the nature, and the sciences of the Universe hold the best conceptual views for Afrokhan peoples. The problem today however, is that Black peoples the world over have been subjected to the White-European worldview and its system of thinking. And, in order for us to open-heartedly accept the Afrokhan worldview, the teaching itself must insist that it is best for us. But how easy is it for an astute Afrokhan scholar to successfully initiate Black concepts into the hearts and minds of prospective Black students? Well, to tackle this issue I've ironically taken on many pseudo-European concepts just as an icebreaker. In fact I must admit that much of MMSN (volumes 1 and 2), includes pseudo-Pleiadian-European-Christian perspectives. This may already be obvious to the more regular readers of the esoteric, who understand and appreciate the many different concepts across the world. I took the latter approaches because I believe readers will find the scientific concepts of western physicists intriguing and thought provoking, which is good for our spiritual nostalgia. And since as a people we have come so far away from our way of life and heritage, it is extremely difficult for us to simply take on the Afrokhan worldview in a flash. For many of us, Afrokhan culture and religion is foreign and alien to that which we currently know. In light of this, the Khemetian Theurgists in their philosophy of the Anatomy of the Universe, as detailed in chapter 2, also had a system of Geometry, now called *'Sacred Geometry,'* to mathematically explain the origin of the Universe. One category of this is called 'The Geometry of Meaning.'[1]

Sacred Geometry; the scientific and mathematical approach to understanding the Universe and its formation is enough to make one say: *"but what if."* The idea however, is for the student to take her/ his own initiative to seek out information from within their own culture and ancestry in order to make the correct link through the right channels, back to the Creator. As stated before, Afrokhan concepts of creation and the nature of the Universe are always rooted in a Reality, verified through meditation or, divining and channelling etc., whereas most westernised concepts of the same are rooted in modern philosophy. I personally prefer scientific proof or evidence of any theory, as opposed to just philosophy. This is the thinking of a true sceptic. The regular Oxford Paperback dictionary defines philosophy as the *'Use of reason and argument in seeking truth and knowledge.'*

As we saw in the previous chapter, philosophy in its Khemetian root meaning is much deeper than this. Our ancient Babylonian and Khemetian Ancestors understood the nature of the Universe at very high degrees, with philosophical concepts, attained through Universal Love, that we cannot even begin to contemplate today – not whilst we continue to conceptualise the Universe with the European's frame of reference anyway. The Ancestors, with their high culture of high intellect and spiritual evolution, which was far more advanced than we have today, has left us with no choice but to marvel at the system and its way of life, its splendour as well as its beauty. The situation at hand is analogous to the contrast between a seventy-year olds' knowledge, as a professional architect and, that of a seven-year old child, playing with Lego pieces. The architect, should she become a teacher of her profession and trade, will have to use simplified concepts that a seven-year old child can gravitate toward and understand. In volume 1, I briefly explained the differences in mindsets of ancient Afrokhans and the mindsets of their modern day European counterparts. As a reminder... the western world and its European peoples are left-brain thinkers whereas ancient Afrokhans and Asiatics are right-brain analysers. The left-brain faculty or aptitude is masculine and logical, and must therefore be convinced of the nature of *things* logically, hence the mathematics of Sacred Geometry✗The right-brain however, is feminine and intuitive as opposed to masculine and logical. The right-brain faculty is able to become Present to what 'Is;' it doesn't need to be convinced logically. It derives its understanding and knowingness of *things* by way of experiencing nature's unifying principle; Spirit. Now, just as the skilled architect has to enter into the current frame of reference of the seven-year old in order to educate, so am I taking into account the current frame of reference of blacks in the Western hemispheres of the world.

The Universe and its nature have been described by many different terms such as: Spider-web effect, the Matrix, the Ovum, the Cosmos etc., all of which can be represented by fantastic geometric systems. But what are we really saying when we say "the Universe?" I mean, are we talking about The All, as in 'All that Is,' or are we just talking about <u>our</u> particular universe? Do you see the problem the very word exhibits? Most of us at first thought, when we hear the word 'Universe' think of the Universe as in 'All that Is.' However, many credible western physicists disagree, and have been disagreeing on this for decades. Many of them have been literally throwing concepts of 'many universes' into the scientific community through magazines, conferences etc., with terms like 'multiverse' and 'omniverse.' I myself first came into the idea of many universes when I learnt of Dr Malachi and his teachings.

The Universe is mathematically Sound

One of the many scientific reasoning regarding the evolution of the Universe postulated by physicists, are indeed its mathematical properties. The Universe is comprehendible, comprehensive and intelligible they say, meaning that it is mathematically sound. And, by this fact, one ontological system says that 'the Universe was created by higher intelligent beings, who simply created a replica of their own Universe, entered it, placed their mark (DNA) and left.' This means that they were able to comprehend the nature of their own Universe mathematically speaking, and thereby spawned their own virtual world using the exact same mathematical principles. Well folks, this is exactly the same thing the Afrokhan Khemetian Masters has been saying for thousands of years. Except of course they were not using modern-day scientific or mathematical terminology or models, to prove their point. Remember the movies, the 13th floor, and the Matrix. I keep referring to these programs[A] because they shed a lot of light and insight on the reality of creation and existence as we have it. In fact the movie Existenz, also gives a good representation of a virtual world (a game) created by scientists of this world, of which participants can actually get caught up and stuck within – and only escape by way of death, both in the virtual reality as well as in this reality.

The mathematics of our cosmos is relatively simple. It is just a matter of time now; thousands, or maybe even as little as a hundred years, before scientists come up with a way of creating and spawning a Universe modelled after ourselves – and why not? But of course – this is assuming that earth carries on as normal for thousands of years forward – with no Nibiru or photon belt phenomena interfering and altering our present course. Is it at all impossible to imagine beings of higher intellect that are perhaps millions of years ahead of us in evolution, that have already performed this fete hundreds of times over? That would be arrogant of us. Surely Leonardo Fibonacci was not the first or the only person within the entire Universe that discovered the pattern of numbers in which nature uses to grow and maintain itself. For a start, the ancient Nilotic blacks enunciated these findings thousands of years ago within the lesser mysteries. And who is to say whether or not, our Nilotic ancestors were taught these mathematical models by EBEs

---

[A] For indeed televised programs are designed to program-in a particular mindset to the audience – us.

(extraterrestrial biological entities). However it was, I invite you now, if you haven't already done so, to spend some time playing with Sacred Geometric models such as: the Fibonacci numbers, the *pi* as well as the *phi* numbers. Bob Frissel in his book *'Nothing in This Book Is True but It's Exactly How Things Are,'* gives us a good place to start as he describes what he was taught by Drunvalo Melchizadeck. Dr Malachi also produced a book called *'Sacred Geometry,'* for the Ancient Egiptian Order neophyte. This book simplifies many of the concepts that western writers try to explain – from their own culture's frame of reference of course. He simply puts the Geometry into an Afro-Egiptian context, which makes them relative to our spiritual development as Afrokhan peoples.

Do not be afraid to entertain what sometimes seem like crazy ideas. Like the notion of scientists creating another Universe, time travelling, or quantum leaping etc., the nature of the Mind is such that whatever can be perceived can actually become a reality; our subjective thoughts can easily become objective manifestations. Be reminded that concepts that are used to explain *things* are only relative truths that aid us along our paths – Mystical or Magical, as we will find throughout the MMSN series…

So how many universes are there?

There are probably as many universes as there are atoms of this Universe, the Cosmos. I am deliberately saying this to further provoke your thoughts, without pun by the way. But for real – and here is the thing: aren't atoms tiny gateways into other dimensions or universes themselves? Well of course they are. You see – it all depends on how far you are willing to take the definition of the word 'Universe.' Some physicists have even gone crazy enough to describe atoms as 'single unit time machines.'[2] The denizens of these time machines, the electrons, whiz throughout space and time at velocities monstrously greater than the speed of light, or 300million meters per second.

Interesting isn't it? It all stands to reasoning with specific usage of words. Again, in volume 1 using semantics, or what Dr Malachi likes to call 'word games,' I wrote of the word 'Universe' meaning to spiral outwards from a single point going against oneness. We have *Uni,* meaning one, and *Verse,* meaning to oppose or to go against. Well this was only relatively true, based on the context of which I was using the definition, which was within the context of explaining Involution toward Evolution (see Ch1 & Ch2), or Big Bang toward Black hole (see Ch8). The idea that atoms are tiny time machines can become clearer if you do a little research on the 'valance electrons' of 'energy bands.' For example, an observed item such as a stool appears to be solid and standing still. Ok, so we already know that the appearance is only so based on our focusing in on particular wavelengths of particles.[A] But guess what... the electrons of the atoms that makes up the stool, are "here" and "over there," at the same time. In fact the particles are in many "over theres" at the same time.[3]

Imagine that there is a three-dimensional template or stencil for the actual stool, positioned in free space. Or more to the point, the stencil itself being invisible to us must therefore be positioned in the fourth dimension, with the intended manifestation to become present in 3-D space. What we have is this: the nature of atoms and their constituents, namely protons, neutrons and the seemingly orbiting electrons, is that they spiral throughout space (like lines of latitude along an orb); ultimately from Nuqta to Big Bang to Black hole. As these particles spiral and pass through the template, they, in a split-second fill the gaps of the template for the stool, thus producing physical and visible images to our optical perception. Bear in mind that the particles are also continuously varying in wavelength as they spiral through open space. So this means that one particular particle can experience manifestation

---

[A] The physical or visible spectrum, or VS, ranges between 400-700 nanometers in wavelength. Any band of waves outside of this range is generally not perceivable by the naked eye. Or is it?

of many objects almost simultaneously, since atoms take on a whole different behaviourism outside of what we call time. An electron can therefore experience many dimensions, universes and *objects* of them in an instant, or in what we call the Now. But God has afforded humans the gift to experience these phenomenons in sequence, this we call life and living, simply time. Life affords us the blessing of not experiencing all of creation and existence all at once. In other words, for the Godhead to experience individual aspects of creation and existence, it had to create bodies, from, and as, differentiated aspects of itself and then place its Consciousness within these entities. Consequently, Consciousness and electrons follow a similar path. I could postulate that the two are one and the same on the highest level. Since particles, by way of their varying degrees of waves experience different aspects of creation and existence, we can use it as an analogy to understanding the path of the Consciousness of humans. As conscious beings we pass through different dimensions, planes, galaxies and planets etc., as we ultimately experience 'All that Is,' never minding the amnesia that we suffer every time we transit from be*ing* to be*ing* or state to state. Therefore full enlightenment lies within the notion of having total recall of the Self.

The Universe is Mental

The ancient Ha Kha teachings of Tehuti, and indeed the teachings of the New Hermetics, (which is based on Freud's and Jung's investigations,) are based upon one very fundamental principle – and that is, the Universe is Mental. The doctrines teach of the Subjective Reality and the objective contexts of the Universe. It states every*thing* that exists within the Universe is held within the Infinite Mind of the Creator, of which we are all mentally and inextricably connected. Every*thing* within the Universe exists as Subjective, and, only becomes objective within the limited minds of humans. That is to say, *things* only become objective or, are only realized or perceived once we put them within a particular context. For example let us take a look at the number two.

2

In Reality – within the Subjective, this is but a glyph that stands alone and paradoxically has no meaning whatsoever. It is therefore empty and meaningless. It just 'Is.' The glyph only becomes objective when we choose to place it within the confines of a context. We place it within the relative truths of one & three; thus we call it 'the number two.'

So the number two now exists as an object, simply because it has become objective, relative to the numbers one and three. And this is exactly how humans perceive the world – in 3D.

123

We have a 3 dimensional perception of Reality, which limits us in our apparent attempts to experience the Subjective Reality of 'All that Is.' The same principle can be used when we analyse a fruit – like an apple for instance. The apple exists within the Subjective as exactly what it 'Is,' for it has no meaning whatsoever within its own Presence. Now, once we bring *it,* the Subjective-fruit, to our awareness, we immediately place it within a context so that we might come to understand and *know* what we are looking at. We place it within a context of: 'something to eat.' And here, we create other contexts, in order to fully appreciate what we are observing. We take into account past experiences such as taste, smell, texture and so on. In fact there are an infinite number of contexts in which we may place *objects,* so that we may satisfy our perceptions of *them.* When it comes to trying to explain a phenomenon such as creation of the Universe, the favourite has always been to create a concept, which is unlike placing creation of the Universe within a context. We cannot truly place The All within a context, for The All already encompasses that said context. And, if such a context existed then we would not be talking about The All; for The

All Is. But the ancients have created concepts such as cosmologies or ontological systems that are often reiterated to us as myths or legends. Remember... *things* and *objects* in Reality have no meaning, they just 'Are.' However, when we apply meaning we actually create geometry in the process. This is to suggest that an *object* or *thing* be created in conjunction with its endless amount of meanings in an instant – and, angles and dimensions, which are both geometric, represent these meanings.

The Geometry of meaning

So what exactly does geometry mean, or what is the geometry of meaning? Everything within our Universe is symmetrical, dual or paired, and is most definitely geometric. And lying deep within these geometric concepts there is great meaning, but perhaps it is not time for us to know these great truths yet, or is it? Well let us see. The first truth about truth is the reality that there is no such thing as 'actual truth' in the objective world – only 'relative truth.' The same implies where questions that require truthful answers are also of an objective inquiry. So if the questions themselves are objective and therefore arbitrary, then so must be the given answers, whether or not we choose to accept the answers as true or untrue.

> *"Anyone who thinks they know it all is just confirming they do not."*
>
> David Icke

And on that note, the more I study is the more I am realizing I know nothing.

> *"Wisdom is knowing how little we know."*
>
> Socrates

And, as I scouted and researched the book *'The Geometry of Meaning,'* by Arthur M. Young, I find more and more that the planet is filled with metaphoric triggers of all sorts. I mean... the information age had been smacking me in the face as hard as I could ever imagine, but this book put extra icing on the cake.

Categories and angles of Knowing

What are the elements that constitute the act of knowing? And how do we know that we really know, or whether are not we are just believing in something? Dr Malachi spared no angle of thoughts as he reiterated over and over the difference between believing and knowing. The world if filled to its brim of persons screaming at the top of their lungs that what they believe in is right and exact. We obviously get the same scenario with the thousands of religions worldwide and ideologies of them, most of which thrive on belief as opposed to knowing. Now, if we could just find one simple principle that can be universal enough as a piece of truth, to be used throughout all these different religions, maybe we can all come to some simple agreements – at least for a start. Well, such a principle exists. It is called mathematics. Mathematics speaks all languages. It does not know race or culture or creed. Mathematics is not concerned about how its student or observer will <u>feel</u> about what it has to say; it is brutally mercy-less with its honesty, and is infallibly 'right and exact' within and without its Self-expression. Mathematics is the genius of God itself. Through the simplicity of mathematics, whether we use algebra, statistics or transpositions of theory, we can find the greatest truths and meanings of any phenomena. The use of the mathematics in Sacred Geometry as a model for acquiring truth is absolutely sound and flawless. Numbers are universal agents of truth; they speak Gods language and can be understood by any persons of any culture or dialect.

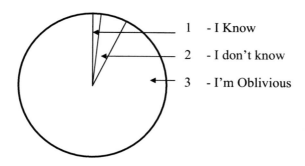

1 - I Know

2 - I don't know

3 - I'm Oblivious

Fig4.1: how much do you know?

Look at the chart of fig4.1, which represents the entire knowledge of our Collective Unconsciousness. The first portion (1) represents that which we know that we know. For example, we know that we have parents and this is a fact. The second portion (2) represents that which we know that we don't know. For example, we know that we don't know how the Universe began. These two portions make up the waking conscious Mind. The third (3) represents that which we don't know that we don't know. (Such as the theories of Freud's Instincts.)

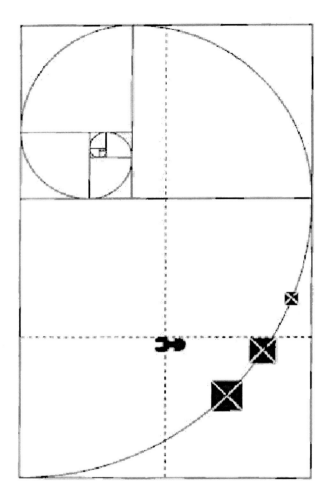

Fig4.2: the geometric positioning of the Great Pyramids

The neophyte on entering the grand lodge is made aware of this model (of fig4.1). It encourages her or him to aspire to become united with the Collective Unconscious, which holds all truths, relevant and actual. Knowing, in this manner, comes with great insight and feeling. Not the illusive feelings we experience within our day-to-day lives, but one that is much, much deeper. As Arthur M. Young says, *"All meaning is an angle."* Two of these angles are immediately obvious: that which is known, and the Consciousness that knows it (fig4.3). Modern science has been forced to accept that in order for an observer to know something about an object observed, she must act in such a way that disturbs the said object.[4]

The act of knowing something about the object is consequently achieved due to the exchanges of energy that occur upon the disturbing of it. This is simile to the beating of a drum, which causes disturbances of the atoms within the atmosphere, (or sphere of atoms), thus producing an on-going chain of disturbances, (or a chain reaction), until the sound vibrations reach the ear. The eardrum is thus disturbed accordingly, thereby informing the listener of the notes that are being played. These are physical exchanges of energy, which can be mathematically calculated. This brings us into the enquiry of two other elements of knowing: the sensed data picked up <u>from</u> the object *observed,* and the rate of projection <u>from</u> the *observer.* The model is called 'the four-fold divisions of knowing,' and obviously, the same principle applies for all 5 senses.

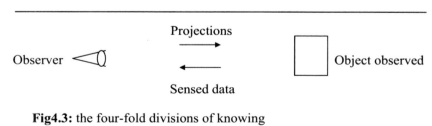

Fig4.3: the four-fold divisions of knowing

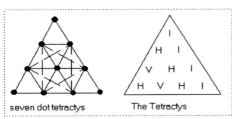

The number equivalents of the letters of the Tetragrammaton are as follows:
I = 10, H = 5, V = 6, H = 5 which is 26
    Then by adding the values of the letters in the following manner:
I = 10; HI = 15; VHI = 21; HVHI = 26
thus 10 + 15 + 21 + 26 = 72, or the Shem ha-meforash.
    By arranging the four letters of the Great Name, (IHVH) in the form of the Pythagorean tetractys, the seventy-two names of God are manifested.

seven dot tetractys   The Tetractys

Fig4.4: the Jewish Tetragrammaton

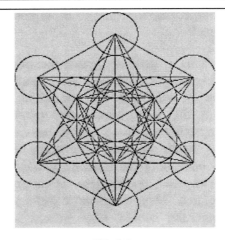

Fig4.5:
The Metatron Cube

This Sacred Geometric symbol represents many possibilities.
If you look close enough you will notice the following:

- The Egg of Life
- The Seed of Life
- The Flower of Life
- The Fruit of Life
- The Tree of Life
- The Vesica Piscis
- The Platonic Solids
- The Merkaba
- Pyramids   and many, many more

Fig4.3: is a re-presentation of a similar diagram found in Arthur Young's work.[5] This four-fold principle can be adopted into almost any system as a model for measuring quantities or qualities. For example, if we are to recognize the measurements of space and time, we may as well employ the ratios of velocity or speed and, the rate of change of velocity with time, which is acceleration. Nature also embodies three-fold and two-fold models. But as we are aspiring fourth dimensional beings we can ignore them as far as this work is concerned.

The Tree of Life system also presents a 2 and 3-way as well as a 4-way model that can be adopted to give meaning and direction in life. The Jewish Kaballists also presented the Jewish Tetragrammaton of YHWH in mathematical and geometric terms (fig4.4). Pythagoras also postulated the Egiptian system of geometry known today as the Pythagorean theorem, which is an announcement of profound Khemetian mathematics. Not forgetting the Great Pyramids (fig4.2) that are positioned along the Golden Mean spiral of which many other holy lands and sites on the planet are situated. These sites are known as **Geodetic** markers. See volume 1 for further information on the Fibonacci sequence of numbers, relating to the Golden Mean/ Golden Section, Proportion.

The Principles of Geodetics
Before proceeding with the principles of geodetics, let us first clinically define the word Geometry:

> *'**Geometry** is a branch of mathematics concerned with the properties of space, usually in terms of plane (two-dimensional) and solid (three-dimensional) figures. The subject is usually divided into **pure geometry**, which embraces roughly the plane and solid geometry dealt with in Euclid's Elements, and **analytical** or **coordinate geometry**, in which problems are solved using*

algebraic methods. A third, quite distinct, type includes the non Euclidean geometries.'

Paraphrased from the Hutchinson Encyclopaedia – 2000 – ISBN 1-85986-288-8

Also, let us look at and take note of two other associated angles of geometry:

*'**Geometric mean**: 'in mathematics, the nth root of the product of n positive numbers. The geometric mean m of two numbers p and q is such that m = √ (p X q). For example, the mean of 2 and 8 is √ (2 X 8) = √16 = 4.'*

*'**Geometric progression** or geometric sequence: 'in mathematics, a sequence of terms (progression) in which each term is a constant multiple (called the common ratio) of the one preceding it. For example, 3, 12, 48, 192, 768,..., is a geometric with a common ratio 4.'*

Both also Paraphrased from the Hutchinson Encyclopaedia above

In nature, many single-celled organisms reproduce by splitting into two so that one cell gives rise to 2, then 4, then 8 cells, and so on, thus forming the geometric sequence of 1, 2, 4, 8, 16, 32,..., in which the common ratio is 2. However, geodetics is:

'Geodetics is a branch of science concerned with determining the exact position of geographical point and the shape and size of the earth.[6]

Graham Hancock

In simplistic terms, 'geometry' means measurements of the earth. According to Graham Hancock in his best selling book, *'Fingerprints of the Gods,'* the Great Pyramid of Egipt serves the foundation of a 'Geodetic Marker.' In the late 18th century, Napoleon Bonaparte, on his invasion of Egipt along with 175 scholars, found that the pyramid was perfectly aligned to true north, and of course, to the south, east and west as well. This meant to them that the mysterious structure made an excellent reference and triangulation point. From this discovery, it was decided to use the meridian passing through its apex as the base line for all other measurements and orientations. Other more recent Egyptologists have found that the mathematical correspondence between the Great Pyramid and the earth is that it represents ratios of specific dimensions of the earth itself; and, that it also geometrically represents the Northern Hemisphere of the earth. But, Could there also be some Universal Mental correspondence herein? Ponder...

Thoughts are *things*

The *things* that make up the material world are the physical manifestations of Divine Thought. We call this phenomenon the Universal Mind. Sacred Geometry, not only does it display fantastic mathematically undisputable equations about *things*, it also informs the observer of the mentality that created the observed. And, as minuscule components of The All, the Afrokhan Mind has the ability to manifest Mental conceptions in exactly the same manner as the Universal Mind does. The Mental Technology of Nuwaubu also tells us that our thoughts are as real as the physical world is around us. Thoughts ultimately effect changes in matter and create reaction after reaction until disturbed in such a manner that changes its angle and therefore direction. Moreover, the science, the mathematics and geometry of the Great Pyramid, indeed, only gives us a glimpse of the mentality that manifested it; for indeed the structure was created mentally and thus manifested from top—down. The mentality of their creation, not only did it perfectly position the three pyramids of Giza to align their shafts with the three stars of Orion's belt, but it also perfectly positioned them along a logarithmic spiral having its roots in some celestial coordinate – as we shall see shortly.

We are taught that through the Doctrine of correspondence, of the Ha Kha philosophy, the adept can transform undesired thoughts into desired ones,[7] by using the higher laws over the lower realms. It is the art of Mental-transmutation. In the 4th dimension, once we make the transition to experience life therein, our thoughts will be instantly manifested to us, unlike in 3rd dimensional reality where there is a delay. This is why thoughts of love, of peace and of harmony; positive thinking, etc., are so important today. Also because, we will, on entering the 4th dimension, be confronted by our demons – the things that we allow to hold us back in life. This is definite; whether we enter the 4th dimension through astral projection or through planetary dimensional shifting, (see Ch8, the Photon belt and Nibiru), or by way of physical death.

In the Highest levels of Mind, we actually become our thoughts. There is no separation between observer and the observed – the 'I Me Presence' and the 'I Am Presence' become One. In the dimensions between Mind and matter, thoughts manifest to us in an instant but externally; and, in the lowest realms, the material world, our thoughts manifest over a period of time – which is a good thing in one sense. This is necessary because it gives us *time* to transform our undesired thoughts into desired ones. Mental thought forms, whether of the Universal Mind or by our human minds, utilize the same substance, and that is the creative essence 'Ether' (some spell it as 'Aethyr'). Ether is the substance of All Mind. It is the elemental (EL Mental) aspects of the Creator also called EL in the Hebrew Torah. These elementals vibrate at velocities greater than light. They, over time, reduce their vibrational (Vibrations of EL) rates down to a speed that can be sensed and experienced by the human faculty – as matter or *things*. The slowing down of the elementals, or the Elements of EL, is the actual becoming of what is to be; it is the process of Involution. The realm of matter however, gives its denizens the ability to manipulate these thought waves into manifesting as that, which is desired. Thoughts are *things* indeed.

Why Sacred Geometry?

If the Creator wants to talk with us, She/ He/ It can reach us anywhere anytime. There was a Christian baiter called Saul who was travelling the road to Damascus. On his way to bait some early Christians, God grabbed him and struck him blind. He later became that misogynistic Paul of the New Testament fame. The Creator can grab our attention in the middle of Trafalgar Square, London, or in the middle of Central Park, New York at anytime. But what if we wanted to contact the Creator at a specific time and place? How would we do it and do it successfully? For a start, experience and ancient knowledge tells us that location is vitally important. It helps to be in the right environment. Spiritual seekers from Mayans through Christians, Native Americans, Egiptians and Hindus, to the Neolithic builders of the stone rings of Britain and Ireland (and many more), are found to have constructed their sacred places (shrines) using certain geometric ratios. With just a small handful of these ratios, these spiritual seekers could more easily contact their Maker, or at least their ancestors. Yes, it is possible to speak to our ancestors and our Creator at *anytime* through prayer etc., however, Scared Geometry makes this easier, and different ratios make different connections easier. The ratios have to do with different spiritual activities like healing, foretelling the future, long-distance communication, levitation and, most important, heightened ability to communicate with our Creator. The ratios help us to vibrate at the appropriate frequency to aid us in accomplishing the particular spiritual activity we have in mind. When we look at sacred enclosures globally, there is a group of 5 basic mathematical ratios that can be observed, from Japan's Pagodas to Mayan temples in the Yucatan, and from Stonehenge to the Great Egiptian Pyramids (fig4.2). These ratios are shown in table 7:

The five basic ratios

Table 7: the 5 basic ratios

Pi ratio	– 3.142
Square root of two	– 1.414
Square root of three	– 1.732
Square root of five	– 2.236
Phi ratio	– 1.618

These are all irrational numbers. They are all ratios of 1, and that is where it all begins – with the One. An irrational number is one that cannot be represented as a ratio of two whole-number integers, and consequently it does not fall into a repeating pattern of any sort when written in decimal notation. A rational number on the other hand, is one that can be expressed as the ratio of two integers (whole-numbers), such as 1/3 or 1/4. All numbers which, when represented in decimal notation, either stop after a finite number of digits or fall into a recurring or repeating pattern, are rational numbers. There are certain kinds of irrational numbers that are called *transcendental numbers*. Such are the five above. Just like irrational numbers, they are defined by what they are not (they are not rational), yet transcendental numbers are so identified because, they are another *sort* of number, known as an *algebraic number*. Any number that is a solution to a polynomial equation is an algebraic number. A polynomial equation is a sum of one or more terms involving the same variable raised to various powers. An advanced mathematics student will show us that 'a transcendental number requires an infinite number of terms to be defined exactly.' Hence God – with an infinite number of descriptions of which none are individually correct in the Subjective. So the beauty of transcendental numbers is that: there are special equations used repeatedly to derive at certain accuracies but the true number is never reached exactly! Formulas like the famous $E=MC^2$ and, nine to the ninth power of nine, provide irrational transcendental results – they represent infinity. *Pi* is found in any circle. In Sacred geometry, the circle represents the spiritual realms. The circle, – since the transcendental number *pi* cannot be described or rationalized with the same degree of accuracy as the physical square. The circle is therefore representative of infinity and is represented by the Yin principle. There are many examples of sacred sites that are circular. It is a good shape to work with and to do all kinds of spiritual activities within. Many circular temples are found throughout the cultures of old Mesopotamia using the *pi* ratio. And in Egipt's old kingdom, The Great Pyramid is a profound expression of Sacred Geometry, as it boasts ratios of *pi* as well as *phi*. On the contrary, In Sacred Geometry, the square represents the physical world as it can be defined totally, using rational numbers. If its side is one, then its perimeter is exactly four, and its area is one square – exactly. The square therefore represents the finite and is represented by the Yang principle. Symbolisms of the square were found in Solomon's temple, in the Holy of Holies, also called the back room. This is where the Hebrews apparently kept the 'Ark of the Covenant' and most other sacred treasures.

In the beginning was the One

The 'One,' in order to observe itself, it cut part of itself away to make *'Other;'* thus having 'One' and 'Other.' This is comparative and simile to the single-celled organism that replicates itself by splitting into two. As the subdivisions continued away from the One, they continued in the *phi* ratio manner. This can be reversed to go back to the One as well. It is in this sense that three is further away from One than two is. Notice how easier it is to go away from One than to go toward it. This is because it is easier to add and multiply than to subtract and divide. This *phi* ratio is derived from the Fibonacci numbers, also known as the *Fibonacci series.* Again, please refer to volume 1 for a more detailed account of this. Geomancers are interested in Sacred Geometry because it is the study of how Spirit integrates into matter. By echoing and amplifying the geometry of nature and planetary movements, we help to align the resonance of Body, Mind and Spirit, with the harmonic frequencies of the above and of the below. Geomancers are also interested because it has been found that certain spaces, with particular ratios, enable the participant to resonate or vibrate at the appropriate rate that maximizes the possibility to connect with the One. For example, fig4.2 shows how a specific point in Egipt represents a central axis, corresponding to the One, of which the Great Pyramids are constructed along its spiral path. The path follows the logarithmic Golden Section proportion or *phi* ratio. Hundreds of other sites across the planet have been built along this exact same spiral path with its terrestrial roots in Egipt. The spot in Egipt that corresponds with the point of the One is strategically placed onto a much larger spiral, which travels throughout our solar system and through outer space. Therefore, through an infinite number of corresponding spirals of specific geometric ratios, the participant can connect with the Creator.

This is just one aspect of Sacred Geometry – that which works with *irrational numbers.* To go to, or to connect with the spiritual, one must go beyond the rational, and ultimately beyond the Mental, and it appears that the above ratios can get us there. By being inside a sacred place that has been constructed using one of these five geometric ratios, the resonance that has been set up can enhance the possibility of rejuvenating the entire body. And so it was, with the Black Pyramid that had been constructed on the sacred land of the United Nuwaubian Nation of Moors, of the AEO, in Eatonton Georgia, USA – we called it Wahanee. It is a sacred site that belonged to our Washitaw and Yamasee Ancestors, whom are also descendants of the Nuwbuns of ancient Tamare – Afrokha.

Fig4.6: Masonic geometric symbolism

Fig4.7: the compass and square symbol

Freemasonry

As well as within the AEO, remnants of Ancient Geometry are also found in other modern day secret orders and societies. There are many of such orders, which all seem to be under one auspice title of, 'Freemasonry.' Herein we have figs4.6-4.8, which shows some of the many masonic symbols, representing the tools of a builder, an architect or a mason, including the well-known 'compass and square symbol.'

The original institution of Masonry however, was consisted of the foundation of the liberal arts and sciences, but more especially in Geometry, says Samuel Pritchard 1730AD. For, at the building of the Tower of Babel, the art and mastery of Masonry was first introduced, and from thence handed down by Euclid, a worthy and excellent mathematician among the Egiptians. Later, it seems, masonry was communicated through many initiates on—down to Hiram, the Master Mason, whom according to history, was concerned in the building of Solomon's Temple in Jerusalem. It can be seen through studying Masonic literature that the operatives, without publicly declaring so, lays claim to some Divine communication with God. This is noted to be in such a manner that is unlike orthodox Christian procedures, and that the foundation of its methods is of other material than the bible. Some say that Freemasonry as we have it today, has its roots in the ancient Druid religion, which in turn has its roots in the ancient magi architects of Persia, and, the priests of Heliopolis Egipt. Just as the Egiptians and Persians paid homage to the Sun as the life-sustaining emblem of the Creator, so it is that the Freemasons pay homage to G.A.O.T.U. – the Grand Architect of the Universe – God (fig4.8).

The Freemason magus uses the compass and square symbol with the letter 'G' in the middle (fig4.7). The 'G' is symbolic of the circle and square; or a half circle and a half square, which equals 360degrees – but it also represents God. The symbol represents a tool for master builders, of which the master of all builders is the G.A.O.T.U.

Fig4.8: the G.A.O.T.U. symbol

The G.A.O.T.U.

The reverence of the Sun as the Great visible agent of a Great invisible 'Cause,' spread itself across Afrokha and parts of Asia, from thence to Greece and Rome, through ancient Gaul, and into Britain and Ireland. The symbolism of the ancient mystical orders of Egipt and indeed their doctrines have followed this same path right through to the modern day Babylons of the USA and Britain. The Great visible agent (the Sun) is symbolised by the eye, sitting at the apex of many a pyramid structure, as found printed on American paper currency. As well as standing for God, the 'G' within the compass and square also stands for 'Genitalia,' 'Grandmaster,' 'Geometry;' and it probably has many other meanings. Note also that the letter 'G' is the 7th letter of the alphabet,[8] where the number seven is the mystical number within western religion and culture.

The term 'Algebra,' which has its roots in Latin, is actually a transposition (or an anagram) of the old Khemetian triad-principle Geb-Ra-El, more commonly called the Archangel Gabriel.[9] We have Geb, the Khemetian Neter of the Earth; we also have Ra or, Re, the Khemetian Solar Neter; then we have the interpolation of the Aramaic 'El,' or Arabic 'Al' meaning God the Source – or the definite article. The Archangel Gabriel, known in ancient Mesopotamia (Sumer) as Nusqu, is also as one of the Grand Architects of the Universe (in that manner of speaking). He was the God that instructed Adam, and later Abraham and Ishmael to construct the Kabbah of Mecca (see Ch2). He provided the necessary Geometry for this remarkable structure to be erected – representing the Tree of Life – the Anatomy of God. The root meaning of the word algebra, in Latin, is 'bone setting,' or, 'the science of reunification.' G.A.O.T.U. also initials the Grand or Great *Architecture* of the Universe.

Fig4.9: the will factor

The G.A.O.T.U. symbol also symbolises the pendulum Principles of duality; of masculinity and femininity; Yin and Yang; positivity and negativity etc. See figs4.9-4.10. Fig4.8 shows the hand of God at the apex of the pendulum – the compass of course representing the two possible extremes of the pendulum-swing. Then look at fig4.9; it presents the *Will* as the Great 'Cause,' and the effect as the dualistic possibilities of manifestation or experience. In life, in practical terms, wo/man is at the apex of her or his own pendulum; therefore you are at the cause of the events within your life. And, through your own volition and will, you decide upon the courses of action to undertake, should it be appropriate or inappropriate, etc. You are the hand that holds the spindle and thus are responsible for all the causes and effects of your experiences of life and living. Know this! – For it is to know Self. Freemasonry teaches that man has to measure up; he must learn to measure himself against the standards of truth and justice that he vowed and pledged to his life by. Tehuti/ Thoth is the Neter/ male-deity of measurement and time, and Ma'at his consort, is the Netert/ female-deity of truth and justice. In this context, the initiate takes on the faculties of both Tehuti and Ma'at. The idea of the hand and pendulum, borrowed from the Egiptian 'Plumb and line' concept, has now found its way over time into modern day Freemasonry. We see this depicted in Egiptian hieroglyphics as the Sun-disc of Aten with thousands of rays showering the earth, where the pharaoh Akhenaton exalted Aten as the God of Gods, and as Grand Architect of the Universe (again, in a manner of speaking). The image of the rays of the sun simulates the rapid to-ing and fro-ing (ebb and fro) of the pendulum swing of possibilities (fig4.9).

> 'The pendulum is the plumb, which is the weight at the end of a line. The inverted pyramid is used by operative masons and carpenters to establish a true vertical and perpendicular line. The plumb line teaches the criterion of rectitude, to avoid dissimulation in conversation and action, and to direct our steps in the path which leads to immortality; to climb the lead line and grip the Holy Hand that holds the power of decision, **Will**.'[10]
>
> Dr Malachi

As stated, we find the symbolism of the pyramid and the all-seeing eye of Ra (some say of Osiris) on the United States paper currency – the dollar bill. Below the pyramid we have the inscription of: NOVUS ORDO SECLORUM, meaning 'New World Order.'[11] But here is the thing. As interesting as all the above sounds, and what a malarkey it all is; but how... do we apply the principles of Sacred Geometry in the 21st century, as laymen? Is it necessary, and can we benefit from its doctrine?

Geometry Today

My eldest son Levelle had been keeping me on my toes for some time now. For the past three years or so, he has been showing great interests in electronics, in particular to do with robotics. I often wandered if he were just trying to follow in daddy's footsteps – me being an electronics design engineer and all? But no, he was genuine. So, what I have tried to incorporate as a learning curve for the both of us, is to create a system of teaching mathematics and of course electronics, in a comprehensive way which can be fun for children. Well, I'm still working on it. However, my son tells me that mathematics in school to him can sometimes be fun, but more often than not can be boring. Children can sometimes shock us with their severe honesty. But honesty works for me. However, at first I was a little disappointed. I was thereby compelled by Conscience to create some extra quality time with my 3 boys, so that I can at least get to know and understand that which is being taught in schools today (the year being 2005). As a spiritual life-coach, which I daily strive to improve, I believe that the education of children about their spiritual nature is a huge task, especially being within a society where the education system does not incorporate metaphysical principles. If you can successfully educate children according to their nature and cultural heritage, then be sure that you can educate almost any adult of the same. But in actual practicality, it can sometimes prove to be a lot simpler and easier to educate children, than trying to educate so-called educated adults. Children are very vivid in their imaginations, and as long as we try to keep things simple we ought to have very little problems. Many adults today find it tedious to even bother about basic mathematical principles in general, let alone ancient Egiptian Sacred Geometry. But as parents, our children often times keep us abreast – for, how else can we be an inspiration for them if we do not know and understand basic educational models? How can we relate to and communicate with our juniors on a level, if we are not kept updated with current education affairs. And, this is not to undermine anyone who has alternative ways of inspiring their children, other than through academic means. I am well aware that there are many parents today who use alternative methods of educating their children; many also educate their children personally, from home, or they hire private tutors.

But, whether we are teaching adults or children, Sacred geometric principles can easily be taught without actually going into the detailed mathematics of it. Simple explanations of the Fibonacci series can easily be given without progressing with the use of numbers. And, we can talk about how the Universe is well ordered in terms of its mathematics, which is good since it informs the observer of the Mentality of its creation. Rationality and irrationality can also be expounded upon without actually using numbers. This is why the ancient ones would use pictures; metaphors or analogies to explain certain *phenomenons*. In my experience as a teacher of the esoteric, adults tend to become moved and inspired when hearing about the science of the pyramids and their geometric relationships to the earth and to the stars, of which their earthly geometric patterns mimic. When it comes to children on the other hand, this is apparently not enough information; they want to know why-how-when-who and if? And, there is always a "but..." As Afrokhan peoples, education for us has to be far more visual than academic. The European system is very academic and consequently lacks spirituality. This has to be the opposite contrast for Afrokhan peoples and their education. As stated several times, the western world and the people of its societies are left-brain thinkers, which is of the rationale, whereas Afrokhan and Eastern peoples are right-brain analysers, which can be considered as irrational. Proceed...

The Irrational World

And what about every-day people whom are often considered as subordinate, due to lack of academic education? Again in my experience as a teacher and coach of the spiritual technology of Nuwaubu and 'Right Knowledge,' I find that the so-called uneducated amongst us are far more receptive to Nuwaubian esoteric philosophy than those that are so-called educated by aspects of mainstream curriculum. Hence why children are also more receptive to the same – society and its indoctrination and education systems have not yet completely duped them into becoming fixed rational thinkers. In nature, there are always two objective possibilities about that which is to be made manifest (fig4.8). If an individual is not going in one particular direction, then by default they must be going in the other. Therefore, if an individual has not been systematically schooled to the point of becoming a fixed rational thinker, then by law and by default they would have developed an inner sense of be*ing* and knowing, thereby shifting their Consciousness beyond the rational on into the irrational. This seems to be almost inevitable every time. Remember... irrational numbers can be algebraic and therefore transcendental, and likewise irrational thinking is also algebraic and transcendental. It is the admonition to think outside of the box. My colleague 'student-teachers' within the AEO call this **outformation**, which is data that is picked up through irrational means – such as meditation, divining, channelling, etc. Many people often pick up messages and visions through trance or through dreaming, which they often find difficult to express through rational means.

This is what determines a true teacher of esoteric philosophy – whether it's of Ancient Egiptian Nuwaubu or of some of the other new age hermetic doctrines. The guru has at hand, the task of transmitting out-formation, using words, analogies or scenarios that are of in-formation. Tricky... Dr Malachi through Nuwaubu (or Nuwaupo, in other dialects) taught us how to transform our selves from In-tellectual to Out-tellectual beings, using Out-formation as opposed to In-formation. For some people, particularly the educated, the idea of Out-tellect, or, out-lect is confronting, since it forces them to address systems and models that are outside of their lect-abilities.

From Intellect to Out-tellect
The Creator is not of the rational world, but is rather of the transcended irrational world. Objects that are created of the material world and therefore of the matrix are rational (symbolised by the *square* and the *yang*), and therefore intellectual. Whereas, objects created and manifested from beyond the matrix are mentally irrational (symbolised

by the *circle* and the *yin*) and therefore Out-tellectual. Therein the irrational, one experiences the Subjective, which is beyond the objectives of Mind. So, Sacred Geometry – rooted in the philosophy of the ancient architects and high priests of the Ancient Egiptian Orders provide us with a transcendental connection to the Creator, NTR.

Yin
Feminine Energy

Yang
Masculine Energy

Fig4.10: the Yin and Yang symbol

The challenge of teaching an outformation doctrine is thus minimised by using geometric models, particularly those with algebraic and transcendental results. The term implies that its data is 'out of formation,' or outside of the norm. This is why people of the esoteric are often considered insane – which is just a play-on-words – it should be out-sane, meaning outside of normal sanity, which gives a whole new meaning to the words sane and insane:

Sane   - one who operates within the sanity of the normal world
Insane   - one who operates in their own sanity (not of the normal world)
Out-sane   - one who operates outside of the sanity of the normal world

Intellectual   - one who operates with the knowledge of the normal world
Out-tellectual   - one who operates with knowledge from beyond this world

'I'm in the world but not of it,' says Christ Jesus of the bible. He was living within the world but operated from within the context of an out-formation doctrine, which (not to put too fine a point on it) he learnt and studied in Egipt. Jesus spent his childhood in Egipt – just like

Moses. The two were familiar with the order of Tehuti (known biblically as the order of Melchizadeck, [Heb 5v8]), where the masters taught them. They studied the principles of Sacred Geometry, of the Healing Arts (known today as the liberal arts), of Mental-transmutation called Alchemy, and of elemental reconfiguration (such as the transformation of water into wine, or the turning of Moses' rod into a snake). Sacred Geometry, a 'Right-Eye of Horus' school, combined with Ha Kha, a 'Left-Eye of Horus' school, unites the two hemispheres of the brain thereby bringing the initiate into Unity-Consciousness. Unity or Christ-Consciousness is a prerequisite for connecting to the Collective Unconscious, which is the Akasha of outformation. The Akastic record, on the other hand, is the physical writing and documentation of transcendental information.

One definition of insanity is, *'Continuing to do the same things over and over and expect to get new or different results.'* And, I learnt through my network-marketing career that the quality of decisions that one make in life are based on the quality of information s/he posses. The religions of Western society base their information on monotheism, the sarcasm of a One-God concept. For the term *monotheism* is combined from the god Monos (god of sarcasm), and Theos (the Greek term for God). It is suggesting that those principalities of high places [Ephesians 3v10] are literally having a laugh in mockery at those of us whom have capitulated to the monotheistic concept of western religion. Monotheism is limited; it creates one-tracked thinking and tunnel vision views of reality. Polytheism on the other hand is vis-à-vis to having a thesaurus of creational concepts and cosmologies, available at the tip of your tongue. This creates open-mindedness, which is necessary in order to receive outformation and to operate within the context of Out-tellect. So the quest is this: religion by its definition is so-posed to elevate the Consciousness of its believers into oneness with Christ and God – but is it? Week after week we do the same things over and over, but the results in terms of quality of life never really change – at least as far as true Human (God in man-form) potential are concerned anyway. Clueless insanity indeed...

Measuring *Up*

In volume 1 I presented the '42 Declarations' and the '42 Confessions' of Ma'at, as the vows and pledges of virtue of which one is to live her or his life in consort. The latter is just one of many of such rectitude[A] however. Throughout the many mystical schools of old and new, there are many declarative instructions so to speak. It doesn't really matter which system of Principles we take on board – they all share common morals, with the objective of transformation and ascension. We are all familiar with the famed 'Ten Commandments' of the Torah (Old Testament). And, the doctrine of Ma'at informs us that: each individual is judged, and can only be judged, by and of the standards of morals, truth and justice s/he takes on (such as the 'Ten Commandments' of the Christian Doctrine). Know this... True Morals are essentially geometric in their meanings, and indeed connect us to our maker through intimate application. Therefore, essentially, you will find that with every religion on that planet, every esoterical doctrine, and every seemingly isolated culture, their codes of conduct transcendentally speaking, all meet at the same point (such is Einstein's $E=MC^2$). The illusion of their differences and separation lies within the actual stories told of their history. I.e., Muslims believe in the stories of Muhammad; Christians believe in the stories of Jesus; and, Jews believe in the stories of Abraham and Moses. But one can never, ever, dispute the moral Principles these characters stood for. It is also very obvious within the three spoken of religions above, that there is even further separation in the form of versions or sects. This is something many believe to be by design – especially where it concerns Black peoples. We are a divided and separated people based upon differences in opinion and interpretation of many a scripture. Please excuse my slight deviation from the subject at hand, but I felt the need to re-mention this

---

[A] A rectitude a code of moral uprightness

situation here, since it is the morals of religion we ought to be concerned about. And, that Sacred Geometry, its mathematics and its rightness, is a means that can unite all religions and esoterical schools.

Moreover, on the subject of Sacred Geometry, how do we really know that the pyramids and the many sacred sites across the world measure up? I mean, do they really merit the integrity to connect one with the Divine, as they are so-posed? The very dimensions of the Great Pyramid confirm this fact – as well as its geodetic position on the planet and, its connection to other galactical geodetic markers, such as Orion, Sirius and Dracos for instance. Scientists speak of the errors found within the calculations of its structure, without blame of its constructors. The error they say is due to the fact that the planet has expanded and contracted in size many times over many thousands of years. This is perfectly understandable. Dr Malachi taught us some of these dimensions as a stepping-stone for our own scrutiny and investigation:

- The height of Pyramid from the top of the platform is 480.95feet
- The thickness of platform is 1.80feet
- The height including platform is 482.75feet
- The perimeter of the Pyramid is 3,023.16feet

These dimensions are in a direct geometric relationship to the planet.

- The perimeter of the Great Pyramid's base is 1/43,200 of the earth's equatorial circumference
- Its height above the top of the base is 1/43,200 of the earth's polar radius

In other words, if a civilisation at some future time were to forget what the equatorial circumference of the earth was, all they would have to do is measure the perimeter of the Great Pyramid's base and multiply it by 43,200. And, if they forgot what the polar radius of earth was, they would similarly measure the height of the Pyramid from its base and multiply by 43,200. The calculations are not 100% as stated, but are close enough if we consider the expansion and contraction of the earth over time.

- If we take the earth's equatorial circumference of 24,920miles and scale it down by 43,200 we get 0.576 of a mile. There are 5280feet in a mile. The next step therefore, is to multiply 0.576x5280 = 3,041.28feet. By comparison we see that the Pyramids perimeter is 3,023.16feet. Close enough?
- Then, if we take the earth's polar radius of 3949.9081miles and scale it down by 43,200 we get 0.0914 of a mile. 0.0914x5280 = 482.59feet. Again by comparison we see that the Pyramid's height is 482.75751feet. Close enough indeed.

Fig4.11 overleaf symbolises the latter. Remember, the earth is not a perfect circle but is rather oblong or oval in nature. However, the symbol helps us to visualise the relationship between earth and pyramid.[12] In light of the geodetic science, the human being and he/r physical make up is also proportional to certain geometric ratios of earth. This in turn connects the human being to the celestial bodies of our solar system, in particular the Sun. To study this relationship, we will next endeavour the science of melanin and its relationship to the stars.

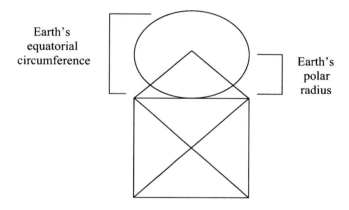

Earth's
equatorial
circumference

Earth's
polar
radius

Fig4.11: the Geometry of the Great Pyramid

~

Notes

[1] Arthur M. Young, *The Geometry of Meaning*, p-xiii (Delacorte Press, USA, 19976, ISBN: 0-440-04987-3)

[2] Marcus Chown, *The Universe Next Door,* p62-81

[3] Ibid, p62-81

[4] Arthur M. Young, *The Geometry of Meaning*, p1-3

[5] Ibid, p2

[6] Graham Hancock, *Fingerprints of the Gods,* p456 (Arrow books, London, 1995, ISBN: 0-7493-1454-0)

[7] Dr Malachi, *The Sacred Wisdom,* p115-116

[8] (a) Ibid, p258 (b) Dr Malachi, *The Ancient Egiptian Sacred Geometry,* p2

[9] Ibid, p4

[10] Ibid, p6

[11] Dr Malachi, *The Spell of Leviathan 666,* p287-292

[12] Dr Malachi, *The Sacred Records of Tamare,* p209

Chapter 5
Melanin and the Nubian Black Box

Power Hormones

The term hormone comes from the Greek word *hormein,* meaning to arouse or to stir up. It is defined as 'an internal secretion, which on reaching some part of a plant or animal body, exercises a specific physiological action.' In humans however, it is the secretion of the endocrine glands, concerned with the control of the body's functions. The major glands are as follows:

Table 8: secretions of the endocrine glands

Pineal gland	-	Melatonin <Serotonin
Pituitary gland	-	Melatonin <Serotonin
Thyroid gland	-	Thyroxine (T4); Triiodothyronine (T3)
Thymus gland	-	T-Lymphocytes
Adrenal gland	-	Adrenaline
Pancreas	-	Glycogen; Insulin
Ovary and Testis	-	Oestrogen/ Progesterone; Testosterone

Hormones bring about changes in the functions of various organs according to the body's requirements. The hypothalamus, which adjoins the pituitary gland, at the base of the brain, is a control centre for overall coordination of hormone secretion; the thyroid hormones determine the rate of general body chemistry; the adrenal hormones prepare the organism during stress for 'fight or flight;' and, the sexual hormones such as oestrogen govern reproductive functions. There are also hormone-secreting cells in the kidney, liver, the gastrointestinal tract, and the placenta. Hormones are therefore known as slow chemical messengers between the body's organs, whereas, the nervous system provides instant communication between the body's sensors and the brain.

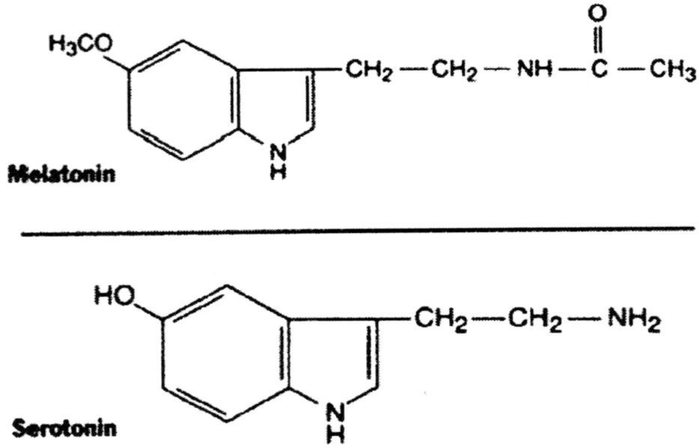

Fig5.1: the Melatonin and Serotonin molecule

Melanin

The word Melanin comes from the Greek word *melas,* meaning black.[1] As a bi-product of '**Melatonin**' and '**Serotonin,**' (fig5.1), Melanin is the most powerful chemical or hormone within the Universe. Given to us as a gift from our Etherian ancestors via their physical descendants, the Anunnaqi,[2] it connects us eternally with them and to the Universe through Universal Love. It is the gift of all gifts, for it controls all Mental and physical activities of the human being, – in

154

particular of the Nubian's anatomy, the Anatomy of God in the flesh. Melatonin, a precursor for Melanin, connects us to the planet through Serotonin making us one with all of nature. In a synergistic fashion, it connects us to the Sun, as well as to the trinity behind the Sun – the Tri Star system Sirius (fig5.2). Sirius in turn is therefore synergistically connected to the centre of the galaxy, of which millions of stars/ suns and planets are also connected. Our galaxy in turn is thus connected to the Central Vortex of our Universe, which is connected to the <u>Great Central Vortex</u> (NTR) where all seven universes are connected.

Our Sun, called *Re*, (pronounced ray) by the ancient Khemetians, and *Shamash*, by the ancient Sumerians is but a reflector for the real Sun, Sirius A of the Canis Major system, etherically called Illiyuwn (fig5.2). The Sun, Shamash, grown specifically for the purpose of sustaining life on this terrain, Ta-Ma-Re – or, *'Planet of land, water and Sun,'* is managed and controlled by the Etherians of the Sirius/ Illiyuwn system. It is therefore a corresponding relay station for 'light-coded' information from Sirius. The Etherians, our guardian angels, whom are also called the **Eluls** by the ancient Ptahites, shower blessing upon us in the form of light, as shown by way of the depiction of Atun as the Sun disk with thousands of *Rays* of tearing light; an anthropomorphic personification of the Ain-Soph-Aur. Since Melatonin is a product of the physical manifestation of all light frequencies combined, Serotonin, it is therefore the most powerful chemical hormone within the Universe.[3] Serotonin and Melatonin is essentially 'light-coded' information, it is of that which comes to us from the chaotic abyss of the Universe, directly from NTR or the Black Dot. Melanin itself, acts as a receiver for the information sent to us from the Black Dot and also acts as storage for the latter – as the downloaded 'Nubian **Black Box**.'

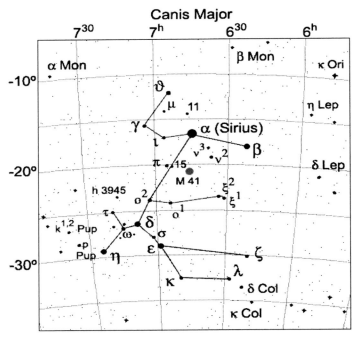

Fig5.2: The Canis Major constellation

Black Box?

The term 'Black Box,' is a coin that represents the fact that Afrokhans and their Nubian descendants have the capability of tapping into the infinite knowledge of the Universe by way of Melanin. I.e., to tap into the historical knowledge of the Ancestors, the Collective Unconscious; of those that are present and indeed of those which are to follow. The Black Box is simply the collective memory of all events since creation – the Akasha.[4] Therefore, Melanin within the skin is not just a pigment hormone; it is a biochemical messenger – the biological *Malachi* of all hormonal messengers [as above so below]. It acts as an absorbent as it is capable of absorbing all spiritual, light and sound frequencies. And thus, as information comes to us from God, from out of chaos via the Ancestors in the form of light, it is subconsciously received by us via our epidermal Melanin. Dear beloved, Universal information is available to all Afrokhan peoples. We must however aspire to exhibit Unconditional Universal Love, as a prerequisite to become One with 'All that Is...' and to become an emblem of the Creator, for the Creator knows All. The Love for our Afrokhan Self, must, inextricably include the Love of Melanin – our essential stuff.

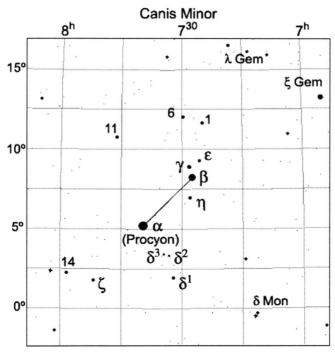

Fig5.3: The Canis Minor constellation

The undermining concept of Black inferiority causes the brain to produce 'death-encouraging hormones,'[5] or 'Melanin inhibiting hormones;' like melanostatin for instance.[A] In other words, by us disliking or hating our very blackness, it becomes an encouragement for the programming of the brain to produce a somatic body that eventually eradicates Serotonin and Melatonin production. This is devastating to the Universal order of be*ing*[6]. It also causes communication malfunctions within the ontological order of be*ing*. As a result, we suffer due to lack of awareness of whom and what we are. We lack the conscientious aspects of our be*ing*, which encourage us to operate under the faculty of the adversary whom lacks Conscience, Universal-knowledge or memory.

Melanin connects us with the Akasha; the Collective Unconscious of 'All that Is,' and it connects us with Amentet, the upper regions of the Astral Light, of which the Halls of Amenta are synergized. Our Universe, **Aum**, with its seventy six trillion years of existence, holds its information and experience by way of light – or, by way of electrical and magnetic currents. Melanin is thus created, utilised and beautifully exhibited by beings of a magnetic nature – as in 9-ether beings, those of the '**Green light**,' the <u>Seraphim</u> or <u>Sarufaat</u>, 'Angels of the 9th Order.' We are connected to the Akashic records, the Divine Astral Light of the Universe by way of our genetic, somatic and spiritual connection to our Ancestors; those who were electro-magnetic melanated peoples. Our Celestial magnetic Ancestors took on the electrical attributes of the physical world when they incarnated in the flesh, and thereby become electro-magnetic beings. Our adversary, are likewise of an electro-radioactive nature, and therefore appears to be in opposition to our

---

[A] Melanostatin, a thirty-six amino acid peptide recently isolated from the frog brain due to its ability to inhibit alpha-melanocyte - stimulating hormone (alpha-MSH) release, is the amphibian counterpart of mammalian neuropeptide Y (NPY). The effect of synthetic melanostatin on the bioelectrical activity of cultured frog melanotrophs was studied in 124 cells by using the whole-cell patch-clamp technique

function. These electro-radioactive beings or, 6-ether beings are destructive in nature, and therefore inhibit the process of communication between 9-ether beings. Their function is to inhibit the communication between the 'I ME Presence,' and the 'I AM Presence,' or, the correspondence between the lower egoic-self and the higher Conscience-Self of 9-ether entities. The devil's program is to cause Afrokhan melanated peoples to go into *'light-code lockdown'* [7] [Phill Valentine]. These Satanic forces function in such ways that is analogous with the damaging effects of free radicals toward Melanin. More on free radicals shortly…

Ancestral communion amongst Afrokhan peoples is done through Melanin, as well as through divining and channelling. Rites of passage are performed effectively by way of Melanin also – to appease the Ancestors and to incite their eternally living spirits to work on behalf of us or through us. Rites of passage enables constant corporeal connection and communication with them, which is necessary since they are closer to the source and are more in tune with the Collective Unconscious than those of us still living. Melanin connects us with the original chaotic Presence of the Universe.

Chaos – the Blackman's Origin of Space

As expressed in chapter 1, chaos is the undifferentiated state of ether (fig1.14), though Pure Ether paradoxically has no state – simply existing without condition and, completely at Peace. Ether herein exists merely as mist, having no definite purpose, shape, form etc. Through objective meditation, NTR, the Creator, *caused* the movement of the first Black Dot or Nuqta to spiral about itself. All frequencies and waves of particles therefore originate from this point of co-ordinate – El Qubt. The physical manifestation of this infinitum of light frequencies geometrically unfolds throughout the Universal matrix as Melanin.

The so-called 'Black Man,' as in the Black Nation, substantially originates from this point – El Qubt, out of chaos as the intended physical manifestation of NTR. Since the Black Nation is the original God-man on the planet, we are properly called 'Nuwbuns,' 'Ptahites,' or 'Melanites,' and, we have our origin within Involution itself. We are both a product of Involution, as well as the manifester of 'All that Is,' – we are the physical manifestation of The All [a microcosm of the macrocosm – as above so below]. Our counter adversary is a bi-product of Involution, physically emerging through the process of evolution. These evolutionary 6-ether entities are Melanin recessive and manifests physically as the 'black-skinned Hindu' of Indonesia – the parents of the Aryan race; the fifth root race of Atlantis. They are the forces of Procyon (fig5.3).

The Black man's origin supersedes the creation of the matrix. Our existence is of a world where none manifested of this world can even begin to imagine. The evolved Universe as we know it, is but a matrix program that is mentally generated – mentally created by Melanite Etherians, existing in and beyond Involution, and are of their own world. Therefore 9-ether conscientious Melanin-dominant beings are of that world. This world however, the matrix, is the home of 6-ether Melanin-recessive beings. These 6-ther beings cannot elevate beyond the spiritual aspects of this world. Why? Simply because they are a product of this world, and therefore do not have the Soul connection to pass through the matrix grids. 9-ether melanated beings however, possess a higher level of energy which we call Soul, that enable us to pass through the matrix grids toward our token home – beyond the Mind of The All. 6-ether beings, or Cherubims, also called Garubaat, do not have a soul, or at least do not possess energy levels of this power. Heaven, for such entities, can only be the highest states of Consciousness attainable within the matrix itself. This is why it is imperative for the European man and his western society to develop a system that inhibits the melanated Afrokhan to aspire to function according to her/ his own nature – NTRU.

Soul Vs Spirit

On the material level, the DNA of the Afrokhan, coated with nucleon-Melanin, is the physical manifestation of her soul. Her spirit is therefore created and thus shaped according to her environment and circumstances. The RNA, which is decoded from the DNA, represents her spiritual characteristics. It is the *self*, as we perceive her, yet the DNA, her Soul, contains all the possibilities she could ever become. The DNA also holds all the possible scenarios of self-expression going all the way back to the first Ancestor – God itself. It has been said much, that, the White man, does not have a soul, and that he functions by way of spirit only. His own scientists scientifically verify this, by the fact that his genes are recessive, and therefore must also be nucleon-Melanin recessive. For, the Soul of the Creator, and indeed the over-Soul of the Afrokhan, cannot degenerate. I.e., God cannot self-destruct, and therefore the Universe cannot create its own demise; it only changes in form or composition. The White race is made in the image and after the likeness of God, which in this context is the melanated Afrokhan. From the dominant DNA of the melanated blacks of old, a degenerative gene was made manifest through gene splicing, in the form of an RNA expression. Thus we have the making or cloning of the Asian race that later fathered the Aryan and subsequent White race. This spliced section of RNA became the sole (not soul) connection for these 6-ether peoples. It is the spirit that governs their Mental and physical faculties, hence them not having a Soul. These are people of the moon, as opposed to the Sun.[8] With the moon being a lifeless body that only reflects the sun's energy, so it is with whites that they can only mimic, or, can only reflect the energy, culture, arts, music and dance etc., of the ancient blacks. And, the reason why whites have to do things like bungee jumping, hand gliding, car racing, hockey, hunting bears, shark diving – you name it, is because they have to work-up a 'high.' Just as how they also drink alcohol, which they call *spirits*, and, also smokes marijuana to get that 'high.' Do you see the connections? They do not naturally have a 'high,' feeling, as Nubians do; we are people of the Sun, and are forever connected through Soul. The whole worth of Asian and Aryan peoples and their make-up is comparative to a piece of degenerated strand of RNA, spliced from the very loins of the Ancient Cyclopean Black Gods; whose Etherian counterparts created the very matrix mankind reside in.

Creation of the Matrix

If we, the melanated Afrokhan Nation even began to understand who we are, the European system of life and living would immediately crash. And, universally speaking, if all the melanated 9-ether Souls of the Cosmos suddenly woke up to the call for ascension, the matrix would immediately collapse, destroying all 6-ether entities therein. How is all of this possible... you may wonder?

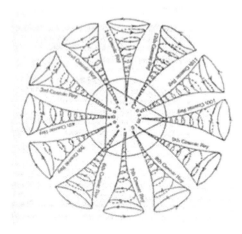

Fig5.4: 12 matrix spirals

The Mental projection of NTR ultimately created the matrix. The first created beings of the Black Dot were intricately interconnected through wavelengths of light frequencies, known collectively as the NTRU, existing as sparks of light within etheric-pockets spiralling throughout pure space. These NTRU, when manifested to us are the so-called Ogdoads, the Enneads or the Orisha-nla etc. They understood exactly who they were, as individual entities of the whole, or as integral parts of NTR, Olodumare etc. They knew that their purpose as 9-ether creative forces was to carry out this great work of creating the matrix of which they would later incarnate into. Together, they mentally projected the relayed information from NTR, in the form of light codes into the void and darkness. Today, we appreciate aspects of these codes as DNA, which back in the beginning of our earth produced and grew the first animals of the matrix, the Amoeba. Prior to the creation of the Amoeba however, the Universe existed predominantly as rings of carbon[9] surrounding semi-nuqta points which themselves encircled larger relay stations of light codes, which we now call stars or suns. Carbon interestingly, is that which creates Serotonin and Melatonin,[10] which originally manifested physically as 'green,' as in the hue of algae. In fact, carbon created the earth and all of its natural parts – animals, insects, trees etc. Pure Melanin would therefore have been green, based on the correspondence and reactions of the light rays from the sun with the naturally produced elements of the planet.

As taught by Dr Malachi, a vital ingredient of Melanin was lost over time. This was magnesium, which has now been replaced by iron.[11] When magnesium oxidises it produces a green hue, and, when iron is oxidised it produces a very dark brown rusty hue. Are you with me on this...? As a matter of fact, some babies are born today with blotches of green pigmentation all over their bodies, which usually clears up after a few days. This indicates the history of our anatomy over its evolutionary growth. The human being in its infancy on earth had a green hue, which over time altered to a dark rusty brown in colour. This is the life history of the ancient Ptahites – those created by Neter Ptah under the auspices of Tehuti who held and recorded the blueprint of the original amoeba.

Destruction of the Matrix

Take a look at planet earth and just imagine what would happen if the NTRU, the creators of this program, were to regroup all of their Mental faculties. I mean, imagine if Ptah, Khnum, Anu, Olodumare, Tehuti, Nkulu-Nkulu, Nyame and all the other Afrokhan melanated creator deities were to simply halt the Mental projection. For a start, the melanated Afrokhan would receive a sudden urge for a paradigm shift. Her/ his mind would immediately open and expand beyond its current egoic limitations. The Afrokhan would achieve almost total recall that this is but a program that we mentally created. It is rather like a virtual reality computer generated game, only appearing real due to our participation and cohesive attachment to the visual effects of the program. It is also like going into a dream state, and enjoying the dream so much that you do not want to be awakened. Then suddenly, your spouse wakes you to come for breakfast. Sometimes we do not want to be awakened. Dreamland is bliss… or at least that is what the ego tells us. The latter is analogous to the fact that the gods – all of them, are simultaneously calling all of their creations to be raptured. There is a Universal re-alignment on all levels – for the gods them selves are also a part of a larger simulation program – the process goes on infinitum. If the Mental projections of these Gods were to suddenly halt, all of their Mental faculties would regroup and those of us that are ready for ascension would be raptured out of the matrix grid program. The rest of us would experience eternal death, as our spirits are recycled back into 9-ether and back into chaos. These un-raptured entities will cease to exist. There will be no means whatsoever to recall any memory of them selves since the Mental Plane would have also been regrouped. Of course, the entire process to us may expand over a period of time, by thousands, perhaps even millions of years. Intriguingly, the creation, Involution, and destruction of an entire Universe occur in the blink of an eye in the Mind of its Creator. But, to those of us that are cohesively trapped within creation itself, it seems like aeons upon aeons of time.

So, the Melanin recessive Europeans, knowing that we are gods, must do everything within their power to prevent us from having total recall. Because, if we remember... KABOOM... and the programs are terminated... and it's all over for them. This scenario is evident where we have many melanated peoples coming forth with Self-enlightening information, for the resurrection of the mentally dead amongst us. The Europeans of the West sought to destroy every Black leader and his organisation that was ever established, over the last one hundred years. We have had leaders amongst us such as these listed below; and of course a whole lot more:

Nat Turner, 1800AD – 1831AD: lead the slave rebellion

Noble Drew Ali, 1886AD – 1929AD: established the Moorish Science Temple

Marcus Garvey, 1887AD – 1940AD: established the Black Star line

Haile Selassie, 1892AD – 1975AD: emperor of Ethiopia

Elijah Muhammad, 1897AD – 1973AD: founder of the Black Muslims

Malcolm X, 1926AD – 1965AD: leader of the Nation of Islam

Martin Luther King, 1929AD – 1968AD: civil rights leader and fighter

Melanin in Action

Over the last one hundred years or so, Melanin has performed and expressed its potential for us in a number of ways including: scholastic aptitudes, professional aptitudes, in sports, as well as general health and well-being. Wherever the system places blacks, we dominate. This is not my arrogance talking; this is a fact. Just look at the history.

Throughout sports we have the likes of:

Jesse Owens	Carl Lewis	Pele
Michael Jordan	Tiger Woods	Daley Thompson
Linford Christie	Serena Williams	Magic Johnson
Muhammad Ali	Florence Joyner	O. J. Simpson
Tessa Anderson	Jackie Robinson	Jackie Kersee

And, scholastically we have the likes of:

John Hanson	Jessie Jackson	Colin Powell
Martin Luther King	James Baldwin	W.E.B. Dubois
Alex Haley	Betty Shabazz	Francis Cress Welsing
KRS One	George G.M. James	Dr Yosef Ben Jochannan
Frederick Douglass	Ben Chavis	Darcus Howe
Arthur A. Schomburg	Johnny Cochran	Clare Holder. OBE

Remember… Melanin controls all Mental and physical activities. Therefore, a Melanin-dominant individual, a Melanite, will have greater responsive potential, in terms of the 5-senses for example, than a Melanin-recessive individual. In the Second World War, it was reported that blacks were often placed at the front lines, not just because they were considered dispensable, but also, primarily since their visual potential was known to be far greater than that of their White brother-soldiers. Blacks are able to see much further distances than whites, and equally are able to see in the dark a lot clearer. The army simply used them for reconnaissance. Nikola Tesla, one of the greatest physicists of the modern world, had created a gadget of some sort that enabled thought patterns of a person to be reflected from the eyes and thereby be projected unto a screen.[12] His theory was based on the fact that images that are picked up by the optic nerves within the eyes are transmitted to the brain for processing, which then creates a Mental image of what is being observed. In reverse, he believed that mental thoughts could create some type of reflex action within the brain that transmits these thoughts down to the optic nerves within the eyes. With an appropriate apparatus, one could pick up and therefore transmit these thought patterns unto a screen to be viewed by others. Other more recent and interesting postulations have since come forth from Europeans, such as remote viewing. The latter, are both natural functions available for Melanin-dominant persons. Remember again, whatever the European can contemplate or reflect through thought, is in fact a reality for the melanite. The above tell us that the Nubian has a larger content of Melanin within her pupils. The abundance of Melanin within Nubians consequently produces dark brown eyes as well as black-skin and black curly hair. An individual, having a reduction in the efficiency of Melanin base amino acids, such as Tyrosine,[A] (see footnote), evidently has light or blond hair, and, blue or hazel eyes; the blue being a reflection of a particular wavelength of light. Also, In a previous chapter we talked about electricity, and the colour blue, being a reflection of an electrical energy that represent transformation and ascension. It is the fastest moving colour in the visible part of the EMS. Here, the Caucasian, with apparently blue eyes, does not have the required Melanin content to absorb and therefore process that energy band, which is associated with ascension.

Melanin as a chemical comes in various qualities and quantities. The highest quality manifests as black in colour, and therefore has the ability to absorb all light and sound frequencies from its immediate

---

[A] There are at least 20 common types of Amino Acids. Most of them are provided by way of the diet; whilst 8, the essential ones, the body's DNA synthesizes.

The synthesised types are:			The essentials are:		
cystein	cystine	tyrosine	tryptophan	isoleucine	lysine
arginine	alanine	glutamic acid	threomine	leucine	methionine
praline	cartinine	glutamine	phenylalanine	valine	
histidine	aspartic acid	glycine			
serine	asparginine	hydroxyproline			

environment. This type of Melanin, found within the epidermal layers of the skin, reflects very little amounts of what it absorbs. Therefore, within its blackness, (a form of darkness), the mentality within it's being creates a Mental image of the energy that it has absorbed. This of course is what actually creates the blackness of the molecule itself. The Mental image is then stored as potential energy, to be used possibly at a later time. So, it is clear to see that since the Nubian has a higher concentration of Melatonin and Seratonin content, and therefore Melanin, her senses of sight, hearing, taste and smell, which are all senses of touch, is dominant over her Caucasian counterpart. But it also suggests that our nervous reactions to external stimuli, our quickness of processing emotions and, the ability to compute the latter is of a dominant nature also. Each Melanin molecule has a mini brain of its own and is thus capable of maintaining independent existence. Also, skin Melanin in its pristine form, can be viewed as solar panels having the ability to absorb and process all types of energy from within and beyond the EMS bands. But, Melanin can also become toxic and distorted if it is not well taken care of. In light of all of this, we must understand the need for us to investigate what types of vitamins and minerals we ought to be consuming in order to maintain optimum Melanin functions. The natural diet of a melanite is indeed different to that of a Melanin-recessive person. The supermarkets of London are filled with foods, whether natural or genetically modified, which are not conducive for the Nubian woman and man. These foods are produced by, and therefore only cater for whites and their physical genetic make-up. They are capable of sustaining life by eating foods that do not have a soul signature. And why would they need to do otherwise since they do not have soul? Whites can live on frozen and other processed foods, which have lost their synergistic connection to nature and the sun. Nubians, Melanites, on the other hand, are not just responsible for nurturing the physical body, but also for nurturing the astral or light body. Therefore, we are best to be consuming live-foods that still have a synergistic connection to the planet and to the sun. This way we are feeding both the physical body with the protein and carbohydrates contained in the food, and, the light body with the light energy of the said food. The year 1970 marked the opening of the seventh seal, the opening, in a manner of speaking, of the Nubian Black Box. It marked a revolutionary turning point for blacks all across the world. People started jumping in leaps and bounds in political arenas, in sports and in entertainment, etc. The year marked the end of the Industrial Age and the birth of the Information Age. This was not because of some Black leader somewhere who promoted this, although there was, but because it was an astrological or, solar biological motivation. We had reached the end of the Piscean era, and were starting to usher in the Aquarian era. Universally speaking, it was time for Melanin to become reactivated within the Black Nations of the earth. 1970 also marked the end of the moon cycle of our planet and, the launch of the new Sun cycle, where Love and Conscience rule. In the 70s, in the entertainment industry, we had the rise to fame of people like:

Aretha Franklin	Bill Cosby	Calvin Lockhart
Oprah Winfrey	Arseno Hall	James Earl Jones
Mario Van Peebles	Richard Prior	Billy Dee Williams
Tracie Chapman	Sidney Pottier	Isaac Hayes
John Amos	Pam Grier	Richard Roundtree

And, in preparation of the oncoming Sun cycle, we have had many astute Black scholars of the esoteric and of ancient Afrokhan spirituality such as:

Dr Malachi	Elijah Muhammad	Marcus Garvey
Haru Hotep T.A.R	Emefie Ikenga Metuh	Aris La Than
Malcolm X	Phill Valentine	Noble Drew Ali
Lliala O. Afrika	Queen Afua	Shaikh Daud
Patricia Newton	Wayne B. Chandler	Sister Marimba Ani
Anthony T. Browder	Ra Un Nefer Amen	Malidoma Patrice Som'e
Louis Farrakhan	Haile Selassie	Bobby Hemmitt
Delbert Blair	Oba T'shaka	John Henrik Clarke

Shades of Melanin

Throughout the Fatherland of Afrokha there are many different shades of Black amongst its people – from the darkest of blue-black through reddish brown to yellowish brown. Dr Malachi teaches that there are 7 different types of Melanin, and, Dr Pookrum, a teacher of holistic philosophy talks of 6 types.[13] She says, there are three main types of Melanin, which are amongst blacks and the two extremes are called:

1. EuMelanin, which has a high electrical charge, extremely absorbent and has a high molecular weight. It gives the appearance of dark brown to blue-black
2. Pseudo-Melanin, which has a low molecular structure and has a lesser capacity to absorb and store energy

In her work, *'Vitamins and Minerals from A to Z,'* Dr Pookrum wrote about the 6 different postulated types of Melanin, and gives a brief description of their properties, capabilities and so on. She also says:

> *"Nothing in our world has the power to make us weak, sad or diseased if we adopt a proper attitude, diet and commitment to wellness. Each of us can live in infinite perfection."*[14]
>
> Dr Pookrum

Genetic Annihilation

Deviating from Melanin slightly – what is the objective of the board game of chess? The objective lies within the supremacy of the 'White-king's' obligation to checkmate the 'Black-king.' Symbolically speaking, am I right? For in the game of chess, the white-side always moves first. This means that although both teams have the same objective, the 'White-king' starts out being on the offensive-defensive, whereas the 'Black-king' starts out on the defensive-offensive. Is this not what we experience in society today? The White male is always on the offensive against Melanin dominant males,[15] as a statement that says, *"We cannot have a genetically superior race over us, they must be suppressed or put down."*

In the game of genetics, the White male plays the role of free radicals. They form special groups among them for the purpose of destroying any Black leader or Black organisation that germinates. Over the years I have heard a lot of talk about the 'Alternatives 1, 2 & 3,' where the establishments had planned to control the Black Nation, and other Melanin carrying peoples through mass genocide. Smaller numbers are easier to control and manipulate. William Cooper talked about this in detail in his book *'Behold a Pale Horse.'* Not that he was on any body's side; he was simply exposing the facts of the matter. The White male is literary saying, *"Blacks can genetically annihilate us, they don't need to use weapons like we do. All they have to do is continue to breed amongst them selves, and they will outnumber us in no time; we have o stop them. Their sperm count is far more potent than ours. We have to practice to make babies, but no, no, they produce babies at such a rate as if there is no tomorrow."* Beloved, in reality, we already outnumber whites, at least 6-1, since they are of the lowest type of Melanin, called pseudo-Melanin or, pheo-Melanin.

Free radicals
In volume 1, I spoke briefly about free radicals and their effect on the production of Melatonin and Seratonin, which are pre requisites for Melanin production. The clinical definition for a free radical is:

> *'An atom or molecule that has an unpaired electron and is therefore highly reactive is a free radical. Most of them are very short-lived. They are bi-products of normal cell chemistry and rapidly oxidise other molecules they encounter. Free radicals are*

thought to do considerable damage. They are generally neutralised by protein enzymes.

Paraphrased from the Hutchinson Encyclopaedia – 2000 – ISBN 1-85986-288-8

I would suggest you consult volume 1 of this work for a quick recap on Melatonin and Seratonin production. The work also talks about free radicals, and how they are actually created, and, how household electrical appliances influence them. In society however, there are many relative comparatives that are present. The media system for example, has been set up in such a way that it inhibits the possibility for blacks to aspire to become what was intended by the Black Box. The Black Box, as stated, is a coined term for the Nubians' Collective Unconscious. The archives of the Black Box tell us that, *"Each and every one of us has a purpose here;"* we were not sent, nor did we volunteer, to come down to this school for the sole purpose of working for the White man and his Eurocentric system. That is an illusion. By way of the definition above, it is clear that free radicals can become neutralised by Spirit, since enzymes are a material manifestation of a spirit-life-force that promote cell growth and therefore cell replication. In the analogy of the latter, the enzymes are representative of the many astute Black scholars and esoteric teachers that have entered the world over the last one hundred years. By them setting up and establishing their doctrines, as well as a consequent culture that represents it, White supremacy will degenerate by way of the overwhelming catalyzed Black power that would become evident. So there is a warfare going on – free radicals Vs Enzymes; spirit Vs Soul; White chess pieces Vs Black chess pieces; religion Vs Afrokhan spirituality, etc.

The Worship of Black Gods

Opposite are listed a few well known facts and statements, where White folks worship Black skinned Gods; always have and always will!

- "Negroes were first worshipped in Greece and Rome"
- "The original Gods of Greek & Roman mythology appeared as Negroes" *(such as Jupiter, Bacchus, Hercules, Apollo, Venus, Hecati, Juno, Metis, Ceres, and Cybele.*
- "White masses bowed down to Black deities"
- "The rites of Apollo were founded by Delphos and his Negro mother, Melainis"
- "The worship of Black Isis and Horus were popular in Roman colonies as far north as Britain" *(worshipped as the Black Madonna and Christ)*
- "The chief title of Zeus, the Greatest of the Greek Gods was, 'Ethiops,' which means 'BLACK'
- J.A. Rogers claims that: "The earliest Gods and Messiahs on all the continents were Black"
- Sir Godfrey Higgins Esq says: "The Alma Mater, the Goddess Multimammia, the founder of the Oracles, the Memmon or first idols were always Black"
- "The original depictions of the ancient Druids were Black"
- "The Ancients viewed the sacred image of the Divine as Black. And the holy race of the Gods was African"
- "All the Gods of Antiquity from Greece to Mexico were BLACK"
- "Jesus is described as having hair like lamb's wool, & feet like burnt brass" Rev 1v14-15 *(the pepper-corn hair was a sign of divinity)*
- "Jesus is represented as Black, as: 'the one who sits on the throne there appeared like jasper and carnelian' *(these are both rare stones and are dark in colour)*
- "Buddha was depicted in early Thailand, having pepper-corn hair" *(he was a Dravidian Black man of Ethiopian descent)*

These quotes were paraphrased from Indus Kamit Kush's work (see endnotes).[16]

Silent Weapons for Quiet Wars

The situation has been reversed. Blacks are now worshipping whites and whites are trying to *become* Black – quietly. And, there are many written about conspiracies concerning Black genocide as stated. For instance, I was listening to Sister Francis Cress Welsing, author of the *'Isis Papers,'* on a cassette recording, lecturing on the subject of 'Genetic Annihilation.' And one of the things that struck me was when she mentioned the fact that scientists had known about Aids and HIV since the year 1969. (Or at least, there was a publication on the subject in that year). I mean, to my astonishment, this was all before I was even born! And I remember first hearing about Aids and HIV when I was probably about 12-13 years old, during my Secondary school years. She said on the cassette that the subject and therefore definition of the AIDS virus came within a book (on p322), of over 400pages, entitled *'A survey on chemical and biological warfare.'*

Warfare…??? Yes, just as I stated two pages ago, there is a warfare going on. In his book *'Behold a pale Horse,'* Cooper also talks about 'Silent Weapons for Quiet Wars.' Although he was primarily talking about government systems and models,[17] I believe the subject ought to involve chemical and biological warfare also.

The subject of melanin is a very extensive one indeed; opposite, I have given you the opportunity to simplify what you have learnt into your own revision notes, for quick retrieval…

~

Revision Notes

Notes

[1] Dr Malachi, *The Melanin-ite Children, (Scroll #133)* p8 (Published by the UNNM)
[2] Ibid, p1 – Introduction
[3] Ibid, p11 & 15
[4] Nebu Ka Ma'at, *The Legacy of the Black Gods in Time before Time,* Introduction (Tamare House Publishers)
[5] Queen Afua, 2003 radio show with Mutabaruka
[6] Patricia Newton, *Melanin and the Black Child* (Audio Cassette)
[7] Phill Valentine, *The Matrix* (Audio Cassette)
[8] Dr Malachi, *People of the Sun,* p1 – introduction (Published by the UNNM)
[9] Patricia Newton, *Melanin and the Black Child* (Audio Cassette)
[10] Booker T. Coleman, *Carbon – life's ultimate gift* (Audio Cassette)
[11] Dr Malachi, *The Melanin-ite Children,* p4-7
[12] Dr Malachi, *Man from Planet Rizq,* p45-54
[13] Dr Pookrum, *Vitamins and Minerals from A to Z,* p23-25 (A & B Publishers Group, ISBN: 1-886433-10-0)
[14] Ibid, back cover
[15] Francis Cress Welsing, *Genetic Annihilation* (Audio Cassette)
[16] Indus Kamit-Kush, *What they never told you in History class,* Volume 1, p222-223(A & B Books Publishers, New York, 1993, ISBN: 1-886433-23-2)
[17] William Cooper – *Behold a Pale Horse,* p35-37

 # Chapter 6
Afrokhan Ontology and Cosmology

Afrokhan Creation stories

Throughout Afrokha and her history, as expressed in the 'Saitic Isis,' of Sir Godfrey Higgins (next chapter), there are literary thousands of cultures and thousands of creation stories, mythologies, cosmologies and folklore.[1] Below, I have incorporated just a handful – just five of these concepts, to give the reader an idea of the vastness of Afrokhan religion, ideology and cosmology. Most of the concepts that I have personally come across seem to be an echo from an earlier account – that of the Khemetian cosmology and its integral cosmogonies, which all carry the oldest recorded creation legends. Or, as I expressed in volume 1, the creational-pattern of our earth matrix, seem to repeat itself time after time – over and over again.[2] The concepts, the contexts, and indeed the elements of many a creation story align as though they all follow a set rule of conduct – like a blueprint. When I was a child, I naively believed that Afrokha *(spelled 'Africa' to me at the time)* was one complete place. I did not understand that there was such a vast number of countries, cultures and languages etc. I started realizing this when I first saw the Zulu movie. I had previously seen other movies with *'African'* themes, but this one stood out like a soar thumb. I think it was the way the warriors were dressed and how they conducted themselves in battle. I had never seen anything like it. Remember... I was only a child at the time. In my latter years I had gone on to study and learn more about Afrokhan cultures and their beliefs. In a few pages ahead we will look at the Zulu culture and it's Creator God Nkulu-Nkulu. But here is a quick synopsis.

The Zulu

*'The Ancient One, known as **Nkulu-Nkulu**, (pronounced unkoolen-koolu), is the Creator God of the Zulu culture. He came from the reeds and from them he brought forth the people and the cattle. He created everything – the mountains, streams, snakes, etc. He taught the Zulu how to hunt, how to make fire, and how to grow food. He also taught the men how to prepare for battle.'*

Boshongo (Bantu tribe of Central Africa)

'In the beginning there was only darkness, water, and the Great God Bumba. One day Bumba, in pain from a stomach ache, vomited up the sun. The sun dried up some of the water, leaving land. Still in pain, Bumba vomited up the moon, the stars, and then some animals – the leopard, the crocodile, the turtle, and, finally, humans.'

From this Bantu account, we find a possible source of the biblical account of creation, where Genesis Ch1 starts of by expressing a state of darkness in which the Spirit of God moved upon the face of the waters. The Sumerian Cosmogony of the Ogdoads related this as Apsu and Tiamat as found in the Enuma Elish, (See chapter 1).

Efik (Nigeria)

'The Creator, Abassi, created two humans and then decided to not allow them to live on earth. His wife, Atai, persuaded him to let them do so. In order to control the humans, Abassi insisted that they eat all their meals with him, thereby keeping them from growing or hunting food. He also forbade them to procreate. Soon though, the woman began growing food in the earth, and they stopped showing up to eat with Abassi. Then the man joined his wife in the fields, and before long they had children also. Abassi blamed his wife for the way things had turned out, but she told him

*she would handle it. She sent to earth death and discord to keep
the people in their place.'*

This account reflects the Babylonian story of Zakar and
Nekaybaw, which are related in the bible as Adam and Eve.[3] With a
little interest you will find that the three accounts – that of the
Babylonian, the Efik and the biblical, share a common context.

Ekoi (Southern Nigeria)

*'In the beginning there were two gods, Obassi Osaw and
Obassi Nsi. The two gods created everything together. Then
Obassi Osaw decided to live in the sky and Obassi Nsi decided to
live on the earth. The god in the sky gives light and moisture, but
also brings drought and storms. The god of the earth nurtures, and
takes the people back to him when they die. One day long ago
Obassi Osaw made a man and a woman, and placed them upon the
earth. They knew nothing so Obassi Nsi taught them about
planting and hunting to get food.'*

This concept resembles the Khemetian Ennead cosmogony of Geb
and Nut, god of the earth and goddess of the sky respectively. Earth and
sky then gave birth to man and woman – Asaru and Aset respectively, in
the Ennead cosmogony.

Fans (Bantu)

*'In the beginning there was nothing but Nzame. This god is
really three: Nzame, Mebere, and Nkwa. It was the Nzame part of
the god that created the universe and the earth, and brought life to
it. While the three parts of Nzame were admiring this creation, it
was decided to create a ruler for the earth. So was created the
elephant, the leopard, and the monkey, but it was decided that
something better had to be created. Between the three of them they
made a new creature in their image, and called him Fam (power),*

179

and told him to rule the earth. Before long, Fam grew arrogant, he mistreated the animals and stopped worshipping Nzame.'

Here we have a reflection of the trinity of Heliopolis, the city of On or Annu, namely Asaru, Aset and Haru; reflected in the bible as God the father, God the Sun/ Son and the Blessed Mother Mary. However, the Bantu continues as follows:

'Nzame, angered, brought forth thunder and lightning and destroyed everything that was, except Fam, who had been promised immortality. Nzame, in his three aspects, decided to renew the earth and try again. He applied a new layer of earth to the planet, and a tree grew upon it. The tree dropped seeds, which grew into more trees. Leaves that dropped from them into the water became fish. Those that dropped on land became animals. The old parched earth still lies below this new one, and if one digs deep enough it can be found in the form of coal. Nzame made a new man, one who would know death, and called him Sekume. Sekume fashioned a woman, Mbongwe, from a tree. These people were made with both Gnoul (body) and Nissim (soul). Nissim gives life to Gnoul. When Gnoul dies, Nissim lives on.'

And from here we see how there was a destruction of the world that warranted a replenishing, thus we have the creation of Adam and Eve, after the emergence of life in the waters followed by land life. Notice the expression *'the old parched earth'* – possibly the result of a pre-historic meteorite shower. According to Dr Malachi we had a meteorite shower some 17,250,000years ago, which wiped out the remainder of the pre-historic dinosaurs.[4]

Creation myths the world over

My reason for expressing these stories here is based upon that fact this work is designed to attract all people – Afrokhans as well their children; Orientals, Asiatics, Native Americans and Europeans etc. There is a distinction to be made toward the end of this chapter, regarding the oneness of Black or, Afrokhan Culture and religion. Below is a synopsis of five more creational myths from across the world.

Ainu

'In the beginning, the world was nothing but a quagmire. Nothing could live there, but in the six skies above and in the six worlds below dwelled Gods, demons, and animals. In the foggy and hanging skies of the lower heavens, demons lived. In the star-bearing and high skies of the clouds lived the lesser Gods. In the skies of the most high lived Kamui, the creator God, and his servants. A mighty metal wall surrounded his realm and, the only entrance was through a great Iron Gate. Kamui made this world as a vast round ocean resting on the backbone of an enormous trout. This fish sucks in the ocean and spits it out again to make the tides. When it moves it causes earthquakes. One day Kamui looked down on the watery world and decided to make something of it. He sent down a water wagtail to do the work. When the poor bird arrived and saw what a mess everything was in, it was at its wit's end to know what to do. However, by fluttering over the waters with its wings and by trampling the sand with its feet and beating it with its tail, the wagtail at last created patches of dry land. In this way islands were raised to float upon the ocean in this, the floating world. Even today, the faithful wagtail is still carrying on its work, still beating the ground with its tail. When Kamui created the world, the devil tried to thwart him. One morning, the devil got up *and lay in wait with his mouth gaping wide to swallow the sun. But Kamui sent a crow to fly down the devil's throat and make him choke and cough. That is why the crow is such a bold bird. Because a crow once saved the world, all crows think they can act, as they like, even stealing people's food. When the animals that lived up in the heavens saw how beautiful the world was, they begged Kamui to let them go and live on it, and he agreed. But Kamui also made many other creatures especially for the world. The first people, the Ainu, had bodies of earth, hair of chickweed, and spines made from sticks of willow. That is why when we grow old; our backs become bent. Kamui sent Aioina, the divine man, down from heaven to teach the Ainu how to hunt and to cook. When Aioina returned to heaven after living among the people and teaching them many things, the Gods all held their noses, crying, "What a terrible smell of human being there is!" They sniffed and sniffed to find out where the stink was coming from. At last they traced the smell to Aioina's clothes. The Gods sent him back to earth and refused to let him back into heaven until he left all his clothes behind. Down in the floating world, Aioina's cast-off sandals turned into the first squirrels.'*

Apache

'In the beginning nothing existed – no earth, no sky, no sun, no moon, only darkness was everywhere. Suddenly from the darkness emerged a thin disc, one side yellow and the other side white appearing suspended in mid-air. Within the disc sat a small bearded man, Creator, the One-Who-Lives-Above. As if waking from a long nap, he rubbed his eyes and face with both hands. When he looked into the endless darkness, light appeared above. He looked down and it became a sea of light. To the east, he created yellow streaks of dawn. To the west, tints of many colors appeared everywhere. There were also clouds of different colors.

Creator wiped his sweating face and rubbed his hands together, thrusting them downward. Behold! A shining cloud upon which sat a little girl. "Stand up and tell me where are you going," said Creator. But she did not reply. He rubbed his eyes again and offered his right hand to the Girl-Without-Parents.

"Where did you come from?" she asked, grasping his hand.

"From the east where it is now light," he replied, stepping upon her cloud.

"Where is the earth?" she asked.

"Where is the sky?" he asked, and sang, "I am thinking, thinking, thinking what I shall create next." He sang four times, which was the magic number.

Creator brushed his face with his hands; rubbed them together, then flung them wide open! Before them stood Sun-God. Again Creator rubbed his sweaty brow and from his hands dropped Small-Boy. All four gods sat in deep thought upon the small cloud. "What shall we make next?" asked Creator. "This cloud is much too small for us to live upon." Then he created Tarantula, Big Dipper, Wind, Lightning-Maker, and some western clouds in which to house Lightning-Rumbler, which he just finished. Creator sang, "Let us make earth. I am thinking of the earth, earth, earth; I am thinking of the earth," he sang four times. All four gods shook hands. In doing so, their sweat mixed together and Creator rubbed his palms, from which fell a small round, brown ball, not much larger than a bean. Creator kicked it, and it expanded. Girl-Without-Parents kicked the ball, and it enlarged more. Sun-God and Small-Boy took turns giving it hard kicks, and each time the ball expanded. Creator told Wind to go inside the ball and to blow it up. Tarantula spun a black cord and, attaching it to the ball, crawled away fast to the east, pulling on the cord with all his strength. Tarantula repeated with a blue cord to the south, a yellow cord to the west, and a white cord to the north.

With mighty pulls in each direction, the brown ball stretched to immeasurable size – it became the earth! Creator scratched his chest and rubbed his fingers together and there appeared Hummingbird. "Fly north, south, east, and west and tell us what you see," said Creator. "All is well," reported Hummingbird upon his return. "The earth is most beautiful, with water on the west-side." But the earth kept rolling and dancing up and down. So Creator made four giant posts – black, blue, yellow, and white to support the earth. Wind carried the four posts, placing them beneath the four cardinal points of the earth. The earth sat still. Creator sang, "World is now made and now sits still," which he repeated four times. Then he began a song about the sky. None existed, but he thought there should be one. After singing about it four times, twenty-eight people appeared to help make a sky above the earth. Creator chanted about making chiefs for the earth and sky. He sent Lightning-Maker to encircle the world, and he returned with three uncouth creatures, two girls and a boy found in a turquoise shell. They had no eyes, ears, hair, mouths, noses, or teeth. They had arms and legs, but no fingers or toes. Sun-God sent for Fly to come and build a sweathouse. Girl-Without-Parents covered it with four heavy clouds. In front of the east doorway she placed a soft, red cloud for a foot-blanket to be used after the sweat. The fire inside the sweathouse heated four stones. The three uncouth creatures were placed inside. The others sang songs of healing on the outside, until it was time for the sweat to be finished. Out came the three strangers who stood upon the magic red cloud-blanket. Creator then shook his hands toward them, giving each one fingers, toes, mouths, eyes, ears, noses and hair. Creator named the boy, Sky-Boy – to be chief of the Sky-People. One girl he named Earth-Daughter, to take charge of the earth and its crops. The other girl he named Pollen-Girl, and gave her charge of health care for all Earth-People. Since the earth was flat and barren, Creator thought it fun to create animals, birds, trees, and a hill. He sent Pigeon to see how the world looked. Four days later, he returned and reported, "All is beautiful around the world. But four days from now, the water on the other side of the earth will rise and cause a mighty flood." Creator made a very tall piñon tree. Girl-Without-Parents covered the tree framework with piñon gum, creating a large, tight ball. In four days, the flood occurred. Creator went up on a cloud, taking his twenty-eight helpers with him. Girl-Without-Parents put the others into the large, hollow ball, closing it tight at the top. In twelve days, the water receded, leaving the float-ball high on a hilltop. Girl-Without-Parents led the gods out from the float-ball onto the new earth. She took them upon her cloud, drifting upward until they met Creator with his helpers, who had completed their work making the sky during the flood time on earth. Together the two clouds descended to a valley below. There, Girl-Without-Parents gathered everyone together to listen to Creator.

"I am planning to leave you," he said. "I wish each of you to do your best toward making a perfect, happy world.

"You, Lightning-Rumbler, shall have charge of clouds and water.

"You, Sky-Boy, look after all Sky-People.

"You, Earth-Daughter, take charge of all crops and Earth-People.

"You, Pollen-Girl, care for their health and guide them.

"You, Girl-Without-Parents, I leave you in charge over all."

Creator then turned toward Girl-Without-Parents and together they rubbed their legs with their hands and quickly cast them forcefully downward. Immediately between them arose a great pile of wood, over which Creator waved a hand, creating fire. Great clouds of smoke at once drifted skyward. Into this cloud, Creator disappeared. The other gods followed him in other clouds of smoke, leaving the twenty-eight workers to people the earth. Sun-God went east to live and travel with the Sun. Girl-

Without-Parents departed westward to live on the far horizon. Small-Boy and Pollen-Girl made cloud homes in the south. Big Dipper can still be seen in the northern sky at night, a reliable guide to all.'

Australian Aboriginal: The Dreamtime

'In the beginning the earth was a bare plain. All was dark. There was no life, no death. The sun, the moon, and the stars slept beneath the earth. All the eternal ancestors slept there, too, until at last they woke themselves out of their own eternity and broke through to the surface. When the eternal ancestors arose, in the Dreamtime, they wandered the earth, sometimes in animal form – as kangaroos, or emus, or lizards – sometimes in human shape, sometimes part animal and human, sometimes as part human and plant. Two such beings, self-created out of nothing, were the Ungambikula. Wandering the world, they found half-made human beings. They were made of animals and plants, but were shapeless bundles, lying higgledy-piggledy, near where water holes and salt lakes could be created. The people were all doubled over into balls, vague and unfinished, without limbs or features. With their great stone knives, the Ungambikula carved heads, bodies, legs, and arms out of the bundles. They made the faces, and the hands and feet. At last the human beings were finished. Thus every man and woman was transformed from nature and owes allegiance to the totem of the animal or the plant that made the bundle they were created from – such as the plum tree, the grass seed, the large and small lizards, the parakeet, or the rat. With this work done, the ancestors went back to sleep. Some of them returned to underground homes, others became rocks and trees. The trails the ancestors walked in the Dreamtime are holy trails. Everywhere the ancestors went they left sacred traces of their presence – a rock, a waterhole, a tree. For the Dreamtime does not merely lie in the

distant past, the Dreamtime is the eternal Now. Between heartbeat and heartbeat, the Dreamtime can come again.'

Aztec

'The mother of the Aztec creation story was called Coatlique (the Lady of the Skirt of Snakes). She was created in the image of the unknown, decorated with skulls, snakes, and lacerated hands. There are no cracks in her body and she is a perfect monolith (a totality of intensity and self-containment, yet her features were square and decapitated). Coatlique was first impregnated by an obsidian knife and gave birth to Coyolxanuhqui, goddess of the moon, and to a group of male offspring, who became the stars. Then one day Coatlique found a ball of feathers, which she tucked into her bosom. When she looked for it later, it was gone, at which time she realised that she was again pregnant. Her children, the moon and stars did not believe her story. Ashamed of their mother, they resolved to kill her. A goddess could only give birth once, to the original litter of divinity and no more. During the time that they were plotting her demise, Coatlique gave birth to the fiery god of war, Huitzilopochtli. With the help of a fire serpent, he destroyed his brothers and sister, murdering them in a rage. He beheaded Coyolxanuhqui and threw her body into a deep gorge in a mountain, where it lies dismembered forever. The natural cosmos of the Indians was born of catastrophe. The heavens literally crumbled to pieces. The earth mother fell and was fertilised, while her children were torn apart by fratricide and then scattered and disjointed throughout the universe.'

Chelan

'Long, long ago, the Creator made the world. Then he made the animals and the birds and gave them their names. When he had

finished his work, the Creator called the animal people to him. "I am going to leave you," he said. "But I will come back. When I come again, I will make human beings. They will be in charge of you." The Great Chief returned to his home in the sky, and the animal people scattered to all parts of the world.

After twelve moons, the animal people gathered to meet the Creator as he had directed. Some of them had complaints. Bluejay, Meadowlark, and Coyote did not like their names. Each of them asked to be some other creature. "No," said the Creator. "I have given you your names. There is no change. My word is law. Because you have tried to change my law, I will not make the human being this time. Because you have disobeyed me, you have soiled what I brought with me. I planned to change it into a human being. Instead, I will put it in water to be washed for many moons and many snows, until it is clean again." Then he took something from his right side and put it in the river. It swam, and the Creator named it Beaver. "Now I will give you another law," said the Great Chief Above.

"The one of you who keeps strong and good will take Beaver from the water some day and make it into a human being. I will tell you now what to do. Divide Beaver into twelve parts. Take each part to a different place and breathe into it your own breath. Wake it up. It will be a human being with your breath. Give it half of your power and tell it what to do. Today I am giving my power to one of you. He will have it as long as he is good." When the Creator had finished speaking, all the creatures started for their homes – all except Coyote. The Great Chief had a special word for Coyote.

"You are to be head of all the creatures, Coyote. You are a power just like me now, and I will help you do your work. Soon the creatures and all the other things I have made will become bad. They will fight and will eat each other. It is your duty to keep them

as peaceful as you can. "When you have finished your work, we will meet again, in this land toward the east. If you have been good, if you tell the truth and obey me, you can make the human being from Beaver. If you have done wrong, someone else will make him." Then the Creator went away. It happened as the Creator had foretold. Everywhere the things he had created did wrong. The mountains swallowed the creatures. The winds blew them away. Coyote stopped the mountains, stopped the winds, and rescued the creatures. One winter, after North Wind had killed many people, Coyote made a law for him: "Hereafter you can kill only those who make fun of you." Everywhere Coyote went, he made the world better for the animal people and better for the human beings yet to be created. When he had finished his work, he knew that it was time to meet the Creator again. Coyote thought that he had been good, that he would be the one to make the first human being. But he was mistaken. He thought that he had as much power as the Creator did. So he tried, a second time, to change the laws of the Great Chief Above. "Some other creature will make the human being," the Creator told Coyote. "I shall take you out into the ocean and give you a place to stay for all time." So Coyote walked far out across the water to an island. There the Creator stood waiting for him, beside the house he had made. Inside the house on the west-side stood a black suit of clothes; on the other side hung a white suit. "Coyote, you are to wear this black suit for six months," said the Creator. "Then the weather will be cold and dreary. Take off the black suit and wear the white suit. Then there will be summer, and everything will grow. I will give you my power not to grow old. You will live here forever and forever."

Coyote stayed there, out in the ocean, and the four Wolf brothers took his place as the head of all the animal people. Youngest Wolf Brother was strong and good and clever. Oldest

Wolf Brother was worthless. So the Creator gave Youngest Brother the power to take Beaver from the water. One morning Oldest Wolf Brother said to Youngest Brother, "I want you to kill Beaver. I want his tooth for a knife." "Oh, no!" exclaimed Second and Third Brothers. "Beaver is too strong for Youngest Brother." But Youngest Wolf said to his brothers, "Make four spears. For Oldest Brother, make a spear with four forks. For me, make a spear with one fork. Make a two-forked spear and a three-forked spear for yourselves. I will try my best to get Beaver, so that we can kill him." All the animal persons had seen Beaver and his home. They knew where he lived. They knew what a big creature he was. His family of young beavers lived with him. The animal persons were afraid that Youngest Wolf Brother would fail to capture Beaver and would fail to make the human being. Second and Third Wolf Brothers also were afraid. "I fear we will lose Youngest Brother," they said to each other. But they made the four spears he had asked for. At dusk, the Wolf brothers tore down the dam at the beavers' home, and all the little beavers ran out. About midnight, the larger beavers ran out. They were so many, and they made so much noises, that they sounded like thunder. Then Big Beaver ran out, the one the Creator had put into the water to become clean. "Let's quit!" said Oldest Wolf Brother, for he was afraid. "Let's not try to kill him." "No!" said Youngest Brother. "I will not stop." Oldest Wolf Brother fell down. Third Brother fell down. Second Brother fell down. Lightning flashed. The beavers still sounded like thunder. Youngest Brother took the four-forked spear and tried to strike Big Beaver with it. It broke. He used the three-forked spear. It broke. He used the two-forked spear. It broke. Then he took his own one-forked spear. It did not break. It pierced the skin of Big Beaver and stayed there. Out of the lake, down the creek, and down Big River, Beaver swam, dragging Youngest Brother after it. Youngest Wolf called to his brothers; "You stay here. If I do not return with Beaver in three days, you will know that I am dead." Three days later, all the animal persons gathered on a level place at the foot of the mountain. Soon they saw Youngest Brother coming. He had killed Beaver and was carrying it. "You remember that the Creator told us to cut it into twelve pieces," said Youngest Brother to the animal people. But he could divide it into only eleven pieces. Then he gave directions. "Fox, you are a good runner. Hummingbird and Horsefly, you can fly fast. Take this piece of Beaver flesh over to that place and wake it up. Give it your breath." Youngest Brother gave other pieces to other animal people and told them where to go. They took the liver to Clearwater River, and it became the Nez Perce Indians. They took the heart across the mountains, and it became the Methow Indians. Other parts became the Spokane people, the Lake people, and the Flathead people. Each of the eleven pieces became a different tribe. "There have to be twelve tribes," said Youngest Brother. "Maybe the Creator thinks that we should use the blood for the last one. Take the blood across the Shining Mountains and wake it up over there. It will become the Blackfeet. They will always look for blood." When an animal person woke the piece of Beaver flesh and breathed into it, he told the new human being what to do and what to eat. "Here are roots," and the animal people pointed to camas and kouse and to bitterroot, "You will dig them, cook them, and save them to eat in the winter. "Here are the berries that will ripen in the summer. You will eat them and you will dry them for use in winter." The animal people pointed to chokecherry trees, to serviceberry bushes, and to huckleberry bushes. "There are salmon in all the rivers. You will cook them and eat them when they come up the streams. And you will dry them to eat in the winter." When all the tribes had been created, the animal people said to them "Some of you new people should go up Lake Chelan. Go up to the middle of the lake and look at the cliff beside the water. There you will see pictures on the rock. From the pictures you will learn how to make the things you will need."

The Creator had painted the pictures there, with red paint. From the beginning until long after the white people came, the Indians went to Lake Chelan and looked at the paintings. They saw pictures of bows and arrows and of salmon traps. From the paintings of the Creator they knew how to make the things they needed for getting their food.'

[Note: The paintings (or pictographs) on the lower rocks have been covered by water since a dam was built at the foot of the lake. Surprisingly, high on the rocks at the north end of the lake, the paintings remained for a long, long time. Then, white folks with guns and little respect for the past ruined them – for fun.]

The Oneness of Afrokhan Religion

Following on from the first synopsis above, regarding the Zulu; – the religion as stated, includes belief in a Creator God (Nkulu-Nkulu), who does not interact in day-to-day human affairs. It is however possible, to appeal to the world of Spirit, but only by invoking the spirits of the ancestors through divination processes. Most Black cultures of antiquity seem to resemble this scenario, as enunciated in Ch3 – where we looked at matriarchal cultures. The diviner therefore, who is almost always a woman, plays a very important part in the daily living of Afrokhan culture. It is believed by the Zulu that all bad things, including death, are the result of evil sorcery or offended spirits. No misfortune is ever seen as the result of natural causes. Another important aspect of Zulu religion is cleanliness. Separate utensils and plates were used for different foods, and bathing often occurred up to three times a day. Christian missionaries often had difficulty gaining a foothold among the Zulu, (and indeed most other Afrokhan tribes,) and whenever they did, it was in a syncretic fashion. The Zulu are best known for their beadwork and basketry. There have also been some figural sculptures questionably attributed to them. Their architecture is quite complex, and the dress or fashion of them has been carefully studied by Europeans in recent years. As is evident by the history of the Zulu, the leader, or chief, is invested with power based on his genealogy. He plays an important part in the internal governing of the Zulu homeland and also acts as a voice for his people on an international level. Although the Zulu are officially ruled by the government of South Africa today, they often act as a dissenting voice on the national scene.

Nkulu-Nkulu

The Zulu have many versions of how Nkulu-Nkulu created the Universe and the world. The Deity is regarded as the First Man; the Great One or; the Great Ancestor. This story tells of how in the beginning, when there was nothing but a vast swamp full of multi-coloured reeds, Nkulu-Nkulu created himself from one of them. He then broke off pairs of reeds, each a different colour, and made the first men and women. Then, after some time, he sent a chameleon to deliver a message to tell man that he would live forever. The chameleon by nature is a slow walker, but despite the importance of the message, it dawdled on its way, eating berries and catching flies with its long, sticky tongue. It often stopped to admire the frequent changes in the colour of its beautiful skin. Meanwhile, the Creator sent another messenger, a lizard, to tell man that he would not live forever. The lizard traveled swiftly and delivered its message before the chameleon arrived. When the chameleon finally reached his destination, it was too late. The lizard had returned to Nkulu-Nkulu, having delivered its message and, some of the people were already dying. The fate of the rest could not be changed. Some Zulu people, who remember the trick played on mankind by the lazy chameleon, regard it to this day as an unlucky animal.

Fig6.1: Zulu Land

PTARE – In Conclusion

According to a lecture by Professor **Molefi Kete Asante**, PTARE is an acronym that symbolises the oneness of Afrokhan Religion and Culture.[5] He argues that, just as Christianity can be viewed as one religion with many branches such as Baptists, Methodists, and Catholics, and as Muslims may be Mourrides, Sunni, or Shiities, so can *African* religion be viewed as one. Therefore we can look at the above cultures of the Zulu, the Boshongo, the Efik, the Ekoi, the Fans, and further more the Igbo, Yoruba, Congo, Asante and others as different branches of Afrokhan religion. PTARE means: Popular Traditional *African* Religion Everywhere.

A Poem for Afrokha

(Africa)

A thousand years of darkness in her face,
She turns at last from out the century's blight
Of laboured moan and dull oppression's might,
To slowly mount the rugged path and trace
Her measured step unto her ancient place.
And upward, ever upward towards the light
She strains, seeing afar the day when right
Shall rule the world and justice leaven the race.

Now bare her swarthy arm and firm her sword,
She stands where Universal Freedom bleeds,
And slays in holy wrath to save the word
Of nations and their puny, boasting creeds.
Sear with the truth, O God, each doubting heart,
Of mankind's need and Africa's gloried part.

Joseph Seamon Cotter

~

Notes

1 Sir Godfrey Higgins, *The Anacalypsis,* Introduction
2 Nebu Ka Ma'at, *MMSN VOL.1,* Ch17
3 Dr Malachi, *The True Story of the Beginning,* p1-2
4 Ibid
5 Professor Molefi Kete Asante, *The Future of African Gods: The Class of Civilizations.* Lecture at W.E.B Du Bois Center, July 10th 1998

Chapter 7
The Anacalypsis revisited

Black History?

The **Anacalypsis**, written over one hundred and forty years ago, in my opinion presents a marvellous account of Black History from a Eurocentric (Westernised) perspective. However, the intention of its author **Sir Godfrey Higgins ESQ**, is to present his many years of study and research toward 'An attempt to draw aside the veil of the Saitic Isis,' or, 'An enquiry into the origins of Languages, Nations, and Religions' etc., as opposed to actual Black History. It is just a matter of clear admittance that the origins of the latter are routed in the history of the blacks of Asia and Afrokha. This Higgins expresses throughout the Anacalypsis. The word *history*, implies his-story – or, in this particular case; *his* version of events that predate his-story, which is pre-his-story – the mysteries of the ancient past. Mystery (or, the mysterious past of pre-history) therefore prefixes <u>my-story</u> from an Afrokhan standpoint. So history as is written by Europeans is relative to events during their reign on planet earth, and, pre-history is relative to events that predate their earthly existence. This they call the *mysteries* of the ancient past...

Although this chapter is called 'The Anacalypsis revisited;' my intention is really to give the reader an introduction to the actual book – which is in two parts. The two accounts are vast; they are collectively over 1000 pages long and should therefore be used as an on-going study – like a reference manual if you like – or at least that is how I personally use it. The book is extremely wordy and can come across as boring to read, which is why I treat it as a reference manual (like a theological encyclopaedia) as opposed to a book to be read from cover to cover. Use your own prerogative though... Go with your own spirit...

'Black History,' has become a very common term, and it is far too cliché in connotation to be used by Nubians who are on the Mystical Path of Self. As Nubians, our history, or rather 'Our Story', predates any age of information that can be materially found on the planet about our legacy. We pre-existed the planet as energy – as Sparks of Light – Chi – Sekhem – or, as Pure Ether (Spirit in its Utopia). We are therefore 'Ether Utopians' – or Ethiopians, meaning to ignite and burn; as in the sparks of Sekhem that burns throughout Creation – the continuum of universes, galaxies and stars etc. We are the substantial essence of the original Nuqta that spiralled throughout Pure Space and created the very planet we now reside on – the Earth, Tamare, Ta, Kush, and even Pangaea, the Greek rendition of our landmass of oneness. Whatever the standpoint we assume, true Black History can only be told or narrated by true Afrokhan peoples – Afrokhans who are bred, born and raised with a foundation of Afrocentric concepts of the origin of *things*. It must be stressed that the Afrokhans' mind has the ability to develop concepts that aid in the understanding of the origin of persons, places and things, and so on. The Afrokhan Mind ontologically develops concepts that encompass the collective. Our Ancestors were rooted in the acknowledgement of the One-ness of Spirit – the interconnectedness of 'All that Is.'

However… the Anacalypsis, for anyone, institutes a good place to start regarding the search for the origins of languages, cultures, nations, governments and religions etc. It must be noted in the interim that the book does not provide the total truth. Well, books never really do anyway. Books only provide pointers toward the total truth – the Reality of what has been; what 'Is;' and what will always be. And that, in this case is – the Black Nation is the founder of all Civilisations, and of Politics, Penal systems, and governmental rule, and of Education, Medicine and Agriculture etc. These truths are found in the ancient

Babylonian cultures as the **'Code of Hammurabi.'** More on
Hammurabi in a bit…

<u>Sir Godfrey Higgins on the Ancient Blacks</u>

Higgins was convinced that a high civilization had flourished prior
to all historical records. He believed that there had existed a most
ancient and Universal religion from which all the later creeds and
doctrines sprang. He attempted to establish the existence of a prehistoric
Universal religion and to trace its development into contemporary times.
He believed this religion possessed accurate knowledge of Universal
and cosmic phenomena and held neither priesthood nor institution as
intermediary in man's communion with the Divine. First published in
1863, this unique work shows that the Celtic Druids were Priests of
Oriental colonies that emigrated from India, and were the Introducers of
the first Cadmean System of Letters, and the Builders of Stonehenge, of
Karnak, and other Cyclopean works in Asia and Europe. This title
contains 4 maps and numerous lithographic plates of Druidical
Monuments. Higgins was engaged in researches for this book nearly ten
hours a day for twenty years. Of his portentous knowledge, his powerful
critical faculty, his fitness to investigate and elucidate the ancient
mysteries of mythology, philology, ethnology,[A] and other ologies, many
persons speak with reverence and rapture. But even men of education
must admit that Higgins collected a large number of curious and
important facts from the archives of ancient Black peoples, of Ethiopia,
Egipt and Indus valley.

Resigning his commission (in the army) round about 1813, he
devoted himself entirely to an unbiased investigation into the history of
religious beliefs. He acquired knowledge of the Aramaic Hebrew
languages, and sometimes pursued his studies in foreign libraries. At the

---

[A] Philology is a comparative study of languages, and, ethnology is a comparative study of
peoples.

date of his death he had apparently projected a journey to Egipt, in search of further clues to religious problems... He had intended to exhibit in a future book – *'the Christianity of Jesus Christ from his own mouth.'* Higgins also claimed to be a Christian; and regarded Jesus as a Nazarite, of the monastic order of Pythagorean Essenes, and, as probably a Samaritan by birth, and leading the life of a hermit. My own research led me to find that the Essenes Brotherhood is an offshoot of the Tat Brotherhood, of which Akhenaton and Tutankhamun were affiliated.[A] The Tat Brotherhood itself is an offshoot of the earlier Arcane and Nacaal mystery schools of Atlantis and Lemuria respectively. All these mystery schools are rooted with the 'Ha Kha' teachings of Tehuti (Thoth). In the words of Higgins:

> *'There is great difficulty in settling the proper places, according to their seniority, of the three sons of Noah, as all divines have allowed. I think it probable that Japhet was the youngest, and Ham the eldest and that the story of uncovering his father was only contrived to justify the claims of Shem to the high priesthood and archierachical sway over the others. The whole history looks as if there had really been such persons as those named, – that the account of them was substantially true, but that it had been accommodated to the system and circumstances of the Jewish priests and government, claiming supremacy from their ancestor, flattering themselves that, however obscure they might then be, a great saviour would come, to place them in the command of the restored Pandaean kingdom. This has, to a very considerable degree, succeeded in placing the Pope at the head of Christianity of modern Judaism, as a reality, though it is lost to the children of Shem.*

[A] In this stance Tutankhamun is regarded as the Jesus of that day and time – just as Horus, being after the order of Tehuti, is regarded as the Jesus of his day also.

Then I should suppose that there have been various races of red and white... that the originals of all the Gods have been of the black race, of the class of followers of Cristna, after a black race had become improved into the shape in which we find him... that the pontifical government did originally consist of this race; and that, in the east, the entire population consisting of this race, it continues back – still retains the rete-mucosum – though for the reasons before given by me, it is improved in shape; but that, in the west, to which it sent out numerous tribes, it mixed with the white races.

If we suppose man to have arrived at a highpoint of mental culture five or six hundred years before the entrance of the sun into Aries, the calculation will shew, that this will give him time to have had a knowledge, from astronomy, of the approach of the comet in twenty-nine centuries. In consequence of prejudice (for it really prejudice) against the negro, or I ought to rather say, against the possibility of a negro, being learned and scientific, arising from an acquaintance with the present negro character, I admit with great difficulty the theory of all the early astronomical knowledge of the Chaldees having been acquired or invented by his race, and that the Chaldees were originally Negroes. [1]

Higgins

Kushites – *(The Ancient Ones)*

According to biblical history, there is only one Kushite tribe of people (called Ethiopians biblically), but according to Higgins there are at least two. The first is the Kushites of Ethiopia and the second, the Kushites of Asia. The term 'Kush' simply means *black,* and therefore Kushites must mean those of the Black lands or simply: Black peoples. The Greek philosopher and historian Herodotus also bear witness to these two groups of blacks as those of 'Ethiopios Kush' and those of 'Indus Kush.' He spoke of the similarities between the two; he said they have a common Ancestor – the Dravidians. These Dravidian blacks are descendants of the people of Atlantis, and according to Dr Malachi, are crossbred with Extraterrestrials from Sirius and Orion – the Neteru and the Anunnaqi. These ETs are the Nubian Black Gods of our scriptures, commonly called angels or messengers of God.

The Ethiopian Kushites and indeed Ethiopia itself were once a part of Egipt. Or better said, North Afrokha was not divided within itself; the people were one with each other, though languages and customs may have varied. The division between so called Egipt; Ethiopia, Nubia, Sudan etc., happened as a result of silent wars during the invasions of North Afrokha by the Persians [525BCE], Greeks [330BCE] and Romans [30BCE].[A]

Written artefacts or relics of the Ancient Ones are indeed difficult to obtain. Ancient Afrokhans, in their cultural development, did not particularly wish to be acknowledged for their works (individually speaking) or for any identifiable developments. They lived a way of life within a context that encompassed the collective; they lived for the Ancestors and for those to come – the continuum of Spirit. Written information only became a necessity for our Ptahite Ether-utopian Kushite Ancestors when they began to forget who they were – as Etherians having a physical experience.

Herodotus on the Ancient Blacks

Impressed by his openness to speak of, and admit that the ancient Kushites and Kuthites were of a high *civilisation* and culture, many modern day astute Black scholars and historians are glad to quote the writings of Herodotus. George G.M. James spared no notes on his haste and excitement to speak and write, on the writings of Herodotus, for he

---

[A] These invasion dates of Egipt are taken from the book *'Stolen Legacy'* by George G.M. James, 1952.

is one of the most honest and fair-minded White historians of Black antiquity. He did not mind talking about blacks as being master shipbuilders, and masters of the seas and sea trading. He wrote that the fastest ships were Phoenician. There are many references of the Egiptians and Ethiopians being black-skinned with broad noses, thick lips and as being woolly-haired. He even speaks of the elder Neolithic Egiptian tribes as being 4-5 feet tall – (such are the Neolithic Kushite-Pygmy tribes). He also said that the Ethiopians are very tall and are the best looking of Black peoples – (such are the Neolithic Kuthite-Watusi tribes). Herodotus, in his writings of the Trojan War describes the Ethiopians as thus:

The famed Greek philosophers	
Pythagoras	(569BCE - 475BCE)
Pindar	(518BCE - 442BCE)
Herodotus	(480BCE - 425BCE)
Socrates	(469BCE - 399BCE)
Plato	(429BCE - 347BCE)
Aristotle	(384BCE - 323BCE)
Alexander	(356BCE - 321BCE)

Table 9: Greek philosophers

'The Eastern Ethiopians – for there were two sorts of Ethiopians in the army – served with the Indians. These were just like the Southern Ethiopians, except for their language and their hair: their hair is straight, while that of the Ethiopians of Libya is the crispiest and curliest in the world.'

Herodotus

The Anacalypsis confers with the above reports on the blacks of Asia in this way:

'It was the opinion of Sir William Jones that a great nation of Blacks formerly possessed the dominion of Asia, and held the seat of empire at Sidon. These must have been the people called by Mr Maurice, Cushites or Cuthites, described in Genesis; and the opinion that they were Blacks is corroborated by the translators of the Pentateuch, called the Seventy, constantly rendering the word Cush by Ethiopia. It is very certain that, if this opinion were well

founded, we must go for the time when this empire flourished to a period anterior to all our regular histories.[2]

Higgins

Fig7.1:
Possible route of Greek expeditionary force to Troy

The objective of the *'Histories'* – one of the many writings of Herodotus, is to discover the origin and basis of the feelings of hostility between the Greeks and Persians. It was all based around commercial trade and trading routes originally. (Whilst some believe it was based around abductions of Phoenician and Greek women).[A] The Persians

---

[A] <u>The Trojan War:</u> One of the Phoenician sailors apparently kidnapped the Kings daughter, Io (and others), of Argos, Greece, and took her (them) to *Egypt*. Some Greeks later entered into Tyre, of Phoenicia, and abducted Europa (and others). This consequently evened the score, but, the Greeks later on, also kidnapped Medea from Colchis. Then some 50years later Paris of Troy abducted Helen, wife of Menelaus, of Argos, and took her to Troy (so the story goes). The Greeks gathered an army and set out to Troy to get her back – they fought for 10years but she was never found, nor did she come forward to halt the war.

initially blamed the Phoenicians for starting the whole thing. They say the Phoenicians were responsible, by their apparent kidnapping of Greek women, which led to the Trojan War. They also had feelings of hate against the Greeks when the Greek army later defeated Troy, since Troy was considered a Persian ally.

The Code of Hammurabi

Fig7.2:
the Hammurabi code

The Five P's known as the five principles of the Caucasian/ Aryan/ European system are namely: *Polytheism, Politics, Penal, Philosophy and Psychology.*[3] These principles are taken from the time of King Hammurabi, the 6th ruler of the Babylonian or Amorite dynasty of Southern Mesopotamia (Old Babylon), and thus are known as the Code of Hammurabi. When Hammurabi took control of Babylon in 1792BCE, Mesopotamia was made up of separate, warring city-states. Hammurabi's goal was to conquer all of Mesopotamia and unite the city-states into one country.

- POLYTHEISM: The belief in and worship of many Deities. This Country (England) specialises in the promotion of freedom of worship; be it Man, Object, or the Creator.
- POLITICS: The science of winning and holding control of the government. The Caucasian race has made very good use of this principle, to the point of giving Nubians the illusion that they have a part in the system.

- PENAL SYSTEM: Relating to the laws and punishments of Nimrod, laid by Hammurabi.
- PHILOSOPHY: An explanation, and or theory of the origin of the Universe, based entirely on conversation, not facts.
- PSYCHOLOGY: The study of the Mind and behaviour of Afrokhan peoples through mis-education. They have been able to program us with courses that had no background, benefits nor meaning in reality, such as their teaching of biology, sociology etc.[A]

So the Code of Hammurabi was a body of laws used to govern his Kingdom, and it is the exact same code, though modified, used today by the new Babylon – the United States of America. This code according to Dr Malachi is consisted of 282 provisions systematically arranged under headings such as: Family, Labour, Personal Property, Real Estate, Trade, and Business.[4] Hammurabi ruled between 1792BCE and 1750BCE, and was the first known administrator of that time period. He was responsible for a high central government and promotion of the welfare of the people of his kingdom. Every citizen was to obey his laws, just the same as in the new Babylon, the USA today; or should I say *'baby-Lon,'* as in baby-London, for the USA is indeed a child of the monarchy of the UK.

The religion of Islam also has a five P system, which they call the five pillars of Islam. Do me a favour and check it out! Nubians today the world over really believe that they have become something special when they are promoted to become Policemen, Politicians, Preachers, Parole officers, Professors, Producers, Philosophers, Paramedics, Pharmacists, Physicians etc., all of which are ultimately governed by the establishments. Those who lived in the image of the evil one introduced the letter P to the Old English language. There is no equivalent to the

---

[A] These 5 definitions are paraphrased from the teachings of Dr Malachi.

letter P in the ancient Cuneiform texts of Old Babylon. The letter P inverted is the number 6 (or 666), that is the number of the beast and the number of a man, as found in Revelations of the New Testament. The Code of Hammurabi over time has evolved into other subsidiary systems of cultural manipulation and control. The 3 definitions below are paraphrased from the Introduction of the book, *'Return To The African Mother Principle of Male and Female Equality - Vol. 1,'* by Oba T'shaka.[5]

(1) COLONIALISM: A system of economic, political, cultural, social and military oppression, where one nation seeks control of another nation's people, land, political system, economy, and military systems, and attempts to distort or destroy the colonised people's culture.

(2) NEOCOLONIALISM: A system of indirect colonialism, where multinational organisations such as the 'World Bank' or the 'international monetary fund' or the 'world health organisation', dictate the value of goods that are sold on the world market. These international bodies impose their will on these countries (such as those of Afrokha, the Caribbean or Latin America), through providing aid, on condition that Western political systems are established in the neo-colony.

(3) INTERNAL COLONIALISM: A system where Afrokhan (in this case African) peoples; and other peoples of colour are racially, culturally, economically and politically oppressed under a system where whites oppress blacks and other people of colour.

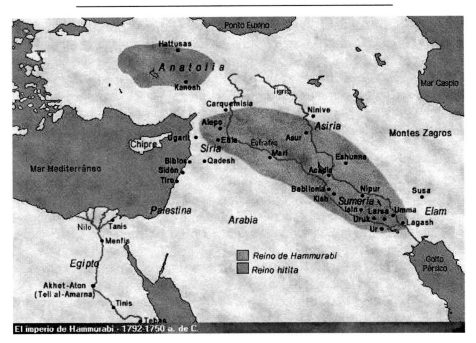

Fig7.3: the Empire of Hammurabi

Nimrod, also known as Sargon, son of Cush and Semiramis, originally created the Code of Hammurabi. Nimrod was a descendant of the Gibborim – those mighty ones who were crossbred from the Anunnaqi (those who from heaven to earth came) *'Kyshites'* and the ancient Ptahites (those of the earth) *'Kushites.'* He was known as a master builder and hunter. His influences created the first 'Freemasonic' societies of the ancient Babylonian world. Gen 2v4 tells us of the generations of the heavens and the earth as a reasonable confirmation of this fact. Also, Gen 6v2-4 tells us about the coming of the sons of god (the Elohim Anunnaqi); going in unto the daughters of man; and Gen 10v8-10 tells us of Nimrod – the mighty hunter before the Lord. Just as

Nimrod's governing body, a Freemasonic lodge headed by King Hammurabi were the dictators of that time, so are today's dictators of secret Freemasonic societies. David Icke spears no hostages in uncovering these truths throughout his series of books such as *'The truth shall set you free.'*

Fig7.4:
Kingdom of Nimrod

The Kushite Origin of Languages

Dr Malachi – as 'Neter Aferti Atum Re,' of the Ancient Egiptian Order, had produced at least two books on the root of earth's North Afrokhan and Middle Eastern languages. The first is called *'First language'* (Scroll #27), and the second, *'God's language'* (Scroll #96). The two titles together display the roots of today's Indo-European languages, and the nations of them.

'When you talk about language, you are talking about overstanding the components of everything, for without language, how would you communicate. Look at this very piece of paper with black ink. Without the black words this paper would be blank; without the so-called black people, the history of the world would

be blank. Black is the source of all information. It's the linguistics or science of language, like overstanding the language of computers. But first, you have to acknowledge the writings on the walls of the Ancient Ones, your family of ancient Khemet (Egipt), ancient Babylon, ancient Accad, and ancient Sumer.' [6]

Dr Malachi

C. Herbert Oliver on the Cadmean system

Speaking of the 'Cadmean System of Letters,' earlier; between 1998 and 1999 I had the privilege of meeting and spending time with Lorna Oliver, and her husband C. Herbert Oliver, who authored the book *'Cadmus and Europa,'* 1994. I spent about 7days on two separate occasions with them at their Brooklyn-New York home. The couple, to me was very dynamic in their approach to life and in what they shared and believed in. They were firm in what they stood for. Herbert, a minister of the Christian faith, spent ten years studying the origins of languages and the racial cultures of them. His book *'Cadmus and Europa,'* presents the facts that the origin of written language and artifacts are of the Black Nation, in particular the Black Phoenicians, the descendants of Noah. Our deep conversations were very inspiring, intriguing and in some cases confronting. We shared many ideals and opinions. My trips to New York were for other reasons at the time; a holiday the first time and business the second; but what I had gained in terms of knowledge and shifts in paradigm was far bigger than my intended reasons for the trips.

This great work, *'Cadmus and Europa,'* gives the reader a viewpoint of literary relics, with the eye of an Afro-American archaeologist. Herbert's thesis is that the basic sciences and tools of learning, the invention of which is often credited to the ancient Greeks, actually originated in Black culture. Such origins, he says however, have been largely and intentionally obscured. To prove his case; Herbert calls upon witnesses from the past for first hand knowledge, I.e., Homer,

Herodotus, Hesiod and Ovid. Their testimony is provided in the context of his authoring dialogue with Cadmus, whose sister Europa abducted by Zeus, (probably just before the Trojan War), brought him from Phoenicia to Greece.[7] The book calls upon the reader to examine evidence that the contributions of ancient Black peoples to Greece and indeed to the world have been denied.

The works and research of Herodotus consisted of three continents, – Asia, Europe and Libya. He was puzzled of the fact that the three areas are named after Black women, and that the lands were actually one landmass. Since history doesn't seem to provide any other evidence of the origins of the names of these continents, we may as well go with what is relatively true for now:

- Asia was named after Asia, wife of Prometheus.
- Europe was named after Europa, sister of Cadmus.
- Libya was named after Libya, daughter of Epaphus.

The Dangers of *Slang*

Dr Malachi in one of his writings, *'Truth bulletin #18,'* addresses the issue of slang. He says:

'Slang destroys a certain portion of the brain making you retarded (slowness of mental development in children). Although slang originated from criminals and tramps, it has now spread to the average person as a common language of everyday life to express hostile emotions.' You may not realise it, Slang affects the way you speak, act, dress and the way you think causing mental deficiency.'[8]

I'm recommending the reader to take a personal look at this three page article as it is very important with regards to today's youth.

The Kushite Origin of Nations

The Ancient Ptahite Ethiopian Kushite, historically routed in all Indo Aryan civilizations, establishers of Afrokhan nations of antiquity, are secretly adorned by the Greek and Roman writers of them, although they try hard to hide their true identity – as in the truth of the Europa-Europe connection. The biblical Noah and his triplet sons, Shem, Ham and Japheth, symbolize the 3 main peoples of earth and their common Ancestor – Noah:

Table 10: evolutionary root-races

Bible	Evolution	Race
Noah	Lares	Nuwbuns (Ptahites, Kushites)
Shem	Gibbon	Negroid (Indus. Asiatics)
Ham	Chimpanzee	Caucasoid (Aryan, Europeans)
Japheth	Orang-utan	Mongoloid (Japanese, Chinese)

The above is symbolic by the way, and is not to be taken literally; it is just a means for thesis comparison – a juxtaposition of biblical history, with anthropological evolution theories and race identification through their physical appearances as well as their genetics. For instance, the Ancient Nuwbuns (Ptahites) are descendants of the Anunnaqi-Kyshites, the Pygmy extraterrestrials that came to earth from the Illiyuwn Tri-Star system millions of years ago; they are not descendants of Anthropoidian monkeys. According to Dr Malachi, these Kyshites or, little Nuwbuns came to earth from the planet *Rizq* of the Illiyuwn system, the 4-D domain of Sirius. See fig5.2, the Canis Major constellation. And, the Indus Asiatics according to their own writings came from a planet called Nirvana in the Procyon solar system of the Canis Minor constellation (see fig5.1). The Caucasoid, according to anthropological scientists, descended from these said Hindus, and is sometimes called the 'lost Aryan Race' of Atlantis through to the Indus Valley. And finally the Mongoloid, again according to Dr Malachi, are descendants of the Indus Asiatics and genetic splicing with extraterrestrial entities called 'Teros' from Sirius. As an extension from the above concepts we find that Noah, a Nubian Ptahite, by way of his sons, also fathered many nations such as:

- **Children of Shem:**   [Gen 10v22]
  - Elam   -
  - Asshur   - Arabia
  - Arphaxad   -
  - Lud   -
  - Aram   - Palestine

- **Children of Ham:**   [Gen 10v6]
  - Cush   - Ethiopia (Kushites)
  - Mitzrayim   - Egipt (Khemetians)
  - Phut   - Libya (Libyans)
  - Canaan   - Gaza (Canaanites)

- **Children of Japheth :**   [Gen 10v2]
  - Gomer   -
  - Magog   -
  - Madai   -
  - Javan   - Greece (Greeks)
  - Tubal   -
  - Meshech   -
  - Tiras   -

Unfortunately my research only enabled me to find so much (2006).

Canaan, (originally called Libana, meaning 'white as milk'), later fathered 11 nations, which accounts for some of the origins of Europe's whites. Let us take a look at a piece of evidence that proves how Europeans erroneously try to hide the truth; that Afrokhans are at the foundation of all European as well as some Eastern, civilisation.

> 'On the south of the Northwest Quadrant lay the teeming black world of Africa, as it does today. It was separated by the Great White Race by the broad stretch of the Sahara desert. The valley of the Nile was the only road leading across the Sahara from south to north. Sometimes the blacks of inner Africa did wander along this road into Egypt, but they came only in small groups. Thus cut off by the desert barrier and living by themselves, they remained uninfluenced by civilisation from the north. The Negro peoples of Africa were therefore without any influence on the development of early civilisation.'[9]
>
> James Henry Breasted

Even down to the grammar used is monstrous in his efforts to undermine the Afrokhan's validity and qualification – the lowercase letters of 'teeming black world' and the uppercase letters of 'the Great White Race.' Breasted has deliberately pursued to obscure the original Kushite inhabitants of North Afrokha and the Kuthites of Asia, with the veiled presence of the so-called 'Great White Race.' In another context, one could say that the Neolithic Nilotic Afrokhans of Ancient Khemet migrated beyond the borders of the Sahara desert.[5] Why? They would avoid having to 'tie into the vine' of the invading White Canaanites (the Hittites, Amorites and Sidonites etc.) and Mulatto Semites etc. There are a number of other Indo-European countries that share their names' sake, with renowned blacks of ancient times, such as Persia, named after

---

[5] I think it is better said that the original Khemetians of Northern Afrokha were pushed out over time, by the invaders, the Hika Kasut and the Tamahu.

Perses, son of the Egiptian *Perseus*, who was son of the Egiptian Black woman *Danae*.

Scholastic Metamorphosis

It is of no doubt that Greek, Roman and European so-called scholars and philosophers have performed a great transformation on Black history and antiquity. This is how Oliver puts it, as he comments on Ovid and his writings regarding Cadmus.

> *'Ovid knew that history has a strange capacity to suffer metamorphoses. Even current history can be very slowly and imperceptibly changed to the point that two thousand years from now Martin Luther King could be perceived as a white man who fought for the under-privileged in blue-eyed, blonde America.'*[10]
>
> Herbert C. Oliver

Biblical chronology has to be the most illusive account of history, written anywhere on the planet. The Bible is but an extrapolation and, an interpolation of information from various cultures, of different time periods, and of different circumstances etc. The reader of the Bible is therefore tricked into believing the illusion that they are reading a true chronological system of events, from the book of Genesis through to the book of Revelations. The Romanticised biblical scholars of the Nicean Council,[A] of 325AD, have made a complete mess of our legacy.

Are the Canaanites Black or White?

Both are correct when looked at within the appropriate context. The original Canaanites are no doubt Black people, Ptahite Kushites, descendants of Ham, properly pronounced Kham. Or at least, the nations of Canaanites that are commonly known today, though are indeed whites, were all originally founded by Black peoples. It is like asking, "Are the Egiptians Black or White?" the original Egiptians,

---

[A] Headed by Emperor Constantine

correctly called Khemites (as in Ham-ites; or Kham-ites), were Black peoples; and todays inhabitants of that area are either White or Mulatto. The same principle applies for the Jews of Israel today, who call themselves *Jewish*, as in – a kind of Jew but not the real Jew. Even Israel is now called the state of Israel, as in the 52nd state of America; oh yes, in fact England is known as the 51st state of the United States of America.

The Kushite Origin of Religions

The origin of the Black man as far as written history can say is unknown. So therefore the origin of the Black man's religion is also unknown. Remember... religion is not what we practice; it is what we are essentially. Our religion has to be our culture; our language; our eating habits etc., simply our way of life, and fundamentally our religion is the expression of our Spirit and Soul through form.

> '*The religion of Buddha, of India, is well known to have been very ancient. In the most ancient temples scattered throughout Asia, where is worship is yet continued, he is found black as jet, with a flat face, thick lips, and curly hair of the Negro.*'[11]
>
> Higgins

And, Higgins on the same page goes on to report:

> '*To what time period are we to allot this Negro? He will be proved to have been prior to the god called Cristna. He must have been prior to or contemporaneous with the black empire, supposed by Sir William Jones to have flourished at Sidon. The religion of this Negro God is found, by the ruins of his temples and other circumstances, to have been spread over an immense extent of country, even to the remotest parts of Britain, and to have been professed by devotees inconceivably numerous.*'

Note from the above quote that Sidon was one of the albino sons of Libana, Canaan, found in Gen 10v15 as his first son. But above, Higgins speaks of the Black empire of Sidon. This must be prior to the people who we know biblically as the Sidonians, found in Deut 3v9.

Religion

Religion,[A] meaning *'to tie back,'* has lost its purpose in the institutions of our modern cultures. To 'tie back' simply means to reconnect, as in, to 'restore our Soul connection' to the Creator, NTR. Beloved Afrokhan people, we are lost, lost in the wilderness of a system of rulership that is not conducive to our spiritual evolution, our soul rapturing, or to our well-being. These radioactive forces must be inhibited if we are to reconnect or 'tie back' to our own Magnetic forces. As stated, religion is what we are, and what we are is analogous to that Apple Mac computer system that has been imposed upon with Windows applications [see Introduction & Ch1]. Our 9-ether physical makeup has become dysfunctional and has been superimposed with 6-ether codes of conduct. The ramification is that we may possibly miss the ultimate rapture; as a result of calling on the wrong gods, breathing incorrectly, eating inappropriately and too often, and we have also forgotten how to properly pray and meditate etc. We have misused 'rites of passage,' libation, and we have overstepped the necessity of acknowledging the Ancestors – those who are renowned and are of high distinction...

The Anacalypsis does acknowledge that religion as we know it today has its roots in ancient Afro-Egipt as well as in Hinduism. Note however, that aspects of Hinduism that we take for granted are also

---

[A] Religion, according to the Oxford paperback Dictionary, 1997 means: (1) belief in superhuman controlling power, esp. in personal God or gods entitled to obedience. (2) Study of religious belief. (3) Particular system of faith and worship. The thesaurus of the same states: (1) belief, faith, theism. (2) Divinity, theology. (3) Creed, cult, denomination, faith, persuasion, sect.

routed in the Egiptian religion or culture, so to speak. Buddha, a Dravidian and Ethiopian by descent, is just one of many people who travelled over to Indus Kush and brought the Afrokhan religion along with them. These highly influential blacks were able, whether deliberately or unintentionally, to interpolate their culture with the Hindus and their own cultures. It was some 2,160years before Buddha (the curly-haired Dravidian God) was succeeded by Krishna, (the straight long-haired Hindu God). This was a time of transition from, a then Ariesian age (Aries), to a Taurusian age (Taurus).

Bearing in mind that these Dravidian blacks are descendants of the agreeable Atlantaens and Lemurians, we clearly see that our most ancient religion was of the 'Law of One.' The religion of the 'Law of One' must be re-established within the Afrokhan communities of the world today. As a Nation of Gods and Goddesses, Neters and Neterts, we have to become the emblem of what true religion is about.

Kushite Gods

Contemporary history books tend to generalise the identity of the so-called mythological gods in some anthropomorphic manner. If they are to represent them in human form, they would most certainly not be depicted as Black. Higgins disagrees; he says:

> *'The Alma Matter, the Goddess Multimammia, the founders of the oracles, the Memmons or first idols, were always black. Venus, Juno, Jupiter, Apollo, Bacchus, Hercules, Asteroth, Adonis, Horus, Apis, Osiris, Ammon, – in short all the wood and stone Deities were black. The images remained as they were first made in very remote times. They were not susceptible of any improvement; and when for any reason they required renewal they were generally made exactly after the former sacred pattern.'*
>
> Higgins – *Anacalypsis* – p286

The Zionists and Khazars

As can be appreciated from above, all cultures of antiquity worshipped Black Gods, whether of celestial or terrestrial origin or habitat. One place in particular, where men would supposedly meet with these Gods, was Mount Zion. The word Zion, in different dialects, also spelled Sion and Siam, is translated in different ways such as:

- The Mount of the Gods, or happy beings;
- The Mount where the Gods reside;
- The triumphing heaven;
- The place of salvation
- The Seat of Speculation

Supposedly then, a Zionist is to be one who worships the Gods of Zion. And, Mount Ararat, of which the Jewish rabbis placed in Ceylon, was also known to be a mystical Zion.[12] Similarly, a Khazar, also supposedly, is one who worships the Gods of Zion. – It is taught by the Arabian historians that Japheth, (a descendant of the original Zionists,) had a son called Khazar,[13] of which sprang the Khozarians of the Caspian Sea. The Roman name Caesar is no doubt a derivative of the word Khazar, says Higgins.

Bill Cooper, in his book *'Behold a Pale Horse,'* talks of the twenty four Protocols of Zion. In this context, he relates it to twenty four codes of conduct, of which the hierarchy of the world-society uses for control and dominance. I suggest that you check this pout for yourself; it is too long a document to be inserted here.

The next chapter takes on a completely different paradigm from the foregoing. It deals with the phenomenon of the Photon belt and Nibiru – from within the context of healing.

~

Notes

[1] Higgins, *The Anacalypsis,* back cover
[2] Ibid, p52
[3] Dr Malachi, *The Nebuchadnezzar Era, (Truth Bulletin #18),* p3-4 (Published by the Holy Tabernacle Ministries)
[4] Ibid, p4-10
[5] Oba T'shaka, *Return To The African Mother Principle of Male and Female Equality,* pX11-X111 (Pan African Publishers and Distributors, California, 1995, ISBN: 1-878557-06-8)
[6] Dr Malachi, *First language,* p1 (Published by the Holy Tabernacle Ministries)
[7] Herbert C. Oliver, *Cadmus and Europa,* p18 (Vantage Press, New York, 1994, ISBN: 0-433-10989-2)
[8] Dr Malachi, *The Nebuchadnezzar Era,* p20-23
[9] James Henry Breasted, *Ancient Times; A History of the Early World,* p133 (Ginn – 1944)
[10] Herbert C. Oliver, *Cadmus and Europa,* p4
[11] Higgins, *The Anacalypsis,* p52
[12] Ibid, p409
[13] Ibid, p613

Chapter 8
The Photon Belt and Nibiru

Crystal Healing – *An Introduction*

Beloved Nubians, as we enter the Monasic ring of Christ-Consciousness energy; the human god-body must be upgraded in order to accommodate the healing forces therein. The transformation of our be*ing*; the transmutation to higher frequency vibration, is of a crystallising nature. Much of our current atomic make up will be transformed into energy, and these energies will thus become crystallised into higher frequency forms – heading toward higher experience – fourth and fifth dimensional. Therefore crystal healing, or the healing of the body assisted with crystals, in practice creates a foundation for the reality to come. Also, the using of crystals to balance or neutralise some of the radioactive, or, free radical producing electrical systems within our household environment, is incumbent. This is especially so for the melanated Afrokhan. It is evident in modern science that the blood, *"the river of life"* [Phill Valentine], is liquidated crystals – or, is blood crystals in liquid form. The blood, containing DNA and RNA acts as a liquidated crystal receiver for higher frequency light-coded information. But, for many of us this peripheral has been distorted and must be repaired if we are to receive information from our Etheric Parents. Conscience, which is <u>above</u>, is in constant communication with that which is <u>below</u>, the human god-body. But, our radioactive 6-ether adversary has promoted our receptors to become dysfunctional as a result of their imposed way of life, since *they* do not have the ability to become crystallised in order to entertain 9-ether light-codes. For us, crystal healing is vital.

As you may have already noticed from the above, there is a distinct difference between *crystal healing* and *healing with crystals*. One may use crystals to compliment or amplify their own healing skills – such as a Reiki practitioner. And, Crystal healing, – which is having our body enwarped within a crystal energy matrix at the right place and at the right time, profoundly creates a harmonious and healthy system of organs. (See Ch9 – Redefining the Merkaba).

> *'When we hold a crystal, we are instantly in touch with the forces that shape our planet and the elements that first formed aeons ago in the heart of distant stars. Current scientific knowledge of the chemical structure and properties of crystals is comparatively recent. Scientific investigations into the properties of crystals have led to our present-day technological dependencies on a variety of both natural occurring and synthesised crystals. Our modern world would not be possible without such crystals. From computers to car engines, lasers to space shuttles – all have vital components that use these unusual bits of stone. The present-day interest in crystal healing is a continuation of mankind's constant fascination with gemstones and minerals through the ages.'* [1]
>
> Simon Lilly

Reiki healing

Practitioners of Reiki utilise crystals for balancing the pranic flow of energy between and within the chakras – much like the purpose of the 7th to 14th Breaths of the Spherical Breathing exercise [see volume 1, Ch9 Part2]. For instance: Zeolite kits, which are assorted pieces of crystals, provide the framework *silicates* (silicon and oxygen based metallic compounds) with interchangeable *cations* (positively charged ions). These kits are excellent for working with Reiki energy. They help release body toxins and dispel bloating. They also help destructive behaviours to fall away as well as create healthy boundaries. Reiki crystals are also essential for people who have environmental sensitivities, and, crystals in general are also ideal tools used when performing affirmations, rituals, integration and transmutation work etc. The seven major talked about chakras are wheels of bio-energetic activity radiating from nerve ganglia (clusters) that start at the base of the spine and continue on to the crown of the head. In retrospect, the vortex of the chakras serves as the etheric sockets of which the actual nerve clusters are plugged.[2] These nerve clusters are the junctions of the major endocrine glands. Relative crystals or stones can be used to compliment working with chakra energy for healing, where each stone simply represent a chakra point, for example see table 11 below.

Table 11: chakra related crystals

Wheel:	Associated with:	Location:	Represented with:
Chakra1:	Earth (Survival)	Base of spine	Garnet
Chakra2:	Water (Emotions and Sex)	Lower abdomen	Carnelian
Chakra3:	Fire (Power and Will)	Solar plexus	Citrine
Chakra4:	Air (Love and Balance)	Heart	Peridot
Chakra5:	Sound (Creativity)	Throat	Blue Topaz
Chakra6:	Light (Intuition)	Brow	Lolite
Chakra7:	Thought (Imagination)	Top of Head	Amethyst

Precious Stones

Precious and semi-precious stones have many qualities beyond their physical attraction, and most have remarkable monetary value. And, in the opinion of most of mankind, from the earliest of recorded times to the present, these gemstones have abilities and characteristics that can only be termed magical. Here, I have presented a small table displaying fourteen very common gemstones, with basic descriptions; and some properties thereof. The topic of gemstones is far too vast to be extended within this work. So, what I am presenting is the means of an introduction only. The table does not include Gold and Platinum since these are considered as precious metals as opposed to precious stones. Note also that crystals are classified as minerals.

Table 12: various types of precious and semi-precious stones

Agate	- Is a type of Quartz
	- It is believed to cure insomnia; and can be used as an antigravity device;
Amber	- Is a yellow translucent fossil resin
Amethyst	- Is a purple/velvet semi-precious stone – type of Crystal
	- It is believed to prevent drunkenness; and can cool sexual passion;
Beryl	- Is a transparent (green) precious stone
	- Helps one in heated situations to become amiable and intelligible
Chalcedony	- Is a type of Quartz
Diamond	- Is a very hard transparent precious stone
Emerald	- Is a bright green Gem
Jasper	- Is a red, yellow or brown opaque Quartz
Ruby	- Is a Crimson or rose-coloured precious stone
	- Believed to help protect fruit trees from tempests
Onyx	- Is a semi-precious variety of Agate with coloured layers
Pearl	- Is a white solid gem formed in shell of certain oysters
Sapphire	- Is a transparent blue precious stone
Sardonyx	- Is a type of Onyx in which white layers alternate with yellow or orange ones
Topaz	- Is a (usually yellow) transparent semi-precious stone – type of Crystal

The Photon Belt – *Revised*

As earth/ Tamare orbits the sun/ Re; our solar system in turn orbits the galactical-center – the Central Sun; called Alcione by our Pleiadian visitors. The photon belt married with a ring of Monasic radiation also orbits this central Sun, but in a perpendicular fashion relative to our orbit. We therefore pass through this ring twice as we make one complete orbit around the centre of the galaxy – Alcione. This cycle, a period of approximately 25,920years is known throughout many ancient cultures under different names such as:

The Annus Magnus
The Great Cycle *(Maya)*
The Great year
The Platonic year *(Plato)*
The Equinox

The phenomenon of this belt is sometimes called the 'Milky Way.' On entering the photon belt via the 'null zone,' earth will go through radical transformations of its entire ecosystem. The 'null zone' or 'null portion' is a region that lay at the very fringe of entering the photon belt. This small section, of which we will encounter over a 3-4 day period, is a region where matter and anti-matter particles clash or merge and become One. This means that 3rd dimensional and 4th dimensional space become overlapped or interfaced, thereby interrupting the electromagnetic grid system of our planet. In fact, the entire solar system and its electromagnetic systems will be disrupted or even completely disabled. In volume 1 Ch9 Part1, I expressed that the Mayan people of old knew of this zone and its implications – positive as well as negative. They call it the 'No Zone!' They wrote of this phenomenon stating that the earth will enter into a zone of pure darkness for 3-4 days. And, that the planet will halt in its rotation and proceed to rotate in the opposite direction. From a modern scientific standpoint this may be due to the fact that the North and South poles reverse completely causing the reversal of the planet's rotation.

Photons
What is a photon?

'The quantum of electromagnetic radiation. It has an energy of (hv) *where* h *is the Planck constant and* (v) *the frequency of the radiation. For some purposes photons can be considered as elementary particles travelling at the velocity of light* (c) *and having a momentum of* hv/c *or* h/λ *(where* λ *is the wavelength). Photons can cause excitations of atoms and molecules and more energetic ones can cause ionisation.*'[3]

Valerie H. Pitt

So as the poles reverse and the planet begin to rotate in the opposite direction, other bizarre things happen. Well, maybe not so bizarre to those who <u>know</u>. On leaving the 'No Zone' and completely entering the photon belt itself, we would have left 3-D space and entered 4-D space in totality. All 3-D objects and synthetically produced *things* would have been diminished, completely annihilated. 4th dimensional objects will begin to appear, colours that we have never seen and couldn't even begin to describe[4] etc. As stated, we take on an energy based crystallised nature; for it is commonly known that crystals are formed either from a liquid or gaseous base element, since the atoms are better to rearrange themselves from that format.

Fourth Dimensional Crystals

Crystals are in general made up of one particular molecule, which repeats itself in precise geometric patterns that make up the whole. This repeating pattern is known as a crystal lattice. A crystal, having fundamental stabilising properties, enables it to maintain a constant electromagnetic signature. Since the crystal is constructed of one repetitive molecule, it has the inherent order and ability to adjust to almost any environment. This means that crystals, as well as other gemstones, based upon their resonating frequencies with the natural elements of the earth, are able to transcend interdimensionally along with the earth – they posses mathematical transcendental properties. They are therefore able to respond to the natural laws of interdimensional transmutation, just like the Giza pyramids, which were originally lined with limestone. The human body, on the other hand, is built up of thousands of different molecules, all having their own unique electromagnetic signatures. Each organ of the body, having its own bio-magnetic field, also has its own unique way or pattern of how it relates to its environment. Any one organ going slightly out of balance at any one time can throw the entire body out of harmony. This is analogous to a large symphonic orchestra, where one of the musicians went completely off-key, causing the band to loose harmony. It may take the bass player for example, to introduce a fundamental note that enables the band members to pattern themselves after this bass note and therefore re-establish harmony. Crystals behave in exactly the same way. They have the ability to re-establish harmony about the organs of the body – in particular the endocrine glands and their nerve clusters – the chakras.

As a bio-electromagnetic balancing tool, crystals help us to maintain integrity and harmony within our body. The 'No Zone' of the photon belt is a region of space where electromagnetic systems can possibly collapse if they are out of balance or disrupted in some way. The book of Revelations, speak of the 'Crystal City' coming down to earth from heaven. But why, and what does it really mean?

> *'And the building of the wall of it was of jasper: and the city was pure gold, like unto clear glass. And the foundations of the wall of the city were garnished with all manner of precious stones. The first foundation was jasper; the second, sapphire; the third, a chalcedony; the fourth, an emerald; The fifth, sardonyx; the sixth, sardius; the seventh, chrysolite; the eighth, beryl; the ninth, a topaz; the tenth, a chrysoprasus; the eleventh, a jacinth; the twelfth, an amethyst. And the twelve gates were twelve pearls; every several gate was of one pearl: and the street of the city was pure gold, as it was transparent glass.'*

Rev 21v18-21
www.audio-bible.com/bible/bible.html

Though the Sumerians speak of such a craft coming down to earth from the planetoid Mothership Nibiru, this quote can also be looked at from within an entirely different context. The crystal city is the photon belt, carrying within it the Christ-Consciousness energy, the Love vibration that heals all *things*, throwing them into perfect harmony and synchronism with all else – with 'All that Is.' Remember… this is just a point of view; further information of the crystal city, Nibiru aka Planet

X is to follow in the next few pages. All of the above phenomena relate to a regrouping or realigning of our Universe. The time is Now.

What Time is Now?

Time and its relationship to entropy, the most illusive aspect of our current 3-D reality, neither travels form behind nor goes forward or vice versa. The phenomenon exists only in 3-D, or, it at least exists according to our perception of the chain of events within the Universe, within creation itself. As far back as the 1960s scientists began to postulate the idea and concept of time in reverse. In his book *'The Universe Next Door,'* Marcus Chown skilfully explained the concept of the *'arrow of time.'*[A]

> *'Physicists have a special way of quantifying disorder. They call it 'entropy.' The entropy of a broken coffee mug is a convenient measure of the total number of ways that the mug can be broken. When a coffee mug breaks, and it becomes disordered, physicists say that its entropy has increased. This statement has in fact been generalised into one of the cornerstones of physics: the second law of thermodynamics. The law states that, overall, entropy can only increase or, at best, stay the same. It can never decrease. The arrow of time, sometimes called the thermodynamic arrow of time, is therefore associated with the direction in which entropy increases.'*[5]

Marcus Chown

Why did I feel the necessity to mention this here? You might wonder... Well, the Universe and its events are expressed in perfect mathematical repetitive cycles. Such as the repeated pattern of our entering the photon belt and the consequent change or shift in

---

[A] The term 'arrow of time' was introduced by the English astronomer Arthur Eddington in his book *'The Nature of the Physical World'* (1928).

Consciousness we experience. The idea that time can be reversed or go backwards may sound absurd at first hearing. But, as for the entities that experience this phenomenon, it is just life as usual. They wouldn't notice that they are actually going backwards. To them, the order and flow of events would appear to be going forward. Imagine travelling around the earth in a straight line, going from north due south for example. Before you know it, you are also travelling due north or, at least travelling back to the point of origin, though you are still going in what seems like a straight line. The law of manifestation works in this exact same manner. The so-called Big Bang, the projection of the Fibonacci spirals from the Nuqta ultimately results in the reversal of the process – The Magical Path followed by the Mystical Path. The exact opposite of the Big Bang is thus the phenomenon of the '**Black Hole**.'[A] But, it doesn't mean that the chain of events, cause and effect etc., actually stop and then reverse upon themselves. It is analogous to the effect of the Black Hole, which is a force that attracts all spiritual energies, regardless of the expressed nature, into itself. Just as the Nuqta, the Black Dot, projects and Involutes Spirit into form and expression, the ongoing continuation of the *phi* ratio of the Fibonacci numbers spiral right back into the exact point of which they emerged – such is the nature of the Black Hole. The process is therefore expressed as: out of Blackness[B] (chaos) came 'Light,' the 'Big Bang,'[C] 'Creation'

[A] A Black Hole is an astronomical body with so high a gravitational field that the relativistic curving of space around it causes gravitational self-closure, i.e., a region is formed, from which neither particles nor photons can escape.

[B] I used the term Blackness as opposed to darkness, since Blackness represents a Presence beyond states.

[C] In 1927, the Belgian priest Georges Lemaitre was the first to propose that the Universe began with the explosion of a primeval atom. His proposal came after observing the red shift in distant nebulas by astronomers to a model of the Universe based on relativity. Years later, Edwin Hubble found experimental evidence to help justify Lemaitre's theory. He found that distant galaxies in every direction are going away from us with speeds proportional to their distance.

and 'Order,' and – back into Blackness (the *Black Hole*) shall The All return. Below is my coined 'cosmological doughnut,' Fig8.1.

A Black Hole in simplistic terms is a star that has collapsed into a tiny point known as a singularity. It is so dense that it sucks in everything near it, including light. Black Holes can be seen via the death-throes of matter being sucked in. Although it becomes invisible past a certain point, an accretion disk, which is visible, develops as the matter swirls toward the centre. However, on the Universal scale, the Universal Black Hole is the collapse of the entire Universe – not just of a star's singularity.

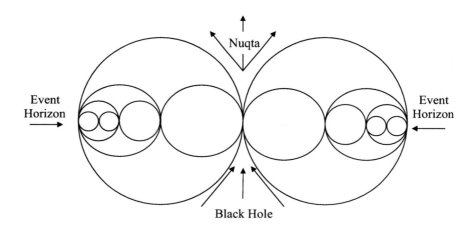

Fig8.1: illustration of the cosmological doughnut

Creation, a 'Flash of Thought'

The photon belt was created and strategically placed in its perpendicular relationship to the cycle of our solar system by our Etherian Ancestors, for very Divine reasons. The Monasic radiation provides the means of cleansing the solar system of negative energy. This is necessary in order for the planets to enter into higher frequency vibration as The All spiral back into the Nuqta, or rather into the Black Hole. So, "what time is it?" The time is Now. Now... is a phenomenon that suggests that the Nuqta, the Black Hole, and All events in between exist simultaneously. In the Mind of the Creator, The All, Creation from Big Bang to Black Hole occurs in the blinking of an eye – as a 'flash of thought.' Everything is everything, All Is in All, existing and not existing at the same time – Now. All that exists in creation will eventually assume the nature of the original creative stuff. Things will take on a crystallised nature of that consistent creative stuff – *ether*, just as crystals are essentially made of one particular molecule. The example of the smashing of the coffee mug is comparative to what happens to creation – things eventually smash or de-materialise back into the essential aspects of atomic structure. Hadrons, such as Protons and Neutrons; Corpuscles, such as Electrons and Ions, will all de-materialise into sub units of Quarks, Bi-apertures and so on into Pure Spirit; into Ether and; into the death-throes of the Universal Black Hole – NTR.

How does the past, present and future exist simultaneously? Well, let us create a scenario together, shall we...? Imagine a reel of film with just three frames. And imagine that we are currently looking at the middle frame, where the first frame has already past us clockwise; the first frame therefore represents the past – the middle frame represents the present and – the third to represent the future. This obviously makes sense according to the general flow of events. Now, imagine a superimposition of all three frames; that is, looking at all three simultaneously. Chaos and confusion will be the first impression of course. But the analogy gives us a simplified comparison of a space—time continuum, where all events are happening at the same instant – at the same space and time. This, and here is the key, is the exact reason why the Creators created the concept of a space—time continuum. It gives us the ability to appreciate creation within time and order, as opposed to within chaos. The perception of all events happening at the same instant is the ultimate Reality though, which ironically is the perception of nothing – no perception – just Presence and awareness of 'All that Is.'

The last two paragraphs should also make obvious the ongoing process of existence through infinite forms of Creation. In other words the front-end of a Nuqta is in fact the back-end of a previous Black Hole and visa versa. This level of truth can only be realised (with the real-eyes) through meditation and Self-realisation. The All exists based upon the principle of change, movement, Involution onto evolution; but *All*, exists without movement or experience. The Universe is paradoxical indeed.

There is one thing that I found to be as intriguing as the photon belt, and that is – the 'Event-Horizon' phenomena. This was already expressed in chapter 1, but here is a quick reminder. An Event-Horizon is the theorised 'one-way ticket' boundary around a Black Hole from which nothing, not even light (photons) can escape. No object except for a Black Hole can have an Event-Horizon, say today's physicists. So evidence for its existence offers resounding proof of Black Holes in space. Once this region has been crossed, that's it, the point of no return. The popular scientific term for the reversed effect of the Big Bang, which is indeed the Black Hole, is called the *'Big Crunch.'* I think the terminology speaks for itself. But here is the token question:

What existed before the first Big Bang?

The one thing that modern physicists agree on regarding the Kaballah is the fact that the Universe began with a Big Bang. However, the physicist community is not able to express what existed prior to the Big Bang phenomena. Well, the Kaballion doctrine presents an answer, or to the least, a comprehendible concept. It presents an existence of Pure Loving Energy in the form of infinite light, our well-known *Ain Soph*. This light, in its anticipation, (which suggests that Infinite Consciousness were Present,) desired to give and to share. But, in a world of all giving and sharing, who is Present to receive? So the light created a vessel. Now, instead of one force in the Universe there are two, the desire to share and the desire to receive – 'One and Other.' The vessel became the desire to receive. Now, imagine that the vessel is a cup shaped out of ice. If we imagine pouring water into the cup, we can indeed see a separation. But, both the water and the vessel are made of exactly the same stuff, H_2O, but are separated by virtue of the difference in vibration. So for a while all was in perfect harmony, a continuous flow of sharing and receiving. Eventually though, the vessel grew frustrated with its role, just like a child who may desire to give gifts to its parent, in return for always receiving, and, desires to create its own fulfilment. The vessel therein desired to become godlike, or, God altogether. So, frustrated with its role as eternal receiver, the vessel eventually pushed back, and just for one moment stopped receiving. It went against the one-ness with the giver and sharer, and then, BANG, the Universe was Created, *Uni*, meaning One and *Verse*, meaning to go against or to oppose. According to the Kaballah this is how the material Universe as we know it was created.

According to popular science, the first Big Bang occurred some 15billion years ago.[6] This created what has been coined the PRIMEVAL FIREBALL, which released radiation at monstrous speeds hurling outwards. The released energy later clumped together in countless groups, thus creating star clusters, which later became galaxies of smaller stars etc. This scientific thesis is in concurrence with the Sumerian account of the creation of Sal, the Central Sun, (so to speak), known as NTR in the Khemetian cosmology, and as the Ain-Soph, to the doctors of the Kaballah. And again, the above thesis also states that Black Holes may reflect Big Bangs, as the Big Crunch. Also, there is a rival theory to the latter, and that is the 'Steady-State' theory. It has not been very popular since it was apparently disproved by the discovery of 'cosmic microwave background.' The theory was to assume that the Universe was originally constant, and that its continued expansion was balanced by the creation of matter.[7]

Black Holes and the Big Crunch
    In order for us to fully appreciate the concept of the Big Crunch, and indeed Black Holes, it is a prerequisite that we must understand the nature of stars – from their birth to their eventual death. The 'birth-days' of stars are based on regions within space where there is a concentration of hydrogen atoms, due to a central gravitational attraction. Or, by the will of Spirit, these first atoms were attracted to each other within very dense clusters of them. Over time, the density of the cluster became so intense that the atoms within begin to collide and bump off of each other, producing tremendous heat and tension. After even further time, the hydrogen atoms actually began to fuse and coalesce, thus producing helium. The production of helium creates a balance within the star itself. I.e., the giving off of helium allows the star to cool, or at best, to stabilise its temperature. I originally learnt through Dr Malachi that our sun produces helium at the rate of 554million tons of hydrogen being converted into 550million tones of helium every second.[8] The remaining 4million tons produced electrical storms and sun spots, and later, caused explosions which hurled balls of energy into its orbit that resulted in the creation of some of our planets. I have since become familiar with many scientific postulations about the said subject. For instance, Stephen

Hawking with his book, *'A Brief History of Time;'* and the previously mentioned Marcus Chown, and his book, *The Universe Next Door.'* Stephen Hawking, being a student of Astrophysics, with many years of experience and study, wrote of the creation and destruction of stars within this, and within many of his other books. Table 13 below, shows the various stages of a star's life cycle. The scientific term however, is 'stellar evolution.'

Table 13: the life cycle of a star (stellar evolution)

Stage	Description
Big Bang	- singularity at point of explosion
Mass of gasses	- mist of hydrogen (H_1)
Red Dwarf	- a 'Main Sequence Star' – conversions of H_1 to helium (H_2)
Red Giant	- at least 10% of H_1 used up
Supernova	- Red Giant collapsed in on itself (theorised point of an event horizon)
White Dwarf	- radius: few thousand miles (100s of tonnes per cubic inch)
Black Dwarf	- final stage of stellar evolution
Neutron Star	- radius: about ten miles (100s of millions of tonnes per cubic inch)
Black Hole	- singularity at point of implosion

The American scientist John Wheeler coined the term 'Black Hole' in 1969. The idea was based on research carried out previously over a period of 100-200years earlier,[9] where scientists were trying to understand the concepts of waves and particles. In other words, some scientists believed that light was constituted of just particles, while others believed it was constituted of waves only. We now know for sure that light, as is all matter, is composed of both waves and particles. This is postulated by the 'wave—particle duality theory' of quantum mechanics. But, the latter research was to find out whether or not light, with its speed of 300million meters per second, was affected by gravity. And, the conclusions were that, the intense gravity of a Neutron star for instance, was so great that it had the ability to slow down waves of particles that were emitted from its mass. This was demonstrated under the theory of light being composed of particles, just like cannon balls and rockets are. And, the Neutron Star, having the possibility to create so strong a gravitation pull, its own emitted particles of light waves would spiral and return to its mass; this lead to the notion that this intense gravitational force, could, also attract external light waves/particles. It was also explained by the said scientists that, the reversal of the light waves back into the Neutron Star, meant that observers such as our-selves today, would not see the light emitted of such a star. Thus, we have the term, Black Hole, where the visible death-throes, represented by the term 'Big Crunch,' demonstrate the entropy and therefore destruction of the Universe.[10]

The term Neutron Star is derived from the fact that, the intense gravitation causes the electrons of the remaining atoms, to be absorbed into the protons, thus producing neutrons. Therefore we have a mass of purely neutrons – a neutral star so to say. Such a fete – the cancelling of positive and negative particles, like yin and yang forces etc., creates the total entropy and therefore total annihilation of the Universe; or at least a part of the Universe at a time. Ultimately, this creates balance and therefore Peace within the Universal Mind, but doesn't do too much good for the observing astronomer who steps too close in inquisitiveness. The gravity on the surface of a Neutron Star is greater than the gravity at its atmosphere's ends, which is an absurd statement since it cannot have a stable atmosphere. But, let's say for example that, the observing astronomer was standing on such a star just before it imploded to form a Black Hole. At the very moment of implosion, the feet and legs of the unfortunate soul would be dragged and stretched inward, in an elastic manner, therefore ripping the body apart down to the very essential stuff, *ether*. The elastic stretch would continue until the gravity at the top of the head increased proportionally thereby sucking the entire body inward. The elastic principle produces the so-called death-throes, which is sometimes reproduced in movies such as

'Lost in Space,' and the new version of 'Planet of the Apes;' and numerous times in television episodes of 'Star Trek,' and 'Star Gate.' I invite you to go and take another look at these movies, if you can only vaguely remember at this time.

Although I have tabulated a stellar evolution sequence above, it is not entirely correct on the face of it. A Red Giant may take one of two paths according to its original size and the rate of how it burns its fuel. In fact, and paradoxically, the more fuel a star starts off with, the sooner it runs out. This is because the more massive the star is, the hotter it needs to be to balance its gravitational attraction.[11] A Red Giant may take the path to become a Neutron Star and ultimately a Black Hole, via a Supernova of course, or, it may take the path of becoming a White Dwarf and ultimately a Black Dwarf. The theory is that, the bigger stars go on to form Black Holes when they collapse in on themselves; this makes sense since the bigger stars have more fuel, and thus they burn faster with extremely fast spins as they collapse. Smaller stars, having slower spins, simply end up as Black Dwarfs; the inward attraction is not strong enough to create a Black Hole. Moreover, the table describes a Red Dwarf as a 'Main Sequence Star.' However, a 'Main Sequence Star' is further categorised into 6 stages from a brown dwarf to a blue star:

(1)   A brown dwarf;
(2)   A red dwarf;
(3)   A yellow star;
(4)   A white star;
(5)   A blue/white star;
(6)   A blue star.

The temperature, colour, brightness, and lifespan of the star depend on its mass. There are literally 1000s of concepts across the planet of creation and entropy; too many to mention within the MMSN series. But I would like to however, talk a bit about the Mayan civilisation and its artefacts. Yes, let us give Egipt and Sumeria; and astronomy, a rest. The Yucatan people have much to share to help enlighten us also.

Mayan Artefacts and Civilisation

Hernan Cortes – excited by stories of the lands that Columbus had recently con-quested, sailed from Spain in 1505AD landing in Hispaniola, which is now called Santo Domingo. After farming there for some years he sailed with Velazquez to conquer Cuba in 1511AD. He was twice elected major of Santiago, then, on 18 February 1519AD, he sailed for the coast of Yucatan with a force of 11 ships, 508 soldiers, 100 sailors, and 16 horses. He landed at Tabasco on the northern coast of the Yucatan peninsular. He met with little resistance from the local population and they presented him with presents including twenty girls. He married Malinche, one of these girls.

Now, the people of the Yucatan peninsular were descendants of the ancient Mayan civilization, which had been in decline from around 900AD. However, it is the mathematical achievements of them that we are concerned with hereon. At the times of these Spanish conquests, the Christian devotees were taken aback by the Mayan religion with its icons and texts written in hieroglyphic form on walls. They perceived it as devil worship and sought to destroy the Mayan's sacred texts and relics. One of these Christian devotees was the Spanish character Diego de Landa. He ordered all Mayan books burned and all idols destroyed. He was however, surprised at the distress caused to the Mayan people by his malice. It is believed that Landa, in remorse of what had happened, regretted his actions and later wrote a book: *'Relacion de las cosa de Yucatan'* (1566AD). In it he describes the hieroglyphs, customs, temples, religious practices and history of the Mayan culture, of which his own actions tried to eradicate.

The Mayan Calendar

The use of the Mayan Calendar is said to dissolve linear, fear-based rigid structures in the minds and souls of those who use it. Engaging ones mind in Mayan Cosmology through use of the calendar breaks the spell of linear sequential time. It opens and introduces the player to the higher timeless potential of these minds and therefore enters new systems. The Mayan calendar is essentially different than our current Gregorian (Georgian) calendar. The Gregorian calendar is said to keep us out of tune with the harmonics of the earth and cosmos by keeping us focused on a linear time, with slogans like: 'time is money,' – a conveyer belt like concept of time. Mayan time however, is depicted as radiating out of the Present-Moment with no intent to take us anywhere other than the Now. For the Mayan's, time has no fundamental reality, but can be conceptualized as an interfacing pattern that weaves itself within the body's various nervous-system circuits. This pattern of time is then projected or superimposed over the eternity of the new moment, creating the apparent illusion of linear sequential time. By properly integrating the different circuits of the nervous system one can learn to stop holographically, the projection of the illusion of linear time, onto the new moment and awaken her or him self to the ever Present eternity that is here and Now.

The Mayan calendar – viewed as a paradigm for the map of both the individual and collective psyche in their co-evolution, represents the evolutionary process that synchronizes life patterns with the earth and Universal cycles. The Mayan calendar represents time as 'a series of some 16 interrelated calendars.' The most important calendars are the 260-day, 13-moon calendar called the **Tzolkin**,[12] and the 365-day, 18-

moon calendar called the **Haab**.[A] Both calendars have 20 days per month, numbering from 0 to 19. The Mayan teach that our current calendar system, the Gregorian system, imposed by Pope George XIII in 1592AD, is out of sync with our own biological rhythms, with planetary electromagnetic fields and many outer celestial cycles. Synchronization with our own unnatural calendar has, according to the Mayan calendars, caused humanity to declare war on them selves, worship materialism and pollute the planet. The Mayan calendar Prophecies the end of our Great Cycle, "AGE OF THE JAGUAR," in late December 2012AD. And, according to Cotterell's sunspot theories, the end of the world will be brought on by the sudden reversal of the earth's magnetic field.

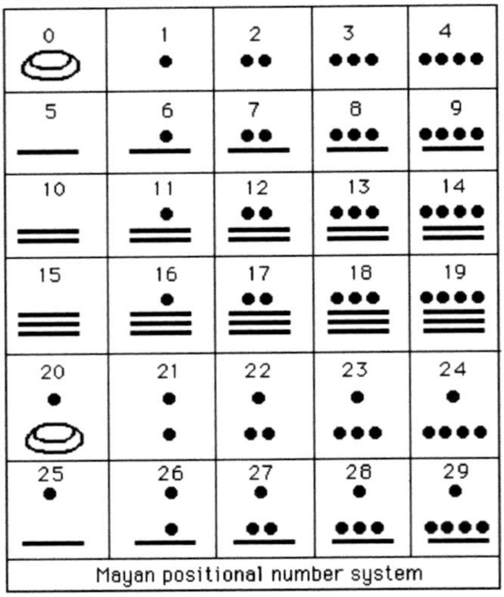

0	1	2	3	4
⬯	•	••	•••	••••
5	6	7	8	9
—	•	••	•••	••••
10	11	12	13	14
=	•	••	•••	••••
15	16	17	18	19
≡	•	••	•••	••••
20	21	22	23	24
• ⬯	• •	• ••	• •••	• ••••
25	26	27	28	29
• —	• •	• ••	• •••	• ••••
Mayan positional number system				

Fig8.2: the Mayan Numerals

[A] The Tzolkin was a ritualistic calendar whereas the Haab was a civil calendar.

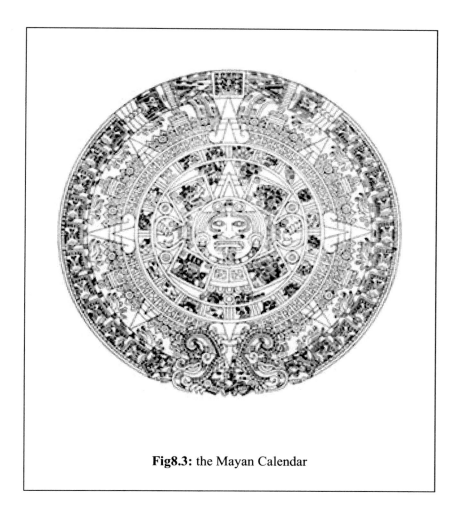

Fig8.3: the Mayan Calendar

Moon cycles of the Maya

The Mayan Sacred Calendar follows a path of thirteen moon cycles. Thirteen moons, instead of twelve months. Twenty-eight days in a moon cycle represents a woman's bleeding cycle. The more my husband and I studied this system, the more their calendar seemed to represent a woman's body. We began to keep a count of days on a device called the Tzolkin. A grid of 260 days repeated over and over. My husband figured out how to use this Tzolkin as a woman's bleeding chart, a MOON MAP. I charted my own bleeding cycles on it and watched as wonderful patterns emerged. The feminine principle oozed forth, the calendar came to life. When we acknowledge thirteen moon cycles, we honor the female cycles.

Fig8.4: Maya moon symbol

I think the ancient women of the Maya enjoyed their moontime bleeding because they followed the true cycle of the thirteen moons. They felt the rhythm of the moon tides pulsing through their bodies and celebrated this joyous time together. They nurtured and cared for each other, making their moontime a special visionary time. When they emerged from their moon lodges, they shared their visions with the tribe.

Our studies continue about these fascinating people and everyday we find more connections to the women of the Maya. If you dig deep and read between the lines, the roles of the females in the Meso-American traditions were ones of power and accomplishment. The female bloodlines were actually the acknowledged lineage of a king or nobleman. The importance of recognizing the female parameters of this society is a step in the worldwide acceptance of women as equals in our world today. The Mayan Calendar has many secrets to discover and Lady Tzolkin is just one of them. Play with her and experience the MOON CYCLES OF THE MAYA for yourself. Happy Mooning...

The document of fig8.4 is an account by an anonymous female writer of the Mayan culture.

Mayan Mathematics and Culture

A common culture, a calendar, and a great cosmology held the Mayan civilisation together, and astronomy played an important part in the religion, which underlay the whole life and customs of the people. Of course, astronomy and calendar calculations require mathematics and indeed the Mayans constructed a very sophisticated number system. The Mayan numbering system was a base twenty system. Almost certain, the twenty system came from the fact that they counted using both their fingers and their toes (see fig8.2). Since I am not including much explanation into how this number system actually works, your own investigative energy will lead you to appropriate and reliable sources. However, you may consult Graham Hancock's book *'Fingerprints of the Gods.'* In it, he gives an account as to how the Maya utilised this base twenty system. But, and indeed, where did the Maya get this remarkable mathematical system from? And what prompted them to develop such a cosmology therewith?

> *'The Maya knew where their advanced learning originated. It was handed down to them, they say, form the First Men, the creatures of Quetzalcoatl, whose names had been Balam-Quitze (Jaguar with the Sweet Smile), Balam-Aceb (Jaguar of the Night), Mahucutah (The Distinguished Name) and Iqui-Balam (Jaguar of the Moon)* [13]

Popul Vuh

The above is taken from the 'Popul Vuh' the creation story of the Mayans. The ancients of the Maya had a complex pantheon of deities whom they worshipped and offered human sacrifices. Rulers were believed to be descendants of the gods and their blood was the ideal sacrifice, either through personal bloodletting or the sacrifice of captives of royal blood. The Maya vision of the Universe is divided into multiple levels, above and below earth, positioned within the four directions of north, south, east and west. After death, the soul was believed to go to the Underworld, Xibalba (shee-bal-bah); a place of fright where sinister gods tested and tricked their unfortunate visitors. But, and also, the Maya, in the Popul Vuh, described their forefathers as:

'Endowed with intelligence; they saw and instantly they could see far; they succeeded in seeing; they succeeding in knowing all that there is in the world. The things hidden in the distance the say without first having to move... Great was their wisdom; their sight reached to the forests, the rocks, the lakes, the seas, the mountains and the valleys. In truth, they were admirable men... They were able to know all, and they examined the four corners, the four points of the arch of the sky, and the round face of the earth. [14]

Popul Vuh

It can be seen by reading several translations of the Popul Vuh, that the Gods were concerned about the fact that Man, had developed in his intelligence to know all that there is to know. The same arousal of concern is also cited in the book of Genesis, where Adam and Eve were expelled from the Garden of Eden, after they partook of the Tree of the knowledge of both 'good' and 'evil.' Correspondingly, the First Four Men, according to the Popul Vuh, were deprived of their ability to see far.[15] Both the Popul Vuh and Genesis therefore tell of the fall of mankind from grace. Grace, in this context, is synonymous with advanced knowledge. The Mayan account however, is far more informative than the biblical version; it talks of how the First Men were so advanced in their wisdom that they were able to astronomically chart various celestial bodies. This obviously includes their accounts of the Photon Belt, of which they lay emphasis on the No-Zone. The Popul Vuh also narrates of the famed Quetzalcoatl, as the father of the First Men, and therefore God of the Maya.

244

Fig8.5:
Quetzalcoatl

Somewhere along my studies I found an account that referred to Enqi, the Sumerian God, as Quetzalcoatl, where he travelled to the far lands of the oceans to set up other civilisations, such as regions of Atlantis. However, Quetzalcoatl is related to many names and incarnations, and plays a prominent role in the pantheons of virtually all the other Meso-American deities. He was a god of such importance and power that nearly no aspect of everyday life seemed to go untouched by him. And, as a historical figure, his actions could not be contained by History, and thus eventually evolved into Myth. And as a legend, he would signal the end of mortal kingship.

When the Spaniards first arrived at the Yucatan peninsula, in the 15hundreds, some of them were not entirely sure who the natives were. But the natives on the other hand, believed that these white visitors were the return of the Gods who gave them civilisation some 900hundred years earlier. It is written in their culture that their Creator, Quetzalcoatl and his pantheon, will return at some future time to redeem them.[16] And, what a coincidence, the Spaniards arrived in the exact year that the Yucatan people were expecting the return of the gods. Sadly, by the time they realised what was happening, the small Spanish army had already established a type of marshal law. Much to the surprise initially though, the Spaniards did not immediately understand why they were welcomed with such warmth and adoration by the Yucatans (Aztecs etc.). But, had these natives known who the visitors were at the outset, the small group of Spanish conquers would not have stood a chance, since they were outnumbered by many thousands to one.[17] However, the

245

Spaniards did have a foreign military advantage over the Yucatan people, of steel swords and armour, gunpowder and cannons etc., as well as frightening horses.[A] The entire Yucatan system of life and living was usurped almost complete, all due to the misidentification of the invaders being the pantheon of Quetzalcoatl.

On the subject of the gods, an interesting phenomenon that distinguished Quetzalcoatl is that, despite the fact he is not the most powerful of gods within the Meso-American pantheon, or one of the eldest, he is nonetheless an integral part of the system. This was partially accomplished by his ability to integrate himself so securely to attributes of his fellow brethren, to such an extent that it is virtually impossible to tell if Quetzalcoatl was the true originator or visa versa. Hence, to establish a single definitive personality to a Mayan god is extremely difficult.

Marvelling at their culture however, historians such as J. Eric Thompson, in 1954, confessed to a deep sense of puzzlement, as to what lead the Mayans to chart the heavens and its celestial bodies. This is because there are a number of disparities identified with the Mayan's abilities. For instance, to grasp the concept of eternity, yet failed to understand basic principles of the wheel; to be able to count in millions, yet never learned to weigh a sack of corn.

According to the Maya, the Great Cycle (25,920year Annus Magnus), began on a date corresponding to mid-August of the year 3114BCE, on our own Gregorian calendar.[18] And, as we have seen above, the end of this Great Cycle, the 'Age of the Jaguar,' will be some time in late-December 2012AD. At the end of this cycle we enter the No-Zone, apparently. Their system of calculating the duration of the cycle is

---

[A] The Aztecs (apparently) thought at first sight, that the horse and rider was one complete animal.

avant-grade in comparison with modern methods. I mean, for a civilisation that does not distinguish themselves in any other way, than that we live within this Great Cycle, which is itself within much larger cycles. All this, and more, display the advanced Mental-technology of the peoples of the ancient Mayan culture, whom descended from the Ancient Olmecs – migrant Nuwbuns of Afrokha before the continental drift. With a pragmatic objective in mind, the Mayans wanted to inform their descendants, the Astecs, the Toltecs, the Chibchas and the Incas etc., of the coming of the end, and therefore of how to prepare. Other prophecies, such as the Mesopotamian ones, speak of similar cycles – from development of culture till end time scenarios, such as the concept of the Nibiru cycle.

Nibiru – *aka Planet-X*

Both the ancient Mesopotamian and the above Meso-American peoples seem to share a common cultural ancestor, and that is the Atlanteans. And, the Sumerians and their Babylonian descendants had a profound cosmology, as is with the Mayans and their descendants, the Yucatan people.

> *'The ancient Sumerians possessed surprising knowledge of the stars and planets, some of it so developed that it must have evolved after many centuries of controlled observation of the heavens. One of their artefacts depicts a figure surrounded by twelve stars or planets, and has been thought by some students of Sumerian sacred and astronomical records to represent the Earth, sun, moon, and nine planets, one more planet than we presently recognise. According to Sumerian cosmology, this tenth "dark" planet could not be seen by observers on Earth because of its specialised orbit and was visible at 3600-year intervals.'*[19]
>
> Charles Berlitz

This citing, by Charles Berlitz in 1983, tells me that Zecharia Sitchin must have had rivals, in the pursuit to decipher ancient artefacts of the Sumerian and Babylonian cosmologies, as we shall see shortly. The cosmogonies of the latter also tell us of the binary nature of our own Sun and indeed of the Suns of other solar systems. But today, the notion that our Sun is a binary star, may sound too far fetched to be a matter of fact to most people. Well, the fact is, it is. In further fact, 99% of known stars are binary (dual), and the ones with planetary systems may even have binary solar systems also. However, our solar system is unlike most other observed ones, where the most popular binary situation is one where a dead star orbits a live and active 'Main Sequence Star.' This is how we have come to know and understand the Sirius system. Sirius B, a dead star, orbits the Sirius A. As stated in volume 1, the original orbit of Nibiru, Planet-X, (or P-X), was 25,920years according to Dr Malachi and Zecharia Sitchin, known as an *Aam*; and was more recently reduced to a smaller orbit of 3,600years called a *Shar*. The new orbit became relative to a sun in the region of Orion. The popular description of P-X is that it is a planet as opposed to a Merkaba spacecraft as is taught by Dr Malachi. But, Mark Hazelwood, in his book *'Blindsided,'* describes P-X slightly different. He says that P-X is a brown dwarf star (that which was a planet at one time) that orbits between these two suns.[20]

Its orbit is rather long in comparison to the other planets of our solar system; 3,600years give or take 100years, says Hazelwood. Interestingly, it spends about 99.9% of its time going away from either one of its suns, after initially slingshotting around it swiftly. In today's case, once it reaches the critical point of approximately 1,800years of slow travelling away from the dead sun, it then, like a shot, hurls its way toward our Sun, as it is caught by its gravitational pull. It takes about 3years to complete the last 0.1% of its route where it will encounter the earth vicinity. I recalled Dr Malachi expressing that Nibiru, on arriving at the Asteroid Belt, will then take 3years for its shams, including the famed Crystal City, to reach the earth.[21] Well, P-X may have already reached this critical point; and, may therefore have already encountered at least the Asteroid Belt, on its way to pass between the Earth and Sun. I'm not sure of the exact year when it will happen; I don't think anyone is; only God knows. But, when this eventually happens, as it is with the entering of the No-Zone, there will be total geological weathering chaos on the planet.[A]

The Prodigal Child

P-X is like the black sheep, or prodigal child of our solar system. Ostracised by its two parents, it periodically returns to its home environment, our solar system, and causes nothing but disruption and havoc, and then leaves without care of implications. It happens every time, according to the ancients. There are many different modern descriptions of this phenomenon. Other writers, (besides Dr Malachi and Zecharia Sitchin,) such as Robert Temple, Erich Von Däniken and David Icke, have described Nibiru in all kinds of interesting ways – from a Merkaba field to a spacecraft, to a planet, and to a brown dwarf star. But, one should at least be intelligible enough to know that something within the context thereof definitely exists. And, with any controversial situation, such as these two, (P-X and the photon-belt,) there will always be those who have set out to disprove and ridicule them.

Sitchin, in some texts, describes the situation as the un-welcomed intruder. Due to its gravitational effects on the inner planets, Nibiru he says creates an upheaval about the weather patterns of them. Today we experience unaccountable numbers of earthquakes, hurricanes, mini and epidemic scale tsunamis, floods and droughts etc. The fringing attributes of both Nibiru and the No-Zone are the causes of these effects. It can be

---

[A] It must be remembered that doom and gloom can be avoided.

summed that, Nibiru is here to cause the destruction of an era of time and living on earth, whereas the Photon Belt, via the No-Zone, provides the cleansing and cleaning up of the latter. This is just a way to look at it of course; But what a scenario… We have to learn to prepare ourselves for the worst case scenarios of what seems to be inevitable. Some of us, after learning about these two situations, may spend a vast amount of time studying and researching them. Then later, once we are satisfied, we may fall back in line with 'life as usual.' There is nothing wrong with this beloved – because life does go on. We will however, be fully aware of what is to come, and will be blessed with the knowledge of how to prepare ourselves. Every now and then we hear bits of information in the media, or glance at pieces of writings in the newspapers or in some scientific magazine or journal. And so we smile internally with comfort, as we are strengthened with confirmation of that which we know deep within. The book of Malachi makes reference to the great and dreadful day, of the coming of the Lord. So here we are. For some of us, the coming of the above calamities may present a sense of relief, while the majority will experience confusion and dreadfulness. As an analogy, we must consciously decide whether are not we want to be raptured or, remain in the muck and mire of the ignorant. In other words, nature has presented two possible outcomes of the oncoming calamities. The religious community have called them *'Heaven'* and *'Hell;'* so it is simply a matter of <u>choosing</u> where our destiny lays.

The Great and Dreadful Day

End time scenarios, are always told of coming about with great destruction – with cataclysms such as floods, storms, earthquakes, volcanoes, and tsunamis etc. For the majority, the undesirable outcome is that most will not make it. Biblically we are taught that two thirds of the population of all lifeforms, on the planet will die. This of course does exclude us, humans. But the chosen few who subsequently heard the call for rapture, such as the 'Indigo People,'[A] (see footnote) would welcome the coming of the end, as a Great Day.

The Fact of the Matter

We are to be reminded that, <u>In Reality</u>, none of the above information regarding the Photon Belt and Nibiru is actually true. Stunned? Don't be. The Photon Belt and indeed Nibiru only exist within our 3D-matrix programming. The I-Am Presence, the Conscience of the Self, knows that we only experience these celestial activities within the lowest faculties of be*ing*. And therefore, in Reality, one can simply become Present to, or become One with the way things Are. By that I mean, the effects of such scenarios do not affect the I-Am Presence – only the I-Me Presence of our mental reflections is affected. Through meditation and remote viewing, we can experience the reality of the Photon Belt and Nibiru; we can even create the desired outcome, since it is all but a mentally generated program. We may travel interdimensionally to many other parallel worlds or dimensions, and therefore create the desired experiences therein, thus not affecting our current dimension – planet earth 21st century etc. The fact of the matter is that none of this is a fact in matter, nor in Spirit. Truth is consistently changing at velocities greater than the speed of electromagnetic radiation. We, humans of earth, are trapped within one particular dimension – 21st century earth – trapped within a multi-verse of multi-dimensions. We believe that this is the only reality, and therefore through fear of death, we become dreadful of such scenarios as the Photon belt and Nibiru. Through religion we fear the devil; and, we also fear the coming and possible chastisement of God. We are told of past-times when God brought destruction on mankind for his transgressions,

---

[A] The term 'Indigo People,' is adopted here from the term *Indigo Child (or Indigo Children)*. It describes the fact that there are persons born specifically within this era for the sole purpose of assisting the Gods in the ushering in of the New World. These persons are not afraid of death – they are usually highly spiritual and intuitive; they often question authority as they are not very conforming; and they also usually present solutions for common problems and issues.

such as the flood of Noah and the fires of Sodom and Gomorrah. But, none of it is true in Reality. It is all a part of a figment of the mentality that created our particular dimension.

Some entity or entities, understanding that this reality creates and presents the greatest of illusions, saw an opportunity to enter and proceed with the agenda of creating more illusions as a means of control, dominance and power. As stated in a previous chapter, the Earth Plane/ reality, is a dimension of spiritual schooling. The greatest lessons are to be gained once the embodied soul learns to overcome limitation, negativity and illusion. But, on the contrary, or in the process thereof, the adversary has created religion as a means of control. Religion obscures the realities of our dimension, and takes away responsibility for one to be the god of her or his own destiny. Religion blinds us from the relative truths of our 3D program, such as Nibiru, Orion, Sirius, Illiyuwn, The Photon Belt, EBEs etc.

~

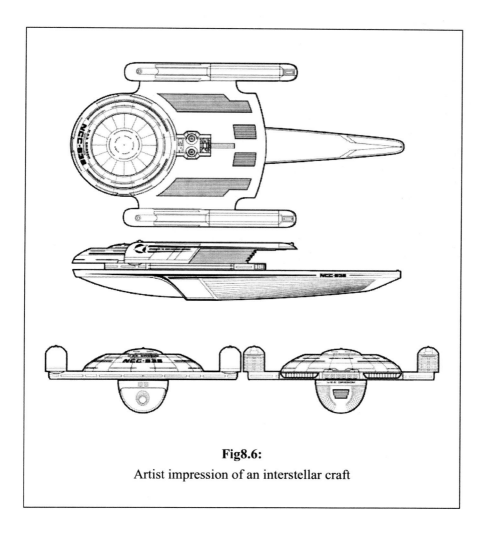

Fig8.6:

Artist impression of an interstellar craft

Notes

[1] Simon Lilly, *Illustrated Elements of Crystal Healing,* p6

[2] Dr Malachi, *The Holy Tablets,* Ch7

[3] Valerie H. Pitt, *The Penguin Dictionary of Physics,* photons, p282

[4] Bob Frissel, *Nothing in This Book Is True, But Its Exactly How Things Are,* p

[5] Marcus Chown, *The Universe Next Door,* p6-7

[6] Dr Malachi, *The Science of Creation,* p35

[7] *The Brockhampton Dictionary of Physics,* p219

[8] Dr Malachi, *The Science of Creation,* p36

[9] Stephen Hawkins, *A Brief History of Time,* p91

[10] Patricia Newton, *Melanin and the Black Child* (Audio Cassette)

[11] Ibid, p93

[12] Graham Hancock, *Fingerprints of the Gods,* p174

[13] Popol Vuh, p167

[14] Ibid, p168-169

[15] Graham Hancock, *Fingerprints of the Gods,* p170

[16] Charles Berlitz, *Atlantis,* p58-59

[17] Ibid, p59

[18] Graham Hancock, *Fingerprints of the Gods,* p174-175

[19] Charles Berlitz, *Atlantis,* p123

[20] Mark Hazelwood, *Blindsided,* p15

[21] Ibid, p17-18

Chapter 9
Merkaba Energy

Preparing for Merkaba Ascension

Preparation for Merkaba Ascension begins with the preparation for self-healing, and self-healing begins with our choosing to be healed in a complete and holistic manner. Most of us tend to believe that life just happens to us and that we do not have much control or influence over our day-to-day affairs. We believe that we are simply going with the motions of whatever we encounter and experience in life. But the fact is—we have the faculty of Choice. We looked at this in some detail in Ch3, concerning choosing a partner – whether in business, or in Love relationships etc. But from hereon, we will try-on the Possibility of choosing the life we love to live, in moment-to-moment continuity. In choosing the life we love to live, we must first choose Love itself – that is, to stand in the Presence of Unconditional Love. From here, we can then choose the life we want to live. This initial stance is also absolutely necessary when creating the Merkaba.

The Power of Choice

Merkaba energy is a very powerful force to work with; it is the energy that warps Consciousness in and out of the fourth and fifth dimensions using both the synergies of the Sacred Breath and the Love Vibration. And Choice, in the context of declaring an agenda is a faculty of Integrity and Power that emanates from the Presence of Unconditional Love, having as its driving force the Sacred Breath. When we choose, we select powerfully and freely – free of conditions (hence unconditional), free of circumstances, of emotions and free of past experiences and memories. To choose then, is to Declare, to Create and to manifest any agenda from the presence or Presence, of *nothing*.

The Presence of *nothing* does not mean loss of Consciousness and awareness – it is the Presence of Be*ing* Present to Consciousness only. From this Presence comes the faculty of Choice, which is neither influenced nor directed, but rather influences and directs the outer world to bring to fruition the intended agenda.

Deciding, as is distinct from choosing, is on the contrary. The making of decisions is therefore conditional – since they are influenced and directed by circumstances, feelings, emotions, expectations etc., which are all subject to change; and will therefore always lack Integrity and Power. But choosing is void of the latter. Most of us who use the word choose when selecting, actually make decisions based upon reasons; as opposed to selecting based upon *nothing*, which is to choose. And, reasons are the very conditions that become the driving force toward manifesting a decided-upon agenda, which lack Integrity and Power. So it can be seen how one looses focus and sight of an agenda due to the constant changing of conditions and circumstances etc. And, if the conditions and circumstances that drove us into deciding change, then the agenda itself will loose its driving force.

Now, in the intention of utilising the Merkaba to raise awareness, with the '17+1 Sacred Breath' exercise, one has to stand in the Space or Presence of Unconditional Love, then choose powerfully and freely, to create her or his own counter-rotating fields if light. The same is true for any other agenda in life. We must choose, not decide. I'm not suggesting that we are to eradicate the mental conceptions of reasons, conditions etc., which tend to arise when selecting. No, but rather to acknowledge these thoughts from an observational point of perspective, then choose freely, from *nothing*. The word 'decide' is synonymous with death. It comes from a group of Latin words with the suffix *cide*, such as genocide, suicide, homicide and so on. But the Power of Choice can only be synonymous with Love, Creation and Life. In the Possibility of living the life we love, we can therefore choose from nothing to be whatever we want to be – whether it is to be wealthy, be famous, be healthy; or to be a good parent, a good wife or husband; – or whatever. We can affirm and declare these possible ways of being with statements like:

I choose to be wealthy
I choose to be famous
I choose to be healthy
I choose to be a parent
I choose to be Present in my relationship

The key words are 'choose' and 'be.' To be is to be. It is a declaration that is created moment-to-moment and is void of circumstance, condition or reason. Prior to performing the '17+1 Sacred Breath' exercise, which is explained in volume 1 of MMSN, the practitioner may choose an outcome of the operation. In other words, the exercise may be used to encourage the manifestation of a created possibility – or, a moment-to-moment chosen way of being. Never mind the conditions. I mean, you may have difficulty understanding how you can choose to be wealthy in the moment and not actually have cash money to substantiate the declaration. The above works because the subconscious-mind will create the necessary conditions in order to attain the actual wealth, and, although this is to be manifested in a future time, (in the world of time,) the feeling, the emotion of being wealthy will be realised moment-to-moment. The philosophy of Spherical Breathing, which is achieved through the counter-rotating fields of the Merkaba moreover, shares the same possibilities of sex magic (refer to Ch3).

The Love Vibration

The benefits of creating the Merkaba field are infinite. The field, created of Unconditional and Universal Love, the Love of the Creator, synergistically connects us in totality with the created Universe. One has to be able to embrace all of life as if she/ he is *One* with All that exist. Understand this beloved: the basis of enlightenment is achieved by firstly expressing Love for Self and kind, and is ultimately attained once we step into the mode of loving *All* aspects of nature without prejudice. The Merkaba in its ultimate purpose encompasses all levels of creative energies throughout The All, as Universal Love, the Supreme Healing Force. Creating the Merkaba field thus begins with creating the Possibility of Holistic Healing.

How difficult or easy do we generally find it to turn to our neighbouring brother and sister and say: *"I love you,"* for no apparent reason? Some of us cringe at the idea, perhaps of being looked at as crazy or strange. This is due to the imposed conditioning of our westernised way of life and living. Our unwilling desire to love each other without reason creates separation and segregation, and inevitably creates fear. Fear in this stance is based on our feelings of being unprotected, unguided, unwanted or unloved. The energy of fear is at the exact polar-opposite of the Love Vibration, within the dance of spiritual embodiment. Love, the Healing Force of the Creator, gives us joy, serenity and comfort. It gives us a sense of belonging and being connected, feeling safe and forever nurtured. Whenever one experiences not being loved by others, or has difficulty in loving others, the sense of being detached sets in. The detachment leads to the fear of being hurt, abandoned, scorned, disowned and even hated etc. These fears are simply emotions felt throughout the nervous system, as the evidence of being in a negative vibration. The Love Vibration through Merkaba Energy forever keeps us in a positive energy state as opposed to the fear energy – liken to good vibes verses bad vibes, high spirit verses low spirit etc.

The polarities of Love and fear are not synonymous with the earthly polarities of like and dislike. Love in this case is achieved at the higher aspects of be*ing*, and fear is induced at the lower aspects of be*ing* – Polarity-Consciousness. As we tune in to Conscience, we experience True Love, Peace and Joy – if we follow the guidance. But, on the contrary the ego-self and the lower natures of be*ing*, creates duality, polarity, separation, limitations as well as negative vibrations, which we translate as fear. (See fig9.1 below).

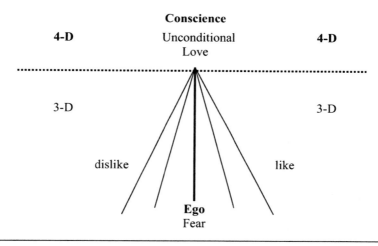

Fig9.1: Love Vs fear

Understanding Chakra, Merkaba, Kaballion and Khundalini energies gives us a sense of interconnectedness with all of life, with all of nature, and, with The All. Therefore the vibrations of Love are forever Present throughout the Universe, called the Spirit of God, the vibrations of God. This energy underpins the very essence of our being and is available to us for healing, in the moment. The lower planes of

Love, the emotions of fear, are apparent in 3-D only, and are eradicated once we step into 4-D, Christ-Consciousness, the dimension where Love rules, not emotions. Please refer to volume 1, where I reiterated the '17+1 Breaths' exercise, as presented by Drunvalo Melchizadeck. The effects of the counter rotating fields of the Merkaba are analogous to the effects of mixing bits of fruit within a fruit blender. Imagine yourself being placed into the blender as a slice of apple. You find that you are accompanied by bits of other species of fruit such as banana, mango, and peach slices. There is also a base present of which you are all soaked – water perhaps. The water may serve as a common medium that will enable the different fruits to be blended into one. This is exactly the way Spirit works, like water, a unifying principle.

The different fruits in this scenario may represent the organs of the body – serving many different functions that compliment the whole of the body. And thus, the spin of the Merkaba once created unifies the organs of the body by way of the chakras into one crystallised matrix field, of Pure Consciousness. The chakras themselves are small vortexes of energy that provide the organs with light-coded information that is picked up by the DNA. Back to the blender – once the fruits are blended into one, a unique sense of taste, of colour and of quality will be entertained. The analogy is clearly metaphoric, but is not far from the reality of what actually happens when one creates the counter rotating fields.

The Sacred Breath (Spherical Breathing)
Drunvalo Melchizadeck as far as I'm aware reintroduced the '17+1 Breaths' exercise in this day and time. I mean, the exercise is very ancient and therefore cannot be attributed to modern men whom have sought out these long forgotten rituals and re-presented them. However, I thank him and those associated with his teachings for bringing this to mainstream attention. As far as the Ancient Egiptian Order is concerned today, within its doctrine, there are several breathing exercises and

rituals, which are intentionally not taught to the general public. Nuwaubian, or Afrokhan spirituality, is very sacred and so the information has always been kept secret/ sacred. (Mums the word...) Sacred information; particular that which is concerned with Ascension has always been kept secret, only to be departed to aspiring students from their personal Kohanes, Gurus or Masters. Many of us of the AEO have thus been blessed, and have sat at the feet of Nuwaubian/ Afro-Spiritual Elders – where knowledge was passed on – in lip to ear fashion. Therefore I am not at liberty to reiterate these high-level spiritual rituals in any of my writings. The '17+1 Breaths,' also called Spherical Breathing (once 4th dimensional awareness is achieved), is more than enough for an inquisitive individual to take-on and apply, to raise her/ his awareness. But, I must still point out that a spiritual coach must be sought out; or perhaps a workshop that deals with sacred breathing and meditation exercises and rituals.

In my experience however, simple breathing techniques can be applied in times of stress and anxiety. For example, if I were confronted with a situation that I wasn't prepared for, I would pause for a moment and take several <u>deep</u> breaths. This powerfully enables me to deal with the situation from a place of, simply becoming Present. That is to not concern myself too much (or at all) about the outcome of the situation, nor indeed its motivation, (its past). Some of us may recall times when we automatically pause to take deep breaths at times of anxiety and uncertainty. This is an involuntary action that is encouraged by the sub-conscious mind. But, conscious application of deep breaths can prove to be far more rewarding, sine it combines the waking-conscious and sub-conscious minds.

Corresponding with Chakra Energy

It is very important to understand and know the Chakra system, as much as it is to understand and know the Kaballah system. In other words, the two are distinctively different doctrines (or systems of initiation), and can easily be applied out of context if the practitioner ignorantly attempts to unify their policies in one complete exercise.

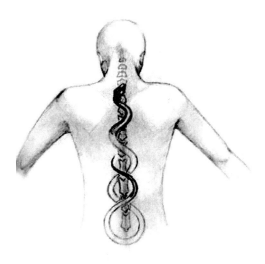

Fig9.2: Khundalini Energy

The Kaballah doctrine teaches of an ontological system where the faculties of the human being (and mankind) are in correspondence with the faculties of the celestial man (God), so to speak. Meaning, just as mankind has a basic set of archetypal tendencies about his behaviour, so is it with his counterpart celestial man, the Deity of which he were created in the image and likeness of. Mankind therefore, in every aspect of his being, mirrors this celestial man, God, according to the teachings of the Kaballion.

The Chakra system however, teaches of a corresponding system also, of which the seven major endocrine glands of the body relate to specific realms of existence. Thus, Merkaba energy, in its ability to raise the Khundalini by way of the 17+1 'Sacred Breath' exercise, allows mankind the opportunity to raise his awareness beyond the physical realm (or plane) and tune in to higher vibratory planes such as:

> The Plane of the Plasmatic Body
> The Plane of the Etheric Body
> The Plane of the Astral (or Light) Body
> The Plane of the Mental Body

Another way to view and compare the two systems is like this. The Kaballah doctrine attempts to explain the embodiment of Consciousness and Spirit into the Human Body (or God in Man form), through Involution, whereas the Chakra doctrine attempts to give man (and mankind) the opportunity to reconnect and establish his awareness at the multiple levels of embodiment in retrospect. This is where the Merkaba field becomes a necessity. Kaballah also explains and teaches how man can, by his understanding of the ten (or eleven) archetypal Mental faculties (see Ch2, the Anatomy of God), combine and utilise in principle a number of them in order to achieve specific goals in life. This is also available through the Chakra—Merkaba doctrine, as well as through sex magic.

Raising the Khundalini

Stretching back into the corridors of time, Asian religions have burrowed from Afrokhan-Kushian Principles of energy vehicles; one of such concepts is the spoken of mystical force called the Khundalini. Throughout history, of many different cultures, many other names have been given to this power. Orgone, esprit, loosh, prana, elan vital, and bio-electricity are some of these names.

'The rise of the Khundalini is linked with a warm liquidly magnetic energy when it rises up the spine. Physical symptoms connected to the opening of the Khundalini may include crackling noises at the base of the neck, and unexplained headaches - but be careful about attributing these symbols to rising Khundalini energies. Often they have a medical cause that needs the attention of a physician.

Khundalini energies are sometimes triggered by a blow to the head or other physical trauma timed by your soul to awaken your psychic journey and innate abilities.

Releasing the Khundalini energy too quickly can have serious emotional effects on a person. One should not attempt to open this thrust of energy if one is not balanced psychologically. This is not for those with manic depression or bi-polar disorder.

The manifestation of the Khundalini energy - frequency of vibration - links with the Sanskrit term 'Chaitanya' - the integrated force of your physiological, mental, emotional and religious bodies.'

Taken from:
www.crystalinks.com/kundalini.html

Preparing to raise the Khundalini through the Merkaba field is like preparing for meditation. You may, in the process, choose to listen to a tape recording of a specific chant, like Aum for instance. Or, listen to natural sounds like the sound of singing birds, rainfall (thunderstorm), blowing wind etc. And, just like preparing for meditation, you must choose an outcome of the operation. Here are some examples of what can be achieved through raising Khundalini Energy:

- Full activation of your DNA;
- Opening of your clairvoyant and clairaudient abilities;
- Feeling connected to the Oneness of the Universe;
- Attaining connection to Higher Awareness and Knowledge;
- Dysfunctioning of the ego, and connection with Conscience;
- Enter the Presence of Unconditional Love, Peace and Joy

Breathing is very important. It is good spiritual practice to focus on your breathing, only, when preparing for meditation, or preparing for Spherical Breathing. Overleaf is a very basic and simple exercise for raising Khundalini Energy and therefore Chakra Awareness. The exercise is also excellent for one who practices living in the Present-Now.

Living in the Now is a simple Decree to make but definitely not an easy one to consistently do. The world of distractions is just as determined to be consistent. The exercise, then, may be used to balance your being on a daily basis, to compensate the imbalances we face in or day-to-day situations.

Exercise

Find a quite place free of distractions

Sit or lie down; find a position that is comfortable for you

Quiet your mind… still your thoughts

Relax your body, completely

Feel at peace

Focus on your breathing, only

Inhale slowly through the nose, deeply to the base of your stomach;
expanding your diaphragm, on counts of nine

Hold your breath for as long as is comfortable

Exhale through the mouth slowly and completely;
again on counts of nine

Repeat nine times, or as is comfortable for you

Now focus your attention on your chakras

Starting from the top of the head, visualise the crown chakra opening

Watch as pure white light enters your crown Chakra
and slowly spirals down through your spine

The white light opens your third eye Chakra

The white light moves down to your throat chakra releasing your blockages
you may feel like chanting Aum

Allow the tones to resonant from your throat
do this as long as is comfortable

The white light now enters your heart Chakra;
you experience a feeling of Unconditional Love and compassion

The white light enters your solar plexus
gently your fears - anger - tensions are released

See the white light enter your spleen Chakra
releasing pain and guilt linked to that Chakra

The white light now enters your Root Chakra, the seat of your Khundalini
energy

As it does, it begins to activate the energy of the base (root) Chakra

Feel the energy suddenly emerge from your Root Chakra,
spiraling up through the base of your spine as if it were a coiled snake

The coiled snake represents the spiraling DNA -
opening, activating; bringing you to Higher levels of Consciousness

Allow the energy to flow through your chakras

See the energy wheels rotating

When you are ready… come back to the physical reality

Relax and balance your energies

You may feel the need to sip some water

Living in the Present-Now

It does not matter what you have experienced in your past, whether joy or pain, love or hurt, wealth or mediocrity; it must be realised that Choice exists as a faculty within the Present-Now, and can be exercised momentarily to create a better life. Many of you live for a future based upon the past; you decide upon a course of action, including its result or outcome, based upon passed experiences. You assume, for example, that because your last three relationships did not work out, the next one wont. Beloved, it does not have to be this way. The Present-Now, this very Moment, void of time and circumstances, gives you the Power of Choice. The Present-Now is a position of Power. To live here, is to first acknowledge and complete the past; for what is done is done.

We often avoid the Present-Now, the Present-Moment. We spend a vast amount of time, (probably 97%>), dwelling on the past and what might have been or, fantasising about a future and either hoping for the best or dreading the worst. As a result we forget the gift of what is available in the moment. The Present-Now can also seem too scary or remote to conceptualise or contemplate. Mistake number-one! The Present-Now cannot be conceptualised. Now, is void of concepts – conceptions do not exist in the Present – only Possibility. This Presence of be*ing* is filled with infinite possibilities for healing, and infinite solutions to problems that constrains our moving forward in life.

Refer to my book, *'The Distinctions of Nuwaubu – 144,000 Human Principles.'* The book outlines 36 very basic human Principles, of which you, the student of Nuwaubu, are encouraged to apply in your own life. The results are that you will break through the constraints of third dimensional living and enter a world of infinite possibilities – the fourth and fifth dimensions. It is not a physical transition, but rather a Mental one. You enter a Presence where you are empowered to create the life you love to live moment-to-moment.

'The beginning of freedom is the realisation that you are not the processing entity – the thinker. Knowing this enables you to observe the entity. The moment you start watching the thinker, a higher level of Consciousness becomes activated'[1]

Eckhart Tolle

By entering the Now, you enter a Higher Presence of being, which is beyond the normal workings of the Mind and ego. You become an observer of your life-situation, – you realise your life-situation is not your True Life. True Life lies in the bosom of the Creator. From the abode of this Reality you are One with the Creator, One with the Universe. Therefore, you are One with the shaping forces of the world. These shaping forces are translated to humans and mankind as Principles of Life and living; hence the Principles of Nuwaubu. In the world of time and circumstance we reiterate these Principles as Distinctions, – rules of thumb, or as codes of conduct. But, in the Present-Now we experience them as Pure Energy – forces that we can utilise by the Power of our Decrees. Merkaba Energy is best utilised from this Presence since it engages Unconditional Love for 'All that Is.'

'The aim of everyone who incarnates on Earth is ascension and enlightenment, which is the total mastery of all the lessons offered here.'[2]

Diana Cooper

When you master the world of limitations of negativity you enter the Present-Now. You become enlightened when you become the One with the ultimate observer, God. You become One with the energy that creates the Merkaba – you are the ultimate time-space vehicle.

Fig9.3: The Merkaba Field

Time—Space Vehicles

Though many European spiritualists speak and write of the Merkaba and its characteristics, the melanated Afrokhan must also know of her/his potential of self-realisation through this vehicle. Matrix vehicles that are created by Europeans are based on spirit only, and only allow time/ space travelling throughout the matrix; Soul-Energy vehicles therefore have greater potential.

The Afrokhan's Merkaba then, is created not just of Spirit, but requires her/his emotional body (Soul) to be intact. The Soul connection allows the melanated Afrokhan to actually transcend this particular matrix creational space and enter into other matrix grids. Otherwise, we may choose to transcend the matrix and elevate further toward the bosom of the Creator, the bosom of The All. In contact with The All, you are introduced to that which is real – REALITY.

Matrix Healing

Merkaba Energy is available to everyone, with varying results according to one's ontological position of course. For the Afrokhan, Merkaba Energy gives us the opportunity to be healed in totality by way of the Universal matrix, – its many faculties, as well as the very mentality of its creation, the Universal Mind.

Matrix healing to the individual is really about aura cleansing though; just as the Universe is described as a macrocosmic matrix in its construction, so it is with the physical body; as above so below. So, matrix healing for the individual is about cleansing the aura of impurities and negative vibrations. The doctrine of the Kaballah provides healing in this way also. In my book, *'The Distinctions of Nuwaubu,'* you are also presented with a list of 36 affirmations, in which they are designed to promote total healing of your be*ing*, – body, Mind and Spirit. The book may therefore serve as a spiritual counter part to the MMSN series.

This volume of the MMSN series has taken you and me through many degrees of study. And, although you may not share the same beliefs and enthusiasm as I do, I'm absolutely certain that the Principles and Distinctions behind this work has been realised. You would have realised the implications of the world's religions and their belief systems; and, the effect they have on our individual as well as Collective-Consciousness. Religion ought to be viewed as selectable systems of healing – matrix healing. But evidently, religion has been set up by man/mankind, for the purposes of dominance and control. Laws are set up to enforce very Divine spiritual Principles it would seem, since mankind have forgotten these Principles – the forces that guide and direct his human function. But it is more to the fact that the laws only serve the best interests of those who propagate them. This book then, has to be looked at, in retrospect, as a course of Mental healing, which leads to matrix healing utilising Merkaba Energy.

I end this volume with the encouragement that you share this information with as many persons as is possible. And, remember, the information only serves as a means of breaking the spell of ignorance and misinformation. You are to use the book: *'The Distinctions of*

Nuwaubu – 144,000 Human Principles,' as a counterpart, which purely deals with the very Principles/forces that govern the human function.

May the Angelic Ones continue to Bless you and Guide you on your quest for 'Right Knowledge,' and Self-Enlightenment...

Hotep... Peace...

Nebu Ka Ma'at

Notes

[1] Eckhart Tolle, *Practising The power Of Now,* p10
[2] Diana Cooper, *A little Light on the Spiritual Laws,* pXIII

Index

Illustrations & Tables

Tables

Glossary

Archetype:	Unconscious animalistic instinct, proposed by Jung
Big Bang:	Singularity before the creation of the Universe
Big Crunch:	Singularity at the end of the Universe
Black Hole:	Region of space—time from which nothing, not even light, can escape
Chakra:	Sanskrit word for wheels of light
Collective Unconscious:	Postulated by Jung as the source of race memory and instincts
Conscience:	Highest aspect of Mind
Entropy:	The 2nd law of thermodynamics, the measurement or rate of the collapsing Universe
Event Horizon:	Point of no return – the boundary of a Black Hole
Geodetic Marker:	Points of triangulating geometric patterns on the ground – the position of sacred sites etc.
I-Am Presence:	Upper ego – Conscience
I-Me Presence:	Lower ego
Kaballah:	Esoteric system of Jewish tradition
Merkaba:	Time-Space matrix vehicle
Singularity:	A point in space—time at which the space—time curvature becomes infinite
Space—time:	The four-dimensional space whose points are events
Subconscious:	That which is below the waking conscious mind
Theurgist:	One who works miracles through supernatural agents
Wormhole:	Thin tubes of space—time connecting distant regions of the universe; might also link to parallel universes

Recommendations and Bibliography

Recommended Books for study

African Mythology, *dictionary of* – Jan Knappert
 (London, England, Aquarian Press, 1995, ISBN: 0-261-66653-3)

Anacalypsis – Godfrey Higgins, ESQ
 (New York, USA: A & B Books Publishers, 1863, ISBN: 1-881316-16-5)

Ancient Egiptian Sacred Geometry, *the* – Dr Malachi
 (Published by the AEO)

Ancient Future – Wayne B. Chandler
 (Georgia USA: Black Classic Press, 1999, ISBN: 1-57478-001-8)

Behold a Pale Horse – William Cooper
 (Arizona USA: Light Technology Publishing, 1991, ISBN: 0-929385-22-5)

Blindsided – Mark Hazelwood
 (all rights reserved by Mark Hazelwood)

Brief History of Time, *A* – Stephen Hawking
 (Great Britain: Mackays and Chatham PLC, 1998, CN: 2570)

Children of the matrix – David Icke
 (USA: Bridge of Love Publications, 2001, ISBN: 0-9538810-1-6)

Coming forth by day – Dr Malachi Z York
 (Published by the AEO)

Dictionary of the Esoteric, *the* – Nevill Drury
 (London, England: Watkins publishing, 2002, ISBN: 1-84293-041-9)

Dictionary of Physics – Valerie Illingworth
 (London England: Penguin Books, 1977, ISBN: 0-14-051-236-5)

Egyptian magic – Murray Hope
  (Northamptonshire, England: Aquarian Press, 1983, ISBN: 0-85030-361-3)

Epic of Gilgamesh, *the* – N.K. Sandars
  (London, England: Penguin Books, 1960)

Fingerprints of the Gods – Graham Hancock
  (London England: Arrow Books, 1995, ISBN: 0-7493-1454-0)

Genesis Revisited – Zecharia Sitchin
  (New York, USA: Avon Books, 1990, ISBN: 0-939680-85-8)

God and Man in African Religion – Emefie Ikenga Metuh
  (London England: Camelot Press Ltd, 1981, ISBN: 0-225-66279-5)

Healing Power of Amino Acids, *the* – Leon Chaitow
  (London, England: Thorsons, 1989, ISBN: 0-7225-1551-0)

Holy Tablets, *the* – Dr Malachi
  (Published by the UNNM)

Illustrated Elements of Crystal Healing – Simon Lilly
  (London, Harper Collins, 2002, ISBN: 0-00-713387-1)

Land of the Fallen Star Gods – J.S. Gordon
  (England: Orpheus Publishing House, 1997, ISBN: 0-9526857-1-X)

Metu Neter, Vol.1 – Ra Un Nefer Amen
  (Brooklyn USA: Kamit Publications, 1990, ISBN: 1-877662-03-8)

Metu Neter, Vol.2 – Ra Un Nefer Amen
  (Brooklyn USA: Kamit Publications, 1994 ISBN: 1-87662-08-9)

Nothing in This Book Is True, But Its Exactly How Things Are – Bob Frissel
  (Berkeley, California: Frog, Ltd. books, 1994, ISBN: 1-883319-01-3)

Rizq and Illiyuwn, (fact or fiction?) – Dr Malachi
  (Published by the HTM)

Sacred Records of Tamare, *the* – Dr Malachi
  (Published by the UNNM)

Sacred Wisdom, *the* – Dr Malachi
  (Published by the AEO)

Something in this Book is True – Bob Frissel
  (Berkeley, California: Frog, Ltd. books, 2003, ISBN: 1-58394-007-4)

Spiritualism – Lyn G. De Swarte
  (Glasgow, England: Thorsons, 1999, ISBN: 0-7225-3818-8)

Stolen Legacy – George G.M. James
  (USA: African American Images, 1954, ISBN: 0-913543-78-0)

Tree of Life Meditation system – Ra Un Nefer Amen
  (New York: Kamit Publications Inc, 1996, ISBN: 1-877662-13-5)

Universe Next Door, *the* – Marcus Chown
  (Headline Book Publishing, London, 2002, ISBN: 0-7472-35287)

7 Habits of Highly Effective People, *the* – Stephen R. Covey
  (New York, USA: Fireside, 1990, ISBN: 0-671-66398-4)

9 Principles of Human Beings, *the* – Dr Malachi
  (Published by the AEO)

12th Planet, *the* – Zecharia Sitchin
  (New York, USA: Avon Books, 1976, ISBN: 75-37875)

Recommended listening Cassettes & CDs for study

African Spirituality & Libation	Sister Marimba Ani
Carbon, 'Life's ultimate gift'	Booker T. Coleman
Nano genetics and mind control	Phill Valentine
The Matrix	Phill Valentine
Genetic Annihilation	Francis Cress Welsing

Recommended Videos and Films for study

Babylon 5	- films
Eloheem – part 1 (Dr Malachi)	- video
Existenz	- film
Independence Day	- film
Matrix trilogy, *the*	- films
No more God games (Dr Malachi)	- video
Predator 1 & 2, *the*	- films
Reptilian Agenda, parts 1 & 2 (David Icke)	- videos
Revelation of a mother goddess (David Icke)	- video
Star Gate (the original movie)	- film
Star wars (both trilogies)	- films
Thirteenth floor, *the*	- film
5th Element, *the*	- film

Other Books by Paul Simons

────── Nebu Ka Ma'at ──────

The Distinctions of Nuwaubu
144,000 Human Principles

Urban Cries
(Volumes 1 & 2)

The Legacy of the Black Gods
In Time before time
(Coming forth from the Akashic Records)

Dictionary of Etymology and
Metaphysical Principles

Contact Paul at:
www.tamarehouse.com
paul@tamarehouse.com